PRAISE FOR *THE DAILY CHAMPION'S MIND*

"Star-ratings and draft positions are meaningless in between the white lines. Mental toughness always precedes physical toughness. I highly recommend reading *The Daily Champion's Mind*."

—Scott Shanle, Super Bowl champion

"High performance is about making the smart choice, not just the emotional one. *The Daily Champion's Mind* gives you the tools to execute under pressure."

—Freddie Crittenden, Olympic track and field athlete

"Having coached at the Olympic and NCAA level, I'm impressed by how practical *The Daily Champion's Mind* is. These daily tools help athletes stay clear, confident, and consistent when the stakes are high."

—Ozzie Quevedo, Olympic and NCAA head swimming coach

"Most people are looking for a big breakthrough, but in my experience it's usually the small things you do consistently that change your life. That's what I appreciate about this book. It reminds us that confidence isn't something you find—it's something you build. A few minutes a day, making better choices, staying in the game in sport or in real life when things get uncomfortable. This book gives you the opportunity to create a mental and emotional practice."

—Gabby Reece, former pro volleyball player, cofounder of XPT, and host of The Gabby Reece Show

"I've always believed that pressure doesn't create character, it reveals it. The question is, what are you doing every day to prepare for those moments? This book gives people practical ways to train the part of themselves that shows up when things get hard. That's useful whether you're competing, running a business, raising a family, or just trying to become a better version of yourself."

—Laird Hamilton, pioneering surfer, waterman, and cofounder of Laird Superfood

"*The Daily Champion's Mind* provides practical steps to consistently train your mind. Small reps that compound over time are exactly what athletes need to stay consistent with this kind of training."

—Edose Ibadin, Olympic track and field athlete

"*The Daily Champion's Mind* allows any athlete to make an incredible investment in the development of their mental game. This practical guide weaves story, science, and—most importantly—daily practice into your life. Phil and Jim have done an outstanding job exploring the mechanics of the mind."

—Henry Barrera, director of performance for the University of Alabama men's basketball

"Adaptability is one of the most crucial strengths in getting where you want to go, no matter the obstacles. It's acquired through years of focus and experience. There is no shortcut to being more adaptable or developing mental fortitude, but this book provides the blueprint for creating a daily mindset practice that will get you there."

—Kai Lenny, world champion paddler, big wave surfer, and waterman

ALSO BY JIM AFREMOW, PHD, AND PHIL WHITE

The Creative's Mind
The Leader's Mind

ALSO BY JIM AFREMOW, PHD

The Champion's Mind
The Young Champion's Mind
The Champion's Comeback

ALSO BY PHIL WHITE

Unplugged
Game Changer
The 17 Hour Fast
Waterman 2.0
Our Supreme Task
Whistle Stop

THE DAILY CHAMPION'S MIND

365 DAYS OF **MENTAL TOUGHNESS** TRAINING WITH THE WORLD'S GREATEST ATHLETES

JIM AFREMOW, PHD,

and PHIL WHITE

BenBella Books, Inc.
Dallas, TX

BENBELLA
BenBella Books, Inc.
8080 N. Central Expressway
Suite 1700
Dallas, TX 75206
benbellabooks.com
Send feedback to feedback@benbellabooks.com

BenBella is a federally registered trademark.

Printed in the United States of America
10 9 8 7 6 5 4 3 2 1

Library of Congress Control Number: 2026024462
ISBN 9781637749647 (trade paperback)
ISBN 9781637749654 (electronic)

Editing by Victoria Carmody
Copyediting by Amy Handy
Proofreading by Martha Gallant and Cheryl Beacham
Text design and composition by Aaron Edmiston
Cover design by Morgan Carr
Printed by Lake Book Manufacturing

For everyone in the arena.
This is for your daily climb.

CONTENTS

INTRODUCTION

IN THE ARENA

"While the greats mastered the body, the greatest mastered the mind."
LeBron James

If you want to compete with courage when fear shows up, stay composed when the pace quickens, and perform freely when it matters most, this book is for you. Mental training isn't theory. It's how you breathe, focus, and respond in the moments that decide the outcome.

In 1910, Theodore Roosevelt delivered a speech that still resonates in locker rooms and arenas today. He reminded the world that it's not the critic who counts, but the person who steps into the arena—face marred by dust, sweat, and blood—risking failure but fully alive in the fight.

More than a century later, those words still guide the best of the best. Serena Williams, Tom Brady, and other champions have lived that truth. Greatness isn't about playing it safe. It's about daring greatly, competing completely, and staying in the fight when comfort calls you out of it.

LeBron James lives by that message. The NBA's all-time leading scorer and four-time champion writes four words on his shoes before every game: *Man in the Arena*. It's not for show. It's a reminder that when the lights hit and the noise builds, talk means nothing. The arena asks only one question: Who are you when your number is called?

THE ARENA WITHIN

Every athlete steps into a physical arena, but the real contest begins in the mind. The body follows where the mind leads. Every movement, every breath, every choice starts there. When your mind is clear, your body performs. When your mind is cluttered, your body tightens.

Your mind is the real arena because it decides how you handle the invisible battles—pressure, fear, doubt, distraction, and frustration. It's what allows you to reset after mistakes, ride momentum, and compete with composure as pressure rises. The physical game tests your fitness. The mental game tests your identity. You win outside only after you win inside.

Mastering the mind isn't about being "mentally tough" once. It's about building strength through daily reps—learning how to notice what's happening and respond with control when it matters. You train the mind the same way you train the body: by showing up, paying attention, and repeating what works.

We've spent our careers inside locker rooms, film rooms, and training centers, helping athletes and performers build the mindset of a champion. Our book *The Champion's Mind* reached competitors around the world who were hungry for practical mental tools. This book is the next step. It brings the best lessons, stories, and strategies from the world's greatest athletes into a daily system you can lean on—one day, one rep, one mindset shift at a time.

The body wins medals. The mind decides who earns them.

HOW TO USE THIS BOOK

Each month, you'll train in a legendary arena—Wimbledon, Augusta, Lambeau, Wrigley, and the Olympic Games. Each month stands on its own, but together they form a year-long mental training journey.

Each week begins with a "Training Partner" day. Here, you'll meet the champion who will guide you for the week. These pages introduce their story, their mindset, and the qualities they'll help you build—no exercises needed. Consider it your warm-up before stepping fully into the work.

The days that follow translate their lessons into actionable mental reps: reflections, cues, resets, and exercises designed to strengthen how you think, feel, and compete. The insights come from the champions. The training comes from applying their mindset in your own arena.

You can move through the book day by day, starting in January, or jump into whichever arena calls to you. Follow it straight through or explore at your own pace. What matters is that you show up. Each time you do, the training adds up. Treat every page like a rep. That's how champions are built.

THE CHAMPION'S SYSTEM

MORNING EDGE

Before the day begins, decide how you're going to show up. Set your standard early, and let your actions honor it all day.

FLIP THE SWITCH

Pressure, doubt, and distraction are part of the game. When they show up, reset fast and get back to the task before one bad moment becomes two.

CHAMPION'S WRAP

A strong day deserves a strong finish. Look back honestly, take what helps you, and leave the rest behind.

Each daily rep takes only a few minutes, but repeated day after day, it compounds. That's how confidence grows and mental toughness becomes instinct.

The tools in this book are your edge.

This isn't a book to admire on a shelf. Keep it close by your bed, in your locker, or in your bag. Hit your Morning Edge before you check your phone.

Flip the Switch instead of flipping through distractions. End your day with the Champion's Wrap instead of letting the world close it for you.

Champions train their minds with intent and consistency. They don't wait for the perfect moment; they create it. They compete with what they have and where they are and turn it into something better. That's what stepping into the arena means. You own every moment and use it to grow.

This book is your mental training ground. Some days will flow; others will test you. Both count. Both build you. The goal isn't to finish the pages. It's to become the kind of competitor who owns pressure, resets fast, and performs with freedom.

Champion the day—or lose it.

CHAPTER 1

JANUARY: OLYMPIA

"The only victory that counts is the one over yourself."
Jesse Owens

Picture Olympia three thousand years ago. The stone track is hot beneath the midday sun, and the air is thick with dust and anticipation. The crowd leans forward shoulder to shoulder, their voices echoing off the surrounding hills.

There were no scholarships, contracts, or cameras. No parents filming from the stands and no scouts searching for the next star. There were only competitors at the line, stripped down to effort, discipline, and the desire to test themselves. Sport existed long before the modern Olympic Games, but Olympia was the first place where competition was recorded, honored, and treated as something sacred.

The spirit of Olympia still matters today. Beginnings set the tone—not just the first stride of a race, but the decision to step up, lock in, and fight through to the finish. This chapter isn't about medals or headlines. It is about becoming the kind of competitor who earns them.

Throughout this chapter, you will train with four Olympic legends: Michael Phelps, Gabby Thomas, Simone Biles, and Mikaela Shiffrin. Their lessons are not highlight reels; they are blueprints for excellence. Your task is to apply their wisdom to your own arena—where it truly matters.

The call is simple: Stop waiting for the perfect opportunity. The arena is already here. The real opponent is the choice in front of you. Your gold medal is today.

Champion the day—or lose it.

DAY 1: MENTAL TRAINING PARTNER

MICHAEL PHELPS

"I want to be able to look back and say, 'I've done everything I can.'"
Michael Phelps

Michael Phelps set a standard the sports world may never see again. Across five Olympic Games, he won twenty-eight medals, including twenty-three gold, and turned the 2008 Beijing Olympics into one of the greatest performances in history. The races were unforgettable, but they were only the visible part. What made Phelps different was the way he prepared.

His edge came from discipline. Diagnosed with ADHD as a child, he found direction in the pool and learned to channel his energy with purpose. Under coach Bob Bowman, he built the kind of consistency that separates champions from everyone else. In the four years leading up to Beijing, he trained every day because he believed one missed day could matter.

Phelps trained his mind the same way he trained his stroke. He visualized every race in detail, including the moments when things might go wrong. So when his goggles filled with water in an Olympic final, he stayed composed, trusted his stroke count, and touched the wall first. That kind of poise did not appear out of nowhere. It was built through thousands of mental reps.

This week, Phelps is your mental training partner. He will show you what discipline looks like when it is lived, not talked about. He will challenge you to prepare with purpose, stay steady under pressure, and follow through when it counts. That is how greatness gets built, one deliberate rep at a time.

DAY 2: LIVE THE CHAMPION DREAM

"You can't put a limit on anything. The more you dream, the farther you get."
Michael Phelps

A dream becomes powerful when it starts shaping how you live. Phelps did not chase medals first. He chased the version of himself capable of winning them. His dream showed up in how he trained, prepared, and responded when the pressure rose. Big dreams do not stay in the future for long. They start asking something of you today.

MORNING EDGE: NAME THE CHAMPION DREAM

Write one clear sentence: "My dream is to ________." Under it, write: "Today I will be the person my dream requires." Put it where you can see it and let it shape the day. A dream gets stronger when your actions start backing it up.

FLIP THE SWITCH: ANSWER THE DREAM

When pressure hits, come back to your breath, your body language, and the next thing that needs to be done well. This is not the dream slipping away. This is the dream asking something of you. Say, "This is what my dream looks like in real time," and step into the next action with purpose.

CHAMPION'S WRAP: WHERE THE DREAM CAME ALIVE

As the day winds down, think about one moment when your actions matched the dream you say you want. That is where the dream came alive. That is how belief starts to settle in. You stop admiring the dream from a distance and start becoming it.

DAY 3: PROTECT YOUR CHAMPION STANDARD

"If you want to be the best, you have to do things other people aren't willing to do."
Michael Phelps

Yesterday, you named the dream. Today, you start living in a way that matches it. Phelps separated himself by how he trained when no one was watching and nothing felt glamorous. The early mornings, the extra attention to detail, the clean finish, and the refusal to bargain with fatigue were all deposits into the competitor he was becoming. A standard remains abstract until your actions prove it.

MORNING EDGE: SET YOUR CHAMPION STANDARD

Say this once: "I live the standard I set." Then choose one action today that proves it. Finish the rep clean, stay locked in when fatigue hits, or bring full effort to the last task instead of fading at the end.

FLIP THE SWITCH: DEFEND THE STANDARD

When resistance shows up, do not give it a microphone. Take one decisive step and begin. The moment you stop negotiating with yourself, you take back control.

CHAMPION'S WRAP: YOU PROTECTED THE STANDARD

At the end of the day, name one moment when you followed through when it would have been easier to ease up. That is how a standard stops being an idea and starts becoming your identity.

DAY 4: THE 3 Cs OF A CHAMPION COMEBACK

"Things won't always go perfect. It's how you adapt that matters."
Michael Phelps

Phelps understood that mistakes and pressure are part of competition. What separated him was his ability to catch himself quickly, reset, and return to the next stroke. That is the comeback skill you are training.

MORNING EDGE: REHEARSE THE COMEBACK

Before the day begins, picture yourself at your best and then imagine something going sideways. See a mistake, delay, or surge of pressure. Now see yourself catching the shift early, settling yourself, and getting back to the next thing that matters.

FLIP THE SWITCH: MAKE THE COMEBACK MOVE

When something throws you off, make the comeback move. First, catch it by noticing the tightening, rushing, or frustration before it takes over. Then blow out the junk with one sharp exhale, clearing the tension, noise, and extra thoughts. After that, take one Return to Zero breath by inhaling through your nose for four seconds and exhaling through your mouth for six. Then champion it by bringing your eyes back to the target and your attention back to the job.

CHAMPION'S WRAP: EARN THE GOLD RESPONSE

Think of one moment today when you got pulled away from your best and made your way back. Bronze means you caught it, silver means you cleared it, and gold means you returned to the task with purpose.

DAY 5: COUNT THE STROKES

"I can only control my own performance. If I do my best, then I can feel good at the end of the day."
Michael Phelps

At the 2008 Olympics, Phelps had water pouring into his goggles in the middle of the race. He could not see the wall, the lane, or the field. So he did what champions do under pressure. He locked in on what he could still trust. He trusted his rhythm, counted his strokes, and stayed with the job right in front of him. Pressure did not call for something extra. It called for steadiness and execution.

MORNING EDGE: KNOW THE JOB

Before the day starts, decide what doing the job means today. It might be staying patient when things get messy, finishing strong when you get tired, or keeping your body language steady when stress rises. One clear job is enough. The tighter the pressure, the simpler the focus.

FLIP THE SWITCH: RETURN TO THE JOB

When tension hits, blow out the junk with one sharp exhale through your mouth, like you are clearing smoke from a room. Then take one Return to Zero breath. Inhale through your nose for four seconds, then exhale through your mouth for six. Let the breath settle you, bring your eyes back to the task, trust your rhythm, and do the job in front of you.

CHAMPION'S WRAP: BACK TO THE JOB

At the end of the day, think of one moment when things went sideways and you brought yourself back to the job. That is how composure gets trained. A champion response is steady, simple, and under control.

DAY 6: LOYAL TO THE STANDARD

"I was willing to do the work that others weren't."
Michael Phelps

Phelps made the decision early and kept honoring it when the work got hard, repetitive, and uncomfortable. That is what commitment really is. Commitment means staying loyal to your standards when your mood, energy, and comfort pull you in different directions. The best performers settle the question early, then spend the day living it out.

MORNING EDGE: MAKE THE CALL EARLY

Before the day gets noisy, decide how you will show up. Choose what you are willing to give today—your focus, your effort, and your follow-through—and commit to delivering it. Make the decision while your mind is clear, so there is nothing to negotiate later.

FLIP THE SWITCH: KEEP THE CALL

When your energy drops or your mind starts looking for an easier way out, stay with the decision you already made. Take one Return to Zero breath. Inhale through your nose for four seconds, then exhale slowly through your mouth for six. Let the breath settle the noise and bring you back to the standard. Then keep moving.

CHAMPION'S WRAP: YOU KEPT THE DEAL

At the end of the day, name one moment when you followed your standard instead of your mood. That is the win. That is what commitment looks like day to day.

DAY 7: OWN THE FINAL STRETCH

"It's not how you start, it's how you finish."
Michael Phelps

Phelps made his biggest moves when the race got tight and the effort got heavy. He understood that the final stretch is not the time to hang on. It is the time to sharpen up, lock in, and become even more intentional. Most people fade when fatigue shows up. Champions treat that moment like an invitation to separate.

MORNING EDGE: SEE YOUR SIGNATURE FINISH

Picture yourself deep in the final stretch, when your body is heavy and the margin is thin. See yourself staying tall, settling your breath, and driving clean all the way through the line. Do not just imagine finishing. Imagine finishing in a way you would be proud to sign your name to.

FLIP THE SWITCH: CLOSE LIKE A CHAMPION

When fatigue or stress hits, take one Return to Zero breath. Let the breath bring you back under control, then lock in your form, your eyes, and your effort. The final stretch is where champions get cleaner and more precise, not less.

CHAMPION'S WRAP: SIGN YOUR NAME TO THE FINISH

At the end of the day, think about how you closed. Did you coast, or did you stay intentional when it would have been easy to fade? The finish is your signature. Make it look like you.

DAY 8: MENTAL TRAINING PARTNER

GABBY THOMAS

"When the stakes rise, I treat pressure like a signal—it's proof I belong in the moment."

Gabby Thomas

Gabby Thomas brings a rare mix to the track. She is a world-class sprinter with a scientist's mind, trained in neurobiology at Harvard and epidemiology at the University of Texas. That shows up in how she competes. Her preparation is precise, her focus is clean, and her confidence is built on what she has done, not what she hopes will happen.

In 2021, just weeks before the US Olympic Trials, doctors discovered a mass on her liver. The uncertainty was real, and the timing could not have been more difficult. She stayed steady, made the Olympic team, and went on to win bronze in the 200 meters and silver in the 4×100 relay at the Tokyo Games. That stretch revealed something important about her. She does not waste energy fighting the situation. She handles it.

By the time Paris 2024 arrived, Gabby had taken her mental game even higher. She used visualization and identity work to train belief with purpose, writing, "I will be an Olympic champion," in her phone until the thought felt lived, not borrowed. Then she went out and backed it up, winning three gold medals in the 200 meters, the 4×100 relay, and the 4×400 relay. She did not just rise to the moment. She arrived ready for it.

This week, Gabby is your mental training partner. She will show you how to build belief on purpose, stay with your race, and treat pressure as proof that you belong. Bring science to your preparation, trust to your execution, and calm to the biggest moments.

DAY 9: THE NEXT MOVE IS YOURS

"A setback doesn't define you. Your response does."
Gabby Thomas

When Gabby learned about the tumor before Trials, the news could have triggered fear, doubt, frustration, and a flood of worst-case thoughts. That is an extreme example, but the same pattern shows up in everyday competition. A mistake, a bad call, a surge of nerves, or one rough moment can quickly set off thoughts that pull you away from your game. The danger is not just that those thoughts show up. It is that you start going with them. Great competitors get better at noticing the first reaction without letting it take over the moment.

MORNING EDGE: THOUGHTS ARE NOT ORDERS

When something goes sideways today, your mind may react fast. It may offer fear, frustration, doubt, or a story about what this means. Let that be the first reaction, not the final word. Say, "Just because it shows up doesn't mean I go with it," and carry that into the day.

FLIP THE SWITCH: RETURN TO ZERO (RTZ)

When the hit comes—a mistake, a doubt, a surge of nerves, or a wave of frustration—relax your jaw, let your shoulders fall naturally, and soften your eyes. Take one Return to Zero breath: Inhale through your nose for four seconds and exhale through your mouth for six. As the exhale ends, silently say, "Back to zero." That means no past, no future, just now. RTZ helps you stop feeding the first reaction so you can get back to what actually matters.

CHAMPION'S WRAP: YOU STAYED WITH THE TASK

When a distracting thought or difficult feeling showed up today, did you go with it or stay with the task? That choice shapes your performance.

DAY 10: BRING YOUR CHAMPION SELF

"I'm building my self-talk. I'm building my confidence in that moment.
I'm telling myself that I am already the Olympic champion."
Gabby Thomas

Gabby builds belief in real time. She does not wait for the result to tell her who she is. She decides to bring her champion self into the moment before it begins and then competes from there. That is a principle you can use anywhere. Do not wait to feel like a champion. Enter as your champion self and let that decision lead.

MORNING EDGE: PRE-DECIDE WHO ENTERS

Before your first rep, decide who you are bringing into the day. Stand tall and feel your body rise into your champion self. See yourself stepping in like you belong at the highest level. Say, "This is a champion moment, and I'm meeting it like one." Let that decision shape your posture, your eyes, and your first move.

FLIP THE SWITCH: RE-ENTER AS YOUR CHAMPION SELF

When pressure rises and your confidence dips, go straight to Return to Zero. Inhale through your nose for four seconds and exhale through your mouth for six. As the exhale lands, lift your chin slightly, bring your eyes up, and let your posture come back to life. That physical shift puts you back into your champion self. Say, "Bring the champion," and step into the next rep with full commitment.

CHAMPION'S WRAP: EVIDENCE OF YOUR CHAMPION SELF

Replay one moment from today when you brought your champion self into it, and notice your body language, your focus, and the way you handled the situation as evidence of who you decided to be.

DAY 11: STAY IN YOUR LANE

"When I focus on my lane and my rhythm, that's when I run my best."
Gabby Thomas

Gabby is talking about staying connected to her own race. Pressure makes you look sideways. You start checking other people's pace, other people's progress, and other people's energy, and that's when your timing gets off. She runs best when she comes back to what she can feel, what she can trust, and what she can do right in front of her.

MORNING EDGE: FIND YOUR PACE

Start with one steady breath and picture yourself moving through the day smooth, composed, and under control. Say, "Run my race." Let that line shape how you walk in, warm up, and begin.

FLIP THE SWITCH: BACK TO MY RACE

When comparison, rushing, or outside noise starts pulling at you, take one Return to Zero breath. As the exhale lands, say, "Back to my race." Feel yourself settle, then go do the next thing with purpose.

CHAMPION'S WRAP: REPLAY YOUR BEST RHYTHM

Think back to one moment today when you stayed patient, trusted your pace, and competed your way. Then picture one moment that pulled you off and see yourself handling it better. Finish with the image of you staying in your own rhythm.

DAY 12: LOCK IN

"There's a lot going on in a race, but I don't let it shake me. I lock in."
Gabby Thomas

Gabby knows pressure does not erase focus. It pulls it in too many directions. The crowd, the clock, the other competitors, and the last mistake all try to grab a piece of your attention. Locking in means choosing what matters most and coming back to it fast. That is how composure holds under pressure.

MORNING EDGE: START FROM ZERO

Start your day with one Return to Zero breath. Inhale through your nose for four seconds and follow the breath up your spine. Exhale through your mouth for six seconds and follow it back down. Let your shoulders drop, your jaw soften, and your eyes settle. Silently say, "Back to zero," and begin the day from there.

FLIP THE SWITCH: SETTLE, THEN CUE

When nerves rise or the moment gets loud, take one Return to Zero breath and let your body get loose and athletic. Then use one simple cue word to direct your focus: "Smooth" when you rush, "Attack" when you hesitate, or "Flow" when you tighten up. Let the breath settle your system and the cue guide your next move.

CHAMPION'S WRAP: CATCH THE RETURN

Replay one moment today when your attention drifted and you brought it back on purpose. Notice what pulled you away, what helped you reset, and how your body responded once you locked back in. That return is the skill. Keep building it.

DAY 13: DO THE WORK ANYWAY

"Be consistent, show up."
Gabby Thomas

Most days won't feel special. You'll wake up flat, tired, or not quite sharp. That is the reality of high-level training. Great performers do not wait for the right feeling before they begin. They go to work, do what is required, and trust the results to follow. Stop waiting for motivation and start honoring the standard you set. Motivation is nice when it's there. The work still has to get done.

MORNING EDGE: STANDARDS BEAT FEELINGS

Some mornings you'll feel ready. Other mornings you won't. Either way, your standard stays the same. Look in the mirror and say, "I show up and do the work." Then prove it with your first action.

FLIP THE SWITCH: TAKE THE NEXT STEP

When motivation dips, take one Return to Zero breath and settle your body. Don't negotiate with how you feel. Take the next small step and start. Momentum follows action, not the other way around.

CHAMPION'S WRAP: YOU KEPT YOUR STANDARD

Before bed, name one moment you showed up when it would've been easier not to. That wasn't just discipline. That was your identity getting stronger.

DAY 14: BE YOURSELF UNDER PRESSURE

"Show up as yourself even if it makes others uncomfortable."
Gabby Thomas

Pressure makes people forget who they are. When the stakes rise, you may feel the urge to change your tone, overthink your decisions, or act "extra" to meet the moment. The best performers don't take that bait. They stay rooted in the same preparation and standards that got them there in the first place. Stop trying to be someone else just because the stakes are high. You don't need a miracle; you just need to be the person who did the work.

MORNING EDGE: STAY ALIGNED

Take one Return to Zero breath—four in, six out—and let outside expectations drop for a moment. Ask yourself, "Who does my dream require me to be today?" Then carry that answer into your first rep, meeting, or interaction. When you're aligned early, the rest of the day feels steadier.

FLIP THE SWITCH: DON'T ABANDON YOURSELF

When pressure tempts you to shrink, fake it, or get away from yourself, take one Return to Zero breath. Reclaim your posture, relax your jaw, and say, "This is my way." Let that bring you back to your game, your rhythm, and your standard. Pressure is not the time to become someone else.

CHAMPION'S WRAP: STAY TRUE TO YOUR WAY

Before bed, recall one moment today when you stayed true to how you compete best. Every time you do that, you build self-trust and strengthen the person your dream requires.

DAY 15: MENTAL TRAINING PARTNER

SIMONE BILES

"Seeing a sports psychologist helped me a lot in my mental training."
Simone Biles

Simone Biles grew up in Spring, Texas, and found gymnastics almost by accident. She was always moving, flipping off couches, climbing everything in sight, and playing with a kind of fearless energy that was hard to miss. Once gymnastics entered the picture, it fit her immediately. She had found the place where her gifts could fly.

By her teens, Simone was already changing the sport with her power, precision, and joy. She went on to become the most decorated gymnast in history, with thirty-seven Olympic and World Championship medals. But her edge was never just physical. She trained her mind deliberately, worked with a sports psychologist, and learned to build confidence, focus, and steadiness under pressure.

What makes Simone such a powerful training partner is the way she changed the conversation around strength. She showed that toughness is not pretending you are fine when you are not. It is being honest, staying connected to yourself, and knowing when to push and when to pause. That kind of courage takes real self-trust.

Simone also built her greatness through relentless work. In the four years leading up to the 2016 Olympics, she trained thirty-two hours a week, six days a week, including holidays and birthdays. Talent gave her a start, but discipline and mental training turned it into something historic. This week, Simone is your mental training partner. She will show you how to value your mind as much as your body and compete from a place of strength that starts within.

DAY 16: LOOK FEAR IN THE EYE

"At the end of the day, we're human too. We get scared."
Simone Biles

Fear shows up when something matters. Simone has felt it before big moments, worked through it, and competed anyway. She has also respected it when it signaled that awareness had to come before action. Courage is not the absence of fear. It is the decision to face it and take the next right step with control.

MORNING EDGE: WALK THROUGH IT

Before your first rep, think of one thing that makes you hesitate. Take a steady breath in through your nose and out through your mouth, then picture fear standing in the doorway. Now see yourself stepping through it. Each time you move toward what scares you, you loosen its grip.

FLIP THE SWITCH: STEADY, THEN CHOOSE

When fear or doubt shows up, take one Return to Zero breath and feel your feet on the ground. Tell yourself, "Choose the response," then do the next right thing on purpose.

CHAMPION'S WRAP: WIN THE CHOICE POINT

At the end of the day, name one moment when fear showed up and you stayed with the moment instead of pulling away. That is courage in action.

DAY 17: BE THE BEST YOU WHEN IT COUNTS

"Be the best me."

Simone Biles

Simone's edge wasn't becoming someone new when pressure hit. It was staying true to who she already was. Pressure doesn't ask you to upgrade your identity. It asks you to trust it. When performers struggle, it's often because they abandon their own game and start forcing something else. Pressure is an invitation to trust your training. You don't need to be better than you are; you just need to be exactly who you are.

MORNING EDGE: THE CHAMPION STANDARD

Before you start your day, look in the mirror and remind yourself of the champion standard. Tell yourself, "A champion executes the plan." You are not trying to be someone new today. You are choosing to honor your training.

FLIP THE SWITCH: CHAMPION RESPONSE

When you feel yourself pressing, reset and clear the noise. Tell yourself, "Champion standard," then shift your gaze to the next technical task. A champion does not dwell. A champion settles in and executes.

CHAMPION'S WRAP: EVIDENCE OF THE STANDARD

Before bed, identify one moment today when you held the champion standard under pressure. Acknowledge that you did not need a miracle. You needed your training. That is how you build proof that your best is already enough.

DAY 18: FIND YOUR FEEL

"You don't have to be serious all the time to do a good job."

Simone Biles

Simone started gymnastics because she loved the feeling of it. There was joy in the movement, freedom in the air, and a kind of play that brought out her best. Tension is the thief of talent. When your body tightens, your timing usually goes with it. Loosen up and let your training show.

MORNING EDGE: FIND THE FEEL

Before your warm-up, lock in the physical sensation of a fast, loose rep. If you're tight, you're slow. Finding that feeling early isn't a bonus; it's a prerequisite for high-speed execution.

FLIP THE SWITCH: LOOSEN FIRST

When you notice yourself pressing or trying too hard, check your body. Is your jaw tight? Are your shoulders creeping up? Take one Return to Zero breath and let the exhale soften you. Come back to feel and tell yourself, "Loose first, then fast." Timing and confidence come back when tension lets go.

CHAMPION'S WRAP: YOU FOUND IT AGAIN

Recall one rep today where the movement felt effortless. That was not a fluke. It came from a loose body and a quiet mind. Acknowledge that connection so you can find it again tomorrow.

DAY 19: CATCH THE SIGNAL EARLY

"I had no idea where I was in the air. I could've hurt myself."
Simone Biles

What happened to Simone at the Tokyo Olympics showed something every athlete, even the best in the world, has to stay on top of. In the middle of competition, her mind and body stopped syncing, and she lost her sense of where she was in the air. That moment highlighted the importance of early signals. Breathing changes, timing slips, and feel disappears before control is lost. Awareness is your early-warning system. Catch the tightness, the rushing, or the drift in focus before it turns into a mistake.

MORNING EDGE: NOTICE FIRST

Start the day by paying attention to your body. How is your breathing? Where are you holding tension? Are you moving smoothly or rushing? When something feels off, take one Return to Zero breath—four in, six out—and recalibrate before you continue. Awareness early keeps problems small.

FLIP THE SWITCH: RESET RIGHT AWAY

When you feel yourself forcing, rushing, or losing feel, stop the spiral early. Take a sharp exhale, relax your jaw, and drop your shoulders. Take one Return to Zero breath and bring your eyes back to the task in front of you. Say, "Reset now." The sooner you reset, the faster control returns.

CHAMPION'S WRAP: YOU CAUGHT IT

Before bed, think of one moment today when you noticed a signal and adjusted instead of pushing through. That moment matters. Each time you catch it early, you build trust between your mind and your body.

DAY 20: PROTECT YOUR EDGE

"I had to put myself first. That's never been done before, and it took strength."
Simone Biles

Commitment isn't just about doing more. It's about knowing what helps you perform and what wears you down. Simone showed that putting yourself first is part of the job when it protects your focus, your energy, and your health. Energy management is a competitive skill. You're protecting your ability to perform.

MORNING EDGE: PROTECT YOUR ENERGY

Before the day starts, decide what you're not going to give your energy to. It might be staying up too late, scrolling too long, or saying yes when you should say no. Make one clear choice to protect your focus today. The way you manage your energy early determines how sharp you are when it matters.

FLIP THE SWITCH: DEFEND YOUR FOCUS

When distraction pulls at you, take one Return to Zero breath. Roll your shoulders back, set your gaze forward, and let the exhale draw a clean boundary around your attention. Tell yourself, "Gold focus." That is your standard, so protect it.

CHAMPION'S WRAP: YOU PROTECTED IT

Before bed, take a few cycles of the Return to Zero breath. As you exhale, let the day settle and appreciate one moment when you protected your focus or energy. That's how you keep your fire strong for tomorrow.

DAY 21: TELL THE TRUTH, STAY STRONG

"It's okay to not be okay. What matters is what you do next."
Simone Biles

Simone changed how toughness is understood. She showed that pretending everything is fine wears you down, while honesty helps you reset and respond with purpose. Real strength is not hiding what's going on inside. It is recognizing it early and doing something useful with it. When you tell yourself the truth, you put yourself back in command.

MORNING EDGE: NAME WHAT YOU NEED

Start today with one honest question: What do I need right now—focus, recovery, or support? Name it, then act on it. Telling yourself the truth does not weaken you. It steadies you and helps you handle what is in front of you.

FLIP THE SWITCH: RESPOND HONESTLY

When nerves, doubt, or frustration show up, do not fight them or try to cover them up. Blow out the tension with one sharp exhale, then reclaim your posture and refocus your eyes on the task at hand. Take one Return to Zero breath and say, "I choose my next move." Honesty does not take you out of the moment. It puts you back in command.

CHAMPION'S WRAP: HUMAN, STILL STRONG

Before bed, recall one moment today when you told yourself the truth under pressure and responded with purpose. That is real strength. If you slipped, say, "How human of me. Still a champion," then reset. Honest moments like that build the kind of strength you can trust.

DAY 22: MENTAL TRAINING PARTNER

MIKAELA SHIFFRIN

"A lot of athletes have said before that pressure is a privilege, and it truly is, to be in the position that I come to the Olympics."
Mikaela Shiffrin

Mikaela Shiffrin learned early that skiing tells the truth fast. Growing up between Colorado and New England, she trained in conditions where even small mistakes showed up right away. At Burke Mountain Academy, the work was simple, demanding, and relentless. She kept coming back to the basics until they became part of her.

That foundation helped turn her into the most successful alpine skier in history. With more than one hundred World Cup wins, three Olympic gold medals, and multiple world titles, Shiffrin has built a career on precision and repeatability. What stands out most is not just what she has won. It is how faithfully she prepares. She builds confidence through daily work, not through wishful thinking.

When the pressure rises, Shiffrin comes back to what is hers. She returns to her breathing, her balance, and the line in front of her. While others rush or force the run, she stays patient and lets the fundamentals carry the day. That is why her skiing looks so clean when the stakes get high.

That mindset resurfaced at the 2026 Winter Olympics. After winning slalom gold, she said, "It just felt like ski racing." On the biggest stage in sport, she brought the moment back to the job. This week, Shiffrin is your mental training partner. She will show you how to stay steady, trust your fundamentals, and let confidence meet you in the middle of the run.

DAY 23: PRESSURE MEANS YOU'RE ALIVE

"I'm not really seeing pressure as a negative."

Mikaela Shiffrin

Nerves are not a sign that something is wrong. They are a sign that your body is getting ready to go. Pressure is raw energy waiting for a direction. Stop trying to calm down and use that extra alertness to sharpen your execution. This is your internal engine revving at the start gate.

MORNING EDGE: BREATHE WITH IT

Before your first rep, notice any nervous energy in your body. Don't try to calm it down or push it away. Take one steady breath and acknowledge, "My body is getting ready to compete." Let the energy stay and move with it.

FLIP THE SWITCH: DIRECT THE ENERGY

When the moment gets bigger and your nerves rise, don't rush or tighten up. Take one Return to Zero breath—four seconds in, six out—and bring your attention back to the task in front of you. Let the energy sharpen your posture, your focus, and your next move.

CHAMPION'S WRAP: BIG-GAME PROOF

At the end of the day, recall one specific moment when you felt the pressure and stayed aggressive anyway. Acknowledge that you handled the nerves and still performed well. That is how you build proof that you are a big-game performer.

DAY 24: TRUST YOUR RUN

"You can't ever make the perfect run, but you can make the best run."
Mikaela Shiffrin

Trying to avoid mistakes pulls athletes out of rhythm. The body tightens, timing slips, and everything starts to feel forced. The best performances come from trusting the work and committing to the line that's there, not the one you wish for. When training leads, movement stays free and decisions stay simple.

MORNING EDGE: GET OUT OF THE WAY

Before you begin, soften your jaw and lower your shoulders. Tension is often a sign that you are overthinking the mechanics. Take a breath and remind yourself, "The skill is in the muscle." Your job is not to create greatness today. It is to get out of the way and let your training show up.

FLIP THE SWITCH: CONVICTION OVER CAUTION

When you start pressing or overthinking, blow out the junk with a sharp exhale—the tightness, the urgency, and the need to get everything right. Take one Return to Zero breath. As you inhale, imagine the breath rising up your spine; as you exhale, feel it settle you into rhythm. Then give yourself a clear cue: "Attack the line." Then go.

CHAMPION'S WRAP: TRUST IN ACTION

Recall one moment today when you trusted your instincts and stayed out of your own way. That was you building trust in your training and in yourself. You do not have to overthink your way into great performance.

DAY 25: DROP THE WEIGHT

"People are allowed to have expectations of me. But I'm allowed to not let that control me."
Mikaela Shiffrin

Carrying other people's expectations is like racing in a twenty-pound weighted vest. It is extra weight that slows you down and drains your tank. Stop chasing approval and start meeting your own standard. When you drop the crowd's expectations, your movement gets freer and your focus gets fierce.

MORNING EDGE: LEAVE IT OUTSIDE THE GATE

Decide what weight you are not carrying today, whether that is the pressure to prove something right now, fear of disappointing someone, or worry about how you look. Ground your feet, lift your posture, and leave that weight outside the gate. Your only job is to attack the next move with all of your available energy.

FLIP THE SWITCH: EXECUTE THE NEXT MOVE

When you feel the vest tightening and the need to prove something to someone else, take one Return to Zero breath and drop the load. Say, "Execute the next move," and answer the pressure with technical precision. Momentum is built by doing, not by seeking validation.

CHAMPION'S WRAP: MOVE LIGHT

Name one moment today when you stopped performing for other people and got back to your own race. That is what lighter looks like, and that is where your best power lives. Let go of any leftover pressure, self-judgment, or outside expectations tonight so your body can recover and your mind can move freely tomorrow.

DAY 26: ADAPT AND ADVANCE

"Things you don't expect come up, and you have to adapt. You can't let it throw you off."
Mikaela Shiffrin

Every athlete runs into things they didn't plan for. A rough start, a bad break, a change in conditions can show up at any time. What matters is how quickly you steady yourself and respond. Adaptation is not backing off or waiting it out. It is staying composed, adjusting on purpose, and continuing to move forward.

MORNING EDGE: OWN THE UNEXPECTED

Something will go sideways today—expect it. When it does, blow out the junk with a sharp exhale, reset your posture, and say, "I adjust and advance." Being ready to pivot keeps you loose, aware, and able to make the most of whatever the day brings. Flexibility is a performance skill.

FLIP THE SWITCH: STEADY IN THE SHIFT

When frustration or resistance builds, take one Return to Zero breath. Let the inhale lift your presence; let the exhale settle your system. Then move with clear intention—one decision, one rep, one step.

CHAMPION'S WRAP: CONTROL IN ACTION

Before bed, recall one moment today when you adjusted instead of tightening up or forcing the issue. That's true self-control—meeting change with composure and direction. That's how a champion advances.

DAY 27: MAKE THE HARD DAYS COUNT

"Every day is an opportunity to work, to improve. Some days it's harder, but that's what makes it matter."
Mikaela Shiffrin

Not every day feels smooth. Some reps drag, some drills miss, and some sessions test your patience. That's part of the craft. The hard days build the belief that lasts. Champions don't need the feeling—they need the follow-through.

MORNING EDGE: MAKE HARD USEFUL

You're not training to feel good; you're training to get better. When the work feels heavy, take one Return to Zero breath and reset your focus. Adjust the plan, not the purpose. Say, "I stay the course." Hard moments are reps too.

FLIP THE SWITCH: STAY IN THE WORK

When frustration spikes, blow out the junk with a sharp exhale and loosen your shoulders. Take one Return to Zero breath and reconnect to your next action. Staying in the work keeps you moving—and movement builds confidence.

CHAMPION'S WRAP: BANK THE DAY

Before bed, recall one moment when you stayed with the work when it would've been easier to check out. That's how greatness is built—one hard day at a time.

DAY 28: BIGGER THAN THE SCOREBOARD

"Skiing is what I do. It's not who I am."
Mikaela Shiffrin

Shiffrin understands a truth most athletes never learn: Outcomes describe performance, not identity. Times, rankings, and medals tell part of the story, but never the whole one. When your sense of self is larger than the results, pressure loses its leverage. You perform freely instead of fearfully.

MORNING EDGE: LEAD WITH IDENTITY

As you enter the moment, take one Return to Zero breath and step into your champion self. Anchor in this truth: "Who I am is bigger than this moment." When identity leads, performance follows.

FLIP THE SWITCH: RETURN TO CORE

When you catch yourself chasing validation, take one Return to Zero breath. As you exhale, place a hand lightly on your chest to steady yourself and say, "Back to who I am." That's your cue to come back to who you are, not what others expect.

CHAMPION'S WRAP: TURN OFF THE SCOREBOARD

Identify one moment today when you acted like the person your dream requires, regardless of the score. Turn off the scoreboard and shift from compete mode into chill mode. That's how you recover and get ready to do it again tomorrow.

DAY 29: PATIENCE WINS UNDER PRESSURE

"The most important thing I've learned? Be patient with the process. It's not always going to be linear."
Mikaela Shiffrin

Progress doesn't climb in straight lines. Some days feel like breakthroughs; others feel like setbacks. What separates champions is their ability to stay calm in the gaps—the stretches where results are slow and doubt gets loud. Patience isn't passive. It's steady, disciplined control while the work takes root.

MORNING EDGE: PRACTICE PATIENCE

Write "RTZ" (Return to Zero) somewhere you'll see it—your water bottle, a piece of equipment, or a small sticky note at your desk. Each time your eyes land on it, take a quiet Return to Zero breath and reset your focus. Patience keeps you present so the work can build.

FLIP THE SWITCH: RESET INSTEAD OF REACT

When frustration spikes, take one Return to Zero breath. Lift your posture and steady your breathing. Let the exhale bring you back into the moment. Tell yourself, "One rep at a time," and move forward without rushing.

CHAMPION'S WRAP: QUIET PROGRESS

End the day by recalling one moment you stayed steady when it would've been easy to hurry or tighten up. That's patience in motion, and it builds more than you realize.

DAY 30: RESET FOR LIFTOFF

"When you have two races in a row, it's really important to keep your mind smooth between runs."
Mikaela Shiffrin

Champions don't stay revved between efforts. They reset with intent so they're ready to launch again. Shiffrin knows the moments between runs are part of the performance. Settle first, then lift off. That's how you stay sharp when it matters most.

MORNING EDGE: SMOOTH LAUNCH

Before your first rep, take a long, steady breath and let your body settle. Feel your posture lift and your mind come online. Ensure a smooth launch into the day so each rep begins with control rather than tension.

FLIP THE SWITCH: RTZ LIFTOFF

When you feel tight or flat, take one Return to Zero breath. Inhale through your nose for four seconds, feeling energy rise like a rocket fueling. Exhale through your mouth for six seconds, letting tension release as your system settles back into control. This is the gear you want before your next run.

CHAMPION'S WRAP: READY FOR THE NEXT RUN

Take one Return to Zero breath before bed and allow the day to settle. Confidence doesn't come from perfect runs. It comes from knowing you can reset and relaunch when it counts. Tomorrow, lift off again.

DAY 31: THE POWER OF RECOVERY

"One thing I've learned from winning an Olympic medal is that it's really exhausting."
Mikaela Shiffrin

Peak performers aren't just worn out from the work. They get worn out from carrying the focus, intensity, and pressure that come with it. Recovery isn't separate from training; it's part of the craft. It's how your mind resets, your emotions settle, and your body absorbs everything you've asked of it. Rest isn't weakness. It's what keeps your edge sharp.

MORNING EDGE: RESPECT THE LOAD

Take one Return to Zero breath and let the exhale feel like setting down the load you've carried all month. Remind yourself, "How human of me . . . and I am still a champion." Fatigue isn't failure. It's proof you've been in it, and a reminder to treat yourself like a teammate, not a problem.

FLIP THE SWITCH: CHOOSE REAL RECOVERY

When you catch yourself numbing out or drifting into mindless distraction, pause for one Return to Zero breath. As you exhale, place a hand lightly on your chest and say, "Back to zero." Then choose one real reset: stretch for two minutes, step outside, drink a glass of water, or get to bed a little earlier. Recovery isn't checking out. It's choosing what actually restores you.

CHAMPION'S WRAP: PARK THE DAY

Let the day be done. Anything worth carrying forward will still be there tomorrow. Take a few slow breaths and let your body know the work is over. Nothing more is required tonight. Great recovery begins when you stop trying to squeeze one more thing out of yourself.

CHAMPION'S TAKEAWAYS: OLYMPIA

Olympia was never about waiting for someday. It was about showing up today. This month asked you to train your mind the way champions always have—through intention, repetition, and response. You visualized your best, settled yourself when things went sideways, and came back to what you could control again and again. Over time, those moments built composure, confidence, and self-trust.

The Return to Zero breath became your anchor. It helped you clear the noise, come back into your body, and return to the present moment with purpose. It reminded you that calm is not weakness. It is control, and it is a reset you can trust when pressure shows up.

As you step off the track, reflect:

- What progress did I make toward my dream through how I showed up each day?
- What response or habit feels more automatic under pressure now?
- What do I trust more about myself than I did a month ago?

That medal is not about the result. It is evidence of how you showed up, what you practiced, and who you are becoming. Bring that composure and self-trust with you into the next arena.

CHAPTER 2

FEBRUARY: WIMBLEDON

"The mental part is the hardest part. Everybody can hit great shots when they're feeling good, but there are days when you're not feeling good and you have to rely on your mental toughness."

Rafael Nadal

Wimbledon is where style meets stress. First played in 1877 at the All-England Club, it is the oldest tournament in the sport and still feels like it. The grass is fast, the bounce stays low, and the silence around Centre Court makes every thought feel louder. There is history in the air, but also nowhere to hide.

That is why Wimbledon is such a pure test of the mental game. Anyone can play freely when timing feels right and the ball is coming clean. The real question is what happens when the skid comes early, the bounce stays low, and the match turns on you. Grass rewards clear minds and punishes tension.

The champions who mastered this place did it with composure. Federer controlled tempo and made pressure look light. Venus brought grace and staying power. Serena turned adversity into force. Djokovic stayed relentless, point after point, until the match bent his way. Different styles, same truth. The mind often decides what the racket can do.

This chapter is about building that kind of poise. Each day gives you three mental reps to help you settle faster, reset cleaner, and compete with more control when the moment speeds up. Your Centre Court is today. Champion the day—or lose it.

DAY 32: MENTAL TRAINING PARTNER

ROGER FEDERER

"I fear no one, but respect everyone."
Roger Federer

Roger Federer did not just win. He changed what winning could look like. Across two decades, he won twenty majors, including a record eight at Wimbledon, and played with a kind of calm that made the biggest moments look smaller than they were. The brilliance was obvious. The discipline behind it was just as real.

As a junior, Federer could run hot. He smashed rackets, lost his cool, and let emotion pull him off his game. The turning point came when he decided composure was a skill he could train. He learned how to settle his breathing, steady his eyes, and carry himself in a way that kept his mind from drifting and his game from unraveling.

On Centre Court, that work showed up everywhere. His footwork stayed light, his tempo stayed smooth, and his decisions arrived right on time. He trusted between-point routines, simple cues, and a clear plan for the next ball. Even when the match got tight, he stayed with his rhythm and trusted that his chance would come.

That is what made Federer so hard to shake and so hard to outlast. He protected his body, respected recovery, and stayed connected to the craft long after others had faded. This week, Federer is your mental training partner. He will show you how to train composure, trust your routines, and compete with calm on the biggest stage.

DAY 33: DANGEROUS WHEN DOWN

"I always believed I could come back."

Roger Federer

A momentum shift is not the end of your edge. It is the moment that reveals who can steady the storm and who starts feeding it. The best competitors do not get rattled when things turn. They get sharper, calmer, and more intentional. When you settle yourself and take command of the next moment, you become dangerous again.

MORNING EDGE: TRAIN THE RESET

Visualize a moment today when you lose rhythm, fall behind, or get hit with adversity. Take one Return to Zero breath—four in, six out—and flush the frustration before it spreads. Remind yourself, "I reset faster than anyone else."

FLIP THE SWITCH: PROJECT PRESENCE

When the score is not going your way, take one Return to Zero breath and say, "Back to zero." Show calm, sharp body language that tells your opponent you are still right here. Stop playing the score and start owning the next move.

CHAMPION'S WRAP: ALWAYS A THREAT

Recall one moment today when things slipped and you chose composure over frustration. That is what keeps pressure on the other side. Say this once before bed: "Up, down, or level, I am always a threat."

DAY 34: BELIEVE FIRST

"A player who wins is a player who thinks he can."
Roger Federer

Confidence is not a gift that drops out of the sky on your lucky days. It is a choice you make before the first rep. It is the quiet, internal decision to trust your hands, your eyes, and your training before the scoreboard gives you a reason to. When you carry that certainty with you, pressure does not change you. You change the pressure.

MORNING EDGE: STEP INTO YOUR POWER

Before you start, take one Return to Zero breath and decide that you own the space you are stepping into. Do not wait for outside signs that you are ready. Say to yourself, "I set the tone today."

FLIP THE SWITCH: RECLAIM THE LEAD

When you feel a flicker of doubt, do not let it settle in. Take one Return to Zero breath, reset your posture, and move like someone who trusts their training. Remind yourself, "I am still the threat here," and attack the next move with total intent.

CHAMPION'S WRAP: BANK THE BELIEF

Recall one moment today when you chose to trust yourself when it would have been easier to doubt. That is how belief gets built. Let the day settle now, knowing your confidence grows every time you choose it on purpose.

DAY 35: LONG VIEW, SHORT FOCUS

"You have to believe in the long-term plan you have, but you need the short-term goals to motivate and inspire you."
Roger Federer

Federer mastered the art of holding a big vision without letting it pull him out of the moment. He did not waste energy chasing the trophy in the middle of the match. He trusted the plan and gave his full attention to the next ball. When you trust your long-term path, you are free to put all your power into the present moment.

MORNING EDGE: OWN THE DETAIL

Acknowledge the big-picture goal, then set it down. Choose one specific, controllable detail you can own today, whether it is a technical cue, a recovery habit, or a mindset shift. Remind yourself, "The plan is set. Now I handle today."

FLIP THE SWITCH: HANDLE THE NOW

When your mind starts racing ahead to the result, take one Return to Zero breath and come back to the present. Ask yourself, "What is the one detail right now?" Then handle it with full attention and elite care. Big wins are built by small moments handled well.

CHAMPION'S WRAP: CHECK THE DETAIL

Look back at the detail you chose this morning. If you showed up for it, you moved the plan forward, regardless of how noisy the day felt. Let the bigger outcome go tonight and rest knowing you handled what was yours to handle.

DAY 36: CONTROLLED FIRE

"I always had the fire in me. But I learned to control it with ice."
Roger Federer

Federer's edge came from mastering his emotions. The fire gave him intensity. The ice gave him precision. Without control, fire burns you. With it, fire powers you. Champions know how to compete with heat in their heart and calm in their mind.

MORNING EDGE: FIRE, THEN ICE

Before practice, choose the heat you want to bring and the calm you want to carry. Fire is your aggression, intent, and competitive edge. Ice is your tempo, patience, and control. Attack the work, but do not rush it. That is controlled fire.

FLIP THE SWITCH: LOCK THE ICE

When frustration spikes, do not try to extinguish the heat. Channel it into your next move. Take one Return to Zero breath, lock in on your technical cue, and let the fire power the effort while the ice dictates the precision.

CHAMPION'S WRAP: COOL THE ENGINE

Identify one moment today when you felt the heat but stayed cool through the finish. That balance between intensity and composure is how high-level performers stay sharp without burning out. Turn the burners off tonight and let your system recover for tomorrow.

DAY 37: LOVE THE GAME

"When you do something best in life, you don't really want to give that up—and for me it's tennis."
Roger Federer

Federer stayed great not just because he was disciplined, but because he never lost his love for the game. He could handle the travel, repetition, pressure, and grind because something deeper kept drawing him back. Love of the game is not soft. It is what keeps your energy alive when motivation dips. It is what makes the work feel worth it again.

MORNING EDGE: FIND THE FEELING

Before practice, take a moment to remember what you love about your game. Maybe it is the rhythm, the challenge, the creativity, the freedom, or the feeling of being fully locked in. Do not just train today. Reconnect with what made you want this in the first place.

FLIP THE SWITCH: BACK TO THE LOVE

When the grind starts feeling heavy, pause and come back to the part of the game you actually enjoy. Feel the movement, the timing, the competition, or the chance to solve problems in real time. The more you reconnect to the game itself, the lighter the work feels.

CHAMPION'S WRAP: PROTECT THE SPARK

Recall one moment today when you felt real enjoyment, even for a few seconds. That feeling matters more than people think. Protect it, because love of the game is part of what keeps greatness going.

DAY 38: HARD DAYS BUILD STRONGER DAYS

"I always believe if you're stuck in a hole and maybe things aren't going well, you will come out stronger. Everything in life is this way."
Roger Federer

Every athlete hits stretches when the rhythm disappears and the work feels heavy. Federer did not panic in those ruts. He trusted that the resistance was doing something for him, not to him. The belief that *this is working for me* is what keeps a bad day from turning into a bad month. When you stop fighting the struggle and start using it, you get harder to shake.

MORNING EDGE: TRUST THE FRICTION

Acknowledge that today might be a grind, and decide you are okay with that. Take a Return to Zero breath and commit to working through the resistance instead of avoiding it. Remind yourself, "The struggle is the training."

FLIP THE SWITCH: SHORTEN THE FOCUS

When frustration hits and you feel stuck, take a Return to Zero breath and cut the panic. Stop trying to solve everything at once and lock in on one small technical task with total precision. Stability is built by winning the next sixty seconds, not by trying to fix the whole season in one rep.

CHAMPION'S WRAP: CLAIM THE GRIT

Identify one moment today when you stayed engaged even though the feel was not there. That is the kind of rep that strengthens your foundation, whether it looked impressive or not. Put the struggle down for the night so you can recover and bring that same grit back tomorrow.

DAY 39: MENTAL TRAINING PARTNER
VENUS WILLIAMS

"Some people say I have attitude. Maybe I do. You have to believe in yourself when no one else does. That's what makes you a winner."
Venus Williams

Venus Williams did not just join women's tennis; she changed it. She changed the look, the feel, and the force of it. She turned pro at fourteen, reached a Grand Slam final at seventeen, and went on to win five Wimbledon titles. Across more than three decades on tour, she became one of the clearest examples of power, poise, and staying power in all of sport.

Her path demanded real adjustment. Injuries tested her body, and Sjögren's syndrome challenged her energy, recovery, and daily rhythm. Venus learned how to train smart, recover well, and respect what her body needed without letting any of it shrink who she was. That is what toughness looks like when it has to keep evolving.

What stood out in competition was the way she carried herself. Between points, she stayed composed, moved with purpose, and kept her attention on the match instead of the noise around it. When tension rose, she came back to simple cues, clear decisions, and the next ball. Her belief showed up in her presence, her discipline, and the way she held her line.

That is what gave Venus such lasting power. She built her career on structure, recovery, and an inner standard that did not depend on circumstances. This week, Venus is your mental training partner. She will show you how to trust yourself, stay steady under pressure, and keep moving forward with strength and class.

DAY 40: STAY ON YOUR LINE

"I don't focus on what I'm up against. I focus on my goals and I try to ignore the rest."
Venus Williams

Venus is talking about disciplined attention. She does not waste energy on opponents, noise, or anything that pulls her off her path. The more locked in you are on what you are building, the less distracted and reactive you become. Stay on your line and let other people spend time on theirs.

MORNING EDGE: PICK THE LINE

Take one Return to Zero breath and picture a straight line from where you are to where you want to go today. Write down one goal that matters and one action that proves it. Say, "This is my line," and start there.

FLIP THE SWITCH: RETURN TO THE PATH

When your mind drifts to someone else, outside noise, or things you cannot control, take one Return to Zero breath. Picture yourself stepping back onto your line. Say, "Back to my path," and put your full attention on the next rep, play, or decision.

CHAMPION'S WRAP: REPLAY YOUR BEST FOCUS

Take a quiet minute and replay one moment today when your attention stayed exactly where it needed to be. See what you saw, feel how steady you were, and notice how clean your mind felt in that moment. End by picturing yourself bringing that same focus into tomorrow.

DAY 41: STAND ON YOUR WORK

"In my mind, I'm always the best. If I walk out on the court and I think the next person is better, I've already lost."
Venus Williams

Venus is not saying to pretend you are better than everyone. She is saying you cannot compete from an inferior mindset. The match starts to slip the moment you mentally place the other person above you. The problem is not a lack of respect for the opponent. The problem is surrendering before the action even begins.

MORNING EDGE: SEE YOURSELF STANDING TALL

Take one Return to Zero breath and picture yourself stepping into the arena calm, tall, and ready. See yourself looking steady, moving with purpose, and meeting the moment without shrinking. Then say, "I trust what I've built," and carry that feeling into your first rep.

FLIP THE SWITCH: RECLAIM THE EDGE

When comparison or doubt shows up, do not argue with it. Take one Return to Zero breath and quickly replay three seconds of your best self competing with strength, rhythm, and presence. Then say, "Back to my game," and attack the next rep with clear intent.

CHAMPION'S WRAP: BUILD THE HIGHLIGHT REEL

Replay one moment from today when you trusted your work and competed with freedom. See it again in your mind like a highlight clip, with your body language, tempo, and mindset exactly how you want them. The more clearly you remember your best moments, the easier they are to return to tomorrow.

DAY 42: NO FINISH LINE FOR EXCELLENCE

"There are no limits for excellence. It's all about what's in your head and how much you're able to put into it."

Venus Williams

Venus never saw excellence as a destination. She treated it as a standard that had to be rebuilt daily. Champions don't wait to feel inspired. They show up with clarity, precision, and discipline. Motivation doesn't start the process—action does. Excellence belongs to those who maintain their standards regardless of mood, comfort, or circumstance.

MORNING EDGE: SET THE BAR

Name one standard that defines how you do things at your best—effort, focus, body language, or preparation. Say, "This is how I do things." Then decide exactly what that standard looks like in action for today.

FLIP THE SWITCH: DON'T LOWER IT

When fatigue or frustration shows up, don't negotiate. Narrow your focus and deliver one rep that matches your standard. Excellence isn't somewhere else—it's expressed right here.

CHAMPION'S WRAP: SAME STANDARD TOMORROW

Before bed, recall one moment today when you honored your standard—even with how you were feeling and regardless of what others were doing. That's excellence in motion. Tomorrow, you do it again.

DAY 43: BACK TO WORK

"When you're a professional athlete, you're always going to have critics. You can't worry about them. All you can do is get better."
Venus Williams

Venus is not trying to silence critics or prove them wrong. She knows they come with the territory. The mistake is thinking they need your attention at all. Every second spent reacting is a second taken from your development. The only response that matters is getting better.

MORNING EDGE: PICK THE WORK

Take one Return to Zero breath and bring to mind one outside voice that has been pulling at you. See it, hear it, and then let it pass without grabbing it. Now choose one part of your game that needs to improve and picture yourself working on it with focus and intent. Say, "This is where my energy goes," and start there.

FLIP THE SWITCH: BACK TO WORK

When criticism, doubt, or noise shows up, don't argue with it and don't analyze it. Take one Return to Zero breath and say, "Back to work." Then immediately put your attention into your next rep with purpose and clean execution.

CHAMPION'S WRAP: BUILD, DON'T REACT

Take a quiet minute and replay one moment today when you chose improvement over reaction. See yourself staying with your craft while the noise stayed outside. The more you see yourself building instead of reacting, the more automatic it becomes.

DAY 44: KEEP BELIEVING

"My parents told us that we could achieve anything. And I believed it. I still do."
Venus Williams

Venus is talking about a belief she chose to keep. As the stakes rose and the pressure grew, her belief stayed strong. A lot of people begin with big belief, then let results, opinions, and hard moments chip away at it. Venus kept hers. She carried it forward and kept building on it.

MORNING EDGE: SET THE STANDARD

Take one Return to Zero breath and bring to mind a goal that matters to you. Picture yourself moving toward it with strength, purpose, and conviction. Say, "I still believe," and take one clear step that matches it.

FLIP THE SWITCH: STAY WITH IT

When your mind gets shaky, take one Return to Zero breath and come back to your standard. Say, "My belief stays with me," and move into your next rep with clear intent. Let your preparation and presence carry the moment.

CHAMPION'S WRAP: SEE IT IN ACTION

Take a quiet minute and replay one moment today when you carried yourself with belief. See your posture, your eyes, your energy, and your choices. Let that image sink in and strengthen the version of you that you are becoming.

DAY 45: PLAY FREE ANYWAY

"When you play unhealthy, it's in your mind too. You get stuck in your mind. So it was nice to be freer."

Venus Williams

Venus understood that when your body feels off, the battle can move quickly into your mind. You get more careful, more controlling, and more aware of every little thing. That tightness can hurt performance as much as the physical issue itself. Her breakthrough was trusting what was still there and playing with more freedom. On imperfect days, a freer mind often gives you your best chance.

MORNING EDGE: TRUST WHAT'S THERE

Take one Return to Zero breath and let your shoulders soften. Picture yourself moving with rhythm, timing, and flow, even if everything does not feel perfect. Say, "I can still play free," and step into the day with that feeling.

FLIP THE SWITCH: FREE UP THE MIND

When tension or overthinking shows up, take one Return to Zero breath. Unclench your jaw, loosen your hands, and let your exhale slow you down. Say, "Free body, free mind," and move into the next rep with rhythm.

CHAMPION'S WRAP: REPLAY THE FREEDOM

Take a quiet minute and replay one moment today when you moved freely instead of carefully. See your body loosen, your mind clear, and your rhythm return. Save that feeling and carry it into tomorrow.

DAY 46: MENTAL TRAINING PARTNER
SERENA WILLIAMS

"I always believe I can beat the best, achieve the best.
I always see myself in the top position."
Serena Williams

Serena Williams did not just dominate tennis. She changed what dominance looked like. She won twenty-three Grand Slam singles titles, four Olympic gold medals, and spent 319 weeks as world number one. For two decades, the sport had to measure itself against her.

Her rise started in Compton, where she chased tennis balls, big dreams, and her sister Venus across cracked courts. Instead of getting lost in comparison, Serena used it as fuel. She saw Venus's success as proof that greatness was possible and kept building her own game, her own belief, and her own identity. That fearless confidence became one of her greatest weapons.

Serena's career tested that belief again and again. She fought through injuries, setbacks, and life-threatening complications, then came back and won more majors. Her power was obvious, but her deeper edge was her way of showing up with hunger, pride, and total conviction. She kept training, kept believing, and kept coming.

That is what made Serena so hard to stop. Her presence never shrank, her fire never left, and her standards stayed high no matter what she was facing. This week, Serena is your mental training partner. She will show you how to believe big, compete free under pressure, and meet setbacks with strength, speed, and swagger.

DAY 47: KEEP THE GAME IN ITS PLACE

"Tennis is just a game. Family is forever."
Serena Williams

Serena is talking about perspective. Tennis meant everything to her, but it was never everything about her. Family gave her a foundation that no result could shake. That is why she could compete so freely. When the game is not your whole identity, pressure has less power over you.

MORNING EDGE: STAY GROUNDED

Take one Return to Zero breath and feel your feet under you. Remind yourself that you are more than your performance today. Say, "I'm grounded, and I'm free to compete," and carry that into your first rep.

FLIP THE SWITCH: PUT IT IN PERSPECTIVE

When pressure builds, take one Return to Zero breath and zoom out. Picture your life beyond this moment—your people, your values, and your bigger world. Then say, "It's a game—go play," and step forward with intent.

CHAMPION'S WRAP: FEEL THE FREEDOM

Take a quiet minute and replay one moment today when you competed with freedom instead of fear. Notice how your body moved, how your mind felt, and how light the moment became. That is what happens when the game stays in its place.

DAY 48: CLOSE THE GAP

"A champion is defined not by their wins but by how they recover when they fall."
Serena Williams

Serena is redefining what it takes to be a champion. Wins matter, but they do not tell the whole story. The deeper test is how you respond when things go wrong. Falling is part of competing. Champions close the gap between the setback and the comeback.

MORNING EDGE: SET THE RESPONSE STANDARD

Take one Return to Zero breath and decide how you will respond today. See yourself handling a mistake, a bad rep, or a tough moment with calm and purpose. Say, "I recover fast and strong," and carry that standard into the day.

FLIP THE SWITCH: RISE QUICKLY

When frustration hits, take one steady breath and lift your posture. Bring your eyes back up and lock in on the next task. Say, "Right here, right now," and move with intent. Let your response be stronger than the moment.

CHAMPION'S WRAP: REPLAY THE RECOVERY

Take a quiet minute and replay one moment today when you got back on track well. See how you reset, what your body language looked like, and how quickly you returned to yourself. That is your edge. Keep strengthening that response until it becomes part of who you are.

DAY 49: MONEY IN THE BANK

"Everything comes at a cost. Just what are you willing to pay for it?"
Serena Williams

Greatness is expensive, and the bill does not arrive all at once. It shows up in workouts, recovery, focus, discipline, and all the little choices most people hope will not matter. Serena's point is that if you want the prize, you have to keep paying into it. Every hard rep, every honest choice, and every time you stay with the work is money in the bank.

MORNING EDGE: MAKE A DEPOSIT

Before training, decide where you will make your deposit today. It might be pushing through fatigue, locking in when bored, eating like a pro, or finishing your work all the way. Tell yourself, "Money in the bank," and handle that part of the day like it counts.

FLIP THE SWITCH: PAY FULL PRICE

When the work starts to sting and your mind looks for a cheaper way out, do not bargain with the moment. Take one steady breath and tell yourself, "Pay full price." Then finish the rep, the drill, or the task knowing you are putting money in the bank for when it matters most.

CHAMPION'S WRAP: CHECK THE ACCOUNT

As you close out the day, think of one moment when you paid for greatness instead of asking for a discount. That is money in the bank, and one day when the pressure is high, you will get to draw from it.

DAY 50: EARN THE SWEET

"Victory is very, very sweet. It tastes better than any dessert you've ever had."
Serena Williams

Victory feels sweetest when you know you earned it. Serena's wins were built on hard days, disciplined choices, and doing the little things well over and over again. The reward at the end means more when you know you did not cut corners to get there. The real sweetness is not just in winning, but in knowing you paid the price first.

MORNING EDGE: PAY THE PRICE UP FRONT

Take one Return to Zero breath and ask yourself, "What is this day going to require from me?" It might require focus, restraint, patience, or the willingness to get uncomfortable. Name the price and say, "I'm willing to pay it."

FLIP THE SWITCH: EARN THIS ONE

When fatigue, doubt, or frustration shows up, take one Return to Zero breath and come back to the task in front of you. You do not need to win the whole day right now. You just need to earn this rep, this point, or this moment.

CHAMPION'S WRAP: THE TASTE OF MORE

Think of one moment today when you leaned into the work instead of backing off or taking the easy way out. That was a taste of something earned, and it always tastes better when you know it came from your effort, your discipline, and your nerve. The best part is that one real taste does not satisfy you. It makes you hungry for more.

DAY 51: OWN YOUR TOO MUCH

"I'm really exciting. I smile a lot, I win a lot, and I'm really sexy."
Serena Williams

Serena is not trying to sound modest here. She is having fun and owning exactly who she is. That is part of the power. A lot of people get uncomfortable when someone is bold, joyful, successful, and fully at ease in their own skin. Serena never made herself smaller to make others more comfortable. She let her presence be her presence.

MORNING EDGE: BRING YOUR FULL SELF

Take one Return to Zero breath and think about the part of you that people notice most—your fire, your joy, your swagger, your intensity. Picture yourself bringing that energy into the day with ease and freedom. Say, "This is part of my edge," and let it show.

FLIP THE SWITCH: LET IT SHOW

When you start to tighten up or hold back, take one Return to Zero breath and lift your posture. Let your face, body language, and energy show who you are. Say, "Full self, full game," and step into the next moment with presence.

CHAMPION'S WRAP: REPLAY YOUR PRESENCE

Take a quiet minute and replay one moment today when you showed up fully and naturally. Notice your energy, your expression, and how your confidence came through. The goal is not to act bigger. The goal is to stop hiding what is already there.

DAY 52: PICTURE IT, THEN PLAY IT

"I am a strong believer in visualization. I really believe in that fantasy world—until it comes true."
Serena Williams

Serena used visualization to make big moments feel familiar before they arrived. She saw success so clearly that her mind and body were ready when the moment came. That is what great imagery does. It gives you a felt sense of the moment before you step into it. When the picture is clear, trust comes easier and play comes freer.

MORNING EDGE: BUILD THE PICTURE

Take one Return to Zero breath, then close your eyes for thirty seconds. Picture one moment you want to handle well today. See the setting, feel your body, and watch yourself finish the play with strength and control. Then open your eyes and carry that image with you.

FLIP THE SWITCH: RETURN TO THE IMAGE

When the moment feels rushed or uncertain, take one Return to Zero breath and bring back the picture you built. See it for a second, then step in and let your body match it. Clear picture, clear action.

CHAMPION'S WRAP: SAVE THE SCENE

Before bed, replay one moment today that looked or felt the way you wanted. Lock in the details like a highlight clip. Then picture one moment you want to bring to life tomorrow and let that image settle in.

DAY 53: MENTAL TRAINING PARTNER

NOVAK DJOKOVIC

"I always try to remind myself why I started playing this sport. It's that pure emotion, love, and passion for the game that drives me."
Novak Djokovic

Novak Djokovic learned early how to stay steady when life around him was not. He grew up in Belgrade during a time of air-raid sirens, uncertainty, and constant disruption, yet he kept training and competing. That environment sharpened his focus, his adaptability, and his nerve. Those qualities helped carry him to twenty-four Grand Slam titles, Olympic gold, and more weeks at world number one than anyone in tennis history.

What makes Djokovic so hard to beat is not just skill. It is the way he keeps rebuilding and refining his edge. When physical struggles began affecting his game, he changed his diet, upgraded his preparation, and trained his mind with the same seriousness as his strokes. Breathing, visualization, and emotional control became part of his daily work.

That work shows up most when the match gets tight. Djokovic knows how to slow things down on the inside even when everything outside is speeding up. He resets after frustration, settles his breathing under fatigue, and keeps bringing his attention back to the next point. He responds with intention instead of giving the moment his emotions.

That is what makes him so relentless. He does not need easy conditions to play great tennis. This week, Djokovic is your mental training partner. He will show you how to steady yourself, reset quickly, and stay dangerous when pressure, fatigue, or chaos try to pull you off your game.

DAY 54: SHORTEN THE STAY

"I probably have more negative thoughts than you. The difference is I don't stay in them long."
Novak Djokovic

Djokovic is not trying to eliminate negative thoughts. He expects them. His edge is how quickly he moves on. Thoughts come and go, but attention decides what stays. The skill is returning to the present again and again.

MORNING EDGE: NOTICE AND RETURN

As you go through your day, catch the first negative thought that shows up. See it for what it is, just a thought, and bring your attention back to what you are doing. That return is the rep.

FLIP THE SWITCH: BACK TO NOW

When a thought grabs you, take one Return to Zero breath and relax your body. Shift your eyes and attention to the next cue in front of you. Say, "Right here," and move with it.

CHAMPION'S WRAP: REPLAY THE RETURN

Take a quiet minute and replay one moment when you caught a thought and came back to the present. Notice how quickly you reset and what helped you return. That is the skill getting stronger.

DAY 55: TRAIN IN THE QUIET

"It's okay to be bored. That's when you're most creative."
Novak Djokovic

Djokovic is talking about what happens when the noise drops. Most people rush to fill quiet moments because boredom feels uncomfortable. He stays there. That is where patience, discipline, and creativity get stronger. If you can stay present when nothing exciting is happening, you will trust your mind more when everything is on the line.

MORNING EDGE: STAY WITH THE QUIET

Sit quietly for two minutes with no phone, no music, and no distractions. Notice the urge to reach for something, then let it pass. Stay with your breath and your body. This is how you build a steadier mind.

FLIP THE SWITCH: USE THE ORDINARY

When the day feels slow, repetitive, or dull, take one Return to Zero breath. Remind yourself, "This is part of the training." Then bring full attention to the rep, the routine, or the task in front of you.

CHAMPION'S WRAP: REPLAY THE STILLNESS

Before bed, think of one moment today when you stayed present without needing extra stimulation. Notice what that felt like in your body and mind, and recognize it as a competitive edge worth building.

DAY 56: DON'T INK THE MISTAKE

"Don't just study the highlights. Study the pain."
Novak Djokovic

Djokovic knows the hard moments have something to teach. Highlights show what worked. Pain shows what tightened up, what broke down, and what still needs work. That is why champions look at the miss, the loss, and the moment that stung. The key is to take the lesson without turning it into your identity.

MORNING EDGE: TAKE THE LESSON

Bring to mind one moment that still stings a little. Look at it with clear eyes. Ask yourself, "What did this reveal?" Take the lesson and leave the label behind.

FLIP THE SWITCH: LEARN, THEN MOVE

When a mistake lingers, take one Return to Zero breath and turn it into useful information. Ask, "What is the next better choice?" Then answer with your body language, your focus, and your next action. That is how pain becomes progress.

CHAMPION'S WRAP: KEEP YOUR IDENTITY CLEAN

Take a quiet minute and think of one hard moment that taught you something valuable. See the lesson clearly and separate it from who you are. Bruises fade. Growth stays.

DAY 57: STAY AVAILABLE

"Injury is the biggest enemy of an athlete. You can't do your job if you're injured. That proves the point of self-care even more—how important it is and how seriously you have to approach it every single day."
Novak Djokovic

Djokovic is talking about a different kind of discipline. Most athletes know how to push. The best also know how to protect what lets them perform. Your body is not something to burn through just to feel tough. It is what makes the work possible. Recovery is part of the job because availability is part of greatness.

MORNING EDGE: CHECK THE EQUIPMENT

Take a few seconds before training to scan your body with honest eyes. Notice what feels strong, what feels tight, and what needs more care. Then adjust your warm-up, your volume, or your approach so you can train well and stay ready.

FLIP THE SWITCH: PROTECT TOMORROW

When fatigue, soreness, or wear starts to build, take one Return to Zero breath and zoom out. Ask yourself, "What helps me stay sharp and available?" Then make the choice that supports your next session, not just this moment. Pros think past today.

CHAMPION'S WRAP: PLAYED THE LONG GAME

Take a quiet minute and think about one thing you did today that helped your body recover, reset, or stay strong. See that choice as part of your performance, not separate from it. The athletes who last are the ones who respect the vehicle.

DAY 58: MAKE IT SOUND LIKE YOUR NAME

"When the crowd is chanting 'Roger,' I hear 'Novak.' It sounds silly, but it's true."
Novak Djokovic

In the 2019 Wimbledon final, Centre Court wanted Federer. Djokovic could feel it in every roar, every surge of noise, every moment the energy leaned the other way. But he did something rare. He decided what the noise meant before it could decide him. Instead of hearing support for someone else, he heard his own name and turned the moment into fuel. That is part of the champion's mind—making any environment feel like it is for you.

MORNING EDGE: BUILD YOUR ARENA

Before the day begins, picture your environment coming alive for you. See the court, field, gym, or road sending energy your way and setting the stage for your best work. Walk in like the moment has been waiting for you and you belong right in the center of it.

FLIP THE SWITCH: HEAR IT YOUR WAY

When pressure rises, take one sharp breath out and settle your body. Then choose what you hear, even if it is not what is actually being said. Let the noise lift you, carry you, and push you into your next clear action.

CHAMPION'S WRAP: TRAVEL WITH THE ENERGY

Take a minute tonight and replay one moment where you made the environment work for you. Notice how you brought your own meaning instead of reacting to what was around you. That ability travels with you, and it is always available when you need it.

DAY 59: WHO YOU BECOME

"What do you want written on your tombstone?"
Dr. Jim Loehr, mentor to Novak Djokovic

Dr. Loehr's question is powerful because it cuts through the noise fast. It pulls your attention away from stats, praise, and quick emotional swings and brings it back to the deeper issue. Sport is always doing more than testing your skills. It is shaping your habits, your character, and the way you carry yourself when things get hard. In the end, the biggest victory is not just what you achieved, but who you became on the way there.

MORNING EDGE: NAME YOUR STANDARD

Before training or competition, ask yourself, "What do I want to be known for today?" Choose two or three words that describe the best version of you, such as steady, disciplined, brave, generous, or composed. Let those words become your target for the day, and carry them with you before anything gets tested.

FLIP THE SWITCH: BEAT THE IMPULSE

When you feel the impulse to rush, react, complain, force, or drift, pause for one second and straighten up. Picture yourself taking one step back and looking at the moment from above, like a leader on the sideline watching the play unfold. Then ask, "What would the person I want to become do here?" and let your next action answer it.

CHAMPION'S WRAP: KEEP THE REP THAT LASTS

Take a minute tonight and replay one moment when you chose your standard over your impulse. Notice what that decision says about the person you are building. Those are the reps that last, because they shape more than performance.

CHAMPION'S TAKEAWAYS: WIMBLEDON

Wimbledon tested your ability to stay composed when conditions were less forgiving. Fast points, awkward bounces, and shifting momentum asked the same question again and again: "Can you stay steady when things don't feel smooth?" This month wasn't about forcing confidence—it was about earning it through calm, reset, and patience.

You learned that poise is a skill. Breath brings you back. Rhythm keeps you grounded. And confidence grows when you trust your preparation instead of reacting to pressure.

Ask yourself:

- Where did I stay calm instead of rushing?
- How did I respond when momentum shifted?
- What part of my composure can I carry forward into the next arena?

Your Wimbledon hardware doesn't shine because it was easy. It shines because you stayed steady when the ground felt fast and uncertain.

CHAPTER 3

MARCH: MADISON SQUARE GARDEN

"The lights are brighter here. The stage is bigger here. This is the Garden."
Clyde Frazier

Madison Square Garden sits in the heart of New York City, and it has been making moments feel bigger for generations. The lights hit harder, the noise closes in, and every possession starts to carry more weight. This place does not hand out comfort. It asks whether you can stay with yourself when the game gets loud, fast, and personal.

That is what this month is about. Anyone can look composed when the game is flowing and the body feels good. The real test begins when your heart rate jumps, your thoughts speed up, and the environment tries to pull you out of your game. Pressure is not the problem. Losing yourself inside it is.

This month, you will train the mental skills that hold up under bright lights. Emotional control keeps feelings from taking over. Present focus keeps your attention on the next play instead of the last mistake or the result you want too soon. Rhythm keeps you loose, clear, and decisive when tension tries to rush you. These skills are simple, but they only show up when you practice them.

The Garden teaches a hard truth. Pressure does not build your habits in real time. It reveals the ones you already have. That is why the work matters. This month, you will train beside LeBron James, Caitlin Clark, Stephen Curry, and Maya Moore, four competitors who trust their preparation, stay where their feet are, and keep showing up when the stage gets big. When the lights come on, that is the standard.

DAY 60: MENTAL TRAINING PARTNER

LEBRON JAMES

"I am LeBron James, from Akron, Ohio, from the inner city. I am not even supposed to be here."
LeBron James, 2013 Finals MVP speech

LeBron James came out of Akron carrying talent, pressure, and expectations that would have crushed most people. He grew up in instability, with his mother fighting every day to build something solid amid uncertainty. That life built more than hunger. It built resilience, perspective, and a kind of strength that had already been tested long before the NBA.

From the moment he entered the league, the spotlight was enormous. Every game was watched, every mistake magnified, and every step met with noise. Over time, LeBron learned to fully immerse his mind in the moment, rather than letting the chaos pull him in every direction. He called that mental fitness, and it became one of the great edges of his career.

LeBron stayed at the top for more than two decades because he kept his inner world stronger than the outside world. He trusted his habits, used his breath, and came back again and again to the play in front of him. Writing "Man in the Arena" on his shoes was part of that mindset. Step in, own the responsibility, and meet the moment head-on.

This week, LeBron is your mental training partner. He will show you how to stay centered when the pressure is big, narrow your focus when the noise rises, and keep your head where your feet are. Your arena may look different, but the job is the same. Step in and own it.

DAY 61: WIN THE INSIDE GAME

"Before you can win the game on the court, you need to win the mental and emotional game in your mind."
LeBron James

LeBron points to a truth most athletes never fully master. Performance is shaped by emotions long before skill shows up. When irritation, rush, or fear takes over, the body tightens, and the mind scatters. Control does not mean suppressing emotions. It means noticing them without letting them take the wheel. When you stay steady inside, your timing improves, your instincts remain online, and your preparation has room to show up.

MORNING EDGE: TAKE THE CONTROLS

Before your first rep, take one Return to Zero breath and say, "I'm in charge of my emotions." Start your day from a place of command, not reaction.

FLIP THE SWITCH: SLOW THE MOMENT

When you feel yourself speeding up under pressure, that's the junk taking over—stress, doubt, and the urge to force the play. Interrupt it with one strong exhale, like wiping a fogged mirror clean. Release the tension in your shoulders and let your body settle. Say, "I'm back in charge." Then lock onto the next play and go.

CHAMPION'S WRAP: BUILD THE INSIDE

Before bed, name one moment today when you slowed yourself down under pressure. That's emotional strength. Build it again tomorrow.

DAY 62: BE HERE NOW

"When the moment arrives, all that stuff needs to disappear. There's no past or future—just you and this shot, in this moment."
LeBron James

Big moments demand one thing most athletes struggle to give them: full attention. The mind drifts to the last play or jumps ahead to what might happen next. LeBron's edge is simple, but trained: When it's time, he brings everything back to what is right in front of him. Just this shot. Just this play. Just this moment. This is not about blocking everything out. It is about putting your attention exactly where it belongs.

MORNING EDGE: BRING IT BACK

Before your first rep, take one Return to Zero breath and ask yourself, "Where are my eyes and attention right now?" Bring both back to the task in front of you. That is where great performance starts.

FLIP THE SWITCH: BRING IT TO ONE THING

When your mind starts drifting, take one Return to Zero breath and choose one thing to focus on right now—your target, your cue, or your next move. Put your attention there and let the rest fall away. Great focus gets simple under pressure.

CHAMPION'S WRAP: STAYED HERE

Think of one moment today when your mind started to drift and you brought it back. That's a mental rep. The more often you do it, the easier it is to come back when it counts.

DAY 63: STAND TALL IN THE NOISE

"People will hate you, rate you, shake you, and break you.
But how strong you stand is what makes you."
LeBron James

As you improve, attention rises with it. Praise, criticism, judgment, and outside opinions start showing up whether you ask for them or not. A lot of that noise has very little to do with your effort, your standards, or the work you are actually doing. The skill is staying rooted in what you have built, so your day is shaped by your standards rather than someone else's reaction.

MORNING EDGE: ROOT INTO YOUR STANDARD

Before your first rep, say, "I trust who I am and how I train." Let that thought settle you and set your tone for the day.

FLIP THE SWITCH: LET THE NOISE PASS

When comments, opinions, or judgment start pulling at your attention, take one Return to Zero breath: Inhale through your nose for four seconds, then exhale through your mouth for six. Say, "That's just noise," then bring your eyes and mind back to the task in front of you.

CHAMPION'S WRAP: STRONG ON YOUR FEET

At the end of the day, think of one moment when you stayed steady instead of reactive. That is what it feels like to hold your ground.

DAY 64: MAKE THE TEAM BETTER

"I think, team first. It allows me to succeed. It allows my team to succeed."
LeBron James

Playing for the group does not mean shrinking your game. It means bringing your game to the group in a way that makes everyone stronger. When everything feels personal, pressure rises, frustration takes over, and your game can get tight. When your focus shifts to helping the team, your mind clears, your decisions get cleaner, and your best instincts come alive.

MORNING EDGE: CHOOSE YOUR IMPACT

Before your first rep, decide how you will help the group today. Pick one clear action you can control, like bringing energy early, talking on defense, making the simple play, or staying locked in between reps. Show up with that role in mind and let your effort lift the team.

FLIP THE SWITCH: TURN OUTWARD FAST

When frustration hits, take one Return to Zero breath: Inhale through your nose for four seconds, then exhale through your mouth for six. Then find a teammate and give them something useful—"I've got you," "Next one," or "I'm here." Turning outward brings you back to the team and back to your best.

CHAMPION'S WRAP: YOU LIFTED THE GROUP

At the end of the day, name one moment when your presence helped the team play better. That is a kind of winning that lasts.

DAY 65: DECIDE BIGGER THAN FATIGUE

"Tired is only in the mind. If you tell yourself you're tired,
you're going to be tired. I don't get tired."
LeBron James

LeBron is not saying the body never feels fatigue. He is saying fatigue does not get to make the decisions. A lot of athletes feel tired and immediately let that feeling shrink their effort, focus, or aggressiveness. LeBron notices the feeling and stays in charge of his response. When your breath stays steady, your posture stays strong, and your mind stays firm, you often find there is more left than you first thought.

MORNING EDGE: SET THE EFFORT STANDARD

Take one Return to Zero breath: Inhale through your nose for four seconds, then exhale through your mouth for six. Stand tall and say, "I decide my effort today." Start the day by choosing how you will show up, not by waiting to see how you feel.

FLIP THE SWITCH: STAY IN CHARGE

When you start to feel drained, take one long exhale and relax your shoulders, jaw, and face. Then tell yourself, "Stay strong," and keep moving with purpose.

CHAMPION'S WRAP: YOU FOUND MORE

At the end of the day, name one moment when fatigue showed up and you stayed in command of your effort. That is mental endurance. Keep stacking it.

DAY 66: FIND YOUR "CLEVELAND"

"Cleveland . . . this is for you!"
LeBron James, 2016 Finals

When LeBron shouted that after ending Cleveland's fifty-two-year title drought, it was more than a celebration. It was a release of years of pressure, loyalty, heartbreak, belief, and unfinished business. It was a kid from Akron delivering on something bigger than a game. Every athlete needs a "Cleveland," a person, place, purpose, or promise that makes the work hit deeper and the moment matter more.

MORNING EDGE: LOCK IN YOUR WHY

Before your first rep, ask yourself, "Who or what is this for?" Choose the person, place, or promise that gives your effort weight. Carry it with you as you begin the day. Let it sharpen your focus and raise your standard.

FLIP THE SWITCH: TURN PURPOSE INTO POWER

When fatigue, doubt, or frustration start creeping in, bring your "Cleveland" back to mind. Say, "This is for _____," and fill in the blank with something that matters to you. Let that thought pull you forward with fresh intent. Then attack the next moment with purpose.

CHAMPION'S WRAP: CARRY A BIGGER REASON

Before bed, think of one moment today when something bigger than comfort, mood, or pressure helped you stay with it. That is what a bigger reason does. It gives your effort heart, your struggle meaning, and your best moments something steady to stand on.

DAY 67: MENTAL TRAINING PARTNER

CAITLIN CLARK

"I just have a lot of confidence in myself. I know how hard I've worked. I've earned the right to have that confidence."
Caitlin Clark

Caitlin Clark grew up in West Des Moines chasing competition. She ran with her older brother, pushed the pace in the driveway, and wanted more than anyone else around her. That edge showed up early. She did not wait for permission to belong. She played like she already did.

That edge turned into something electric at Iowa. Caitlin did not just score points. She stretched the game, lit up the court from deep, and made bold plays look normal. The range, the vision, and the fearlessness grabbed the headlines, but the work built all of it. Her confidence came from reps, corrections, and a belief she earned.

Now in the WNBA, she brings that same blend of joy, fire, and command. She trusts her game because she has lived it over and over again in practice. Her focus stays on what she can control, her effort, her preparation, and the way she shows up. That is what keeps her aggressive and free.

This week, Caitlin is your mental training partner. She will show you how to compete with joy, earn your confidence, and stay bold when the lights get bright. Put in the work, trust what you built, and let it rip.

DAY 68: BRING THE SPARK

"You're not always going to play your best. But you can always bring energy, effort, and a great attitude."
Caitlin Clark

You are not going to have your best stuff every day. But energy, effort, and attitude are always available. When you bring spark, you stay connected to the moment, lift the people around you, and give yourself something real to compete with. Many athletes wait to feel energized before they play well. Champions create the spark that changes the day.

MORNING EDGE: STRIKE THE SPARK

Before your first rep, choose the energy level you want to bring and commit to it. Move with purpose, communicate early, and respond quickly after every action. Set the tone with your presence.

FLIP THE SWITCH: SPARK THE MOMENT

When the pace drops or you feel flat, act fast. Sprint, talk, clap, attack a rep, or make one strong move that wakes you up. Spark comes from action.

CHAMPION'S WRAP: YOU BROUGHT THE SPARK

At the end of the day, ask yourself whether you brought life to the room. Effort creates a spark, and the spark spreads.

DAY 69: WANT THE BALL

"I've always been someone who wants the ball in big moments. I want to take the big shots. I want to make the big plays."
Caitlin Clark

Pressure brings Caitlin to life. Big moments call her forward because she trusts what she has built and welcomes the chance to carry the play. That is the real edge. Champions step toward the risk, the noise, and the responsibility because that is where they get to express their best.

MORNING EDGE: CHOOSE THE RESPONSIBILITY

Picture a moment when you would usually hesitate. Say, "I want the responsibility," then step toward it. The habit of stepping up starts long before the spotlight finds you.

FLIP THE SWITCH: STEP INTO THE SHOT

When your heart starts pounding, take one Return to Zero breath: Inhale through your nose for four seconds, then exhale through your mouth for six. Set your stance, trust your mechanics, and step into the moment with purpose.

CHAMPION'S WRAP: YOU STEPPED UP

At the end of the day, name one moment when you moved toward the pressure instead of away from it. That is how big-moment trust gets built.

DAY 70: OWN THE FILTER

"The outside noise, the expectations—I just use it as fuel. I know who I am."
Caitlin Clark

Noise comes with competing. Opinions, expectations, praise, and criticism all find their way to you. The skill is choosing what earns your attention and what stays outside the gate. Caitlin stays steady by getting clear on how she wants to compete before the noise ever arrives. When that standard is set first, everything else loses power.

MORNING EDGE: SET THE FILTER

Before the day starts, write down two or three short phrases that describe how you want to compete today, such as "calm and aggressive," "free and decisive," or "locked in." That becomes your filter for the day. Let it guide what you focus on and what you leave alone.

FLIP THE SWITCH: BACK TO YOUR GAME

When distractions start pulling at you, take one Return to Zero breath: Inhale through your nose for four seconds, then exhale through your mouth for six. Let your shoulders drop, say, "Back to my game," and put your attention on the next task.

CHAMPION'S WRAP: YOU CHOSE WHAT GOT IN

At the end of the day, ask yourself, "What got my attention today, and did it help my game?" The more clearly you choose what gets in, the more consistently you play your way.

DAY 71: BELIEF GOES FIRST

"When I step on the court, I'm the best player. That's how I think."
Caitlin Clark

Belief is a choice you make before the moment gets loud. Caitlin steps onto the court with a clear internal story, and that story shapes her posture, her decisions, and her aggression. When belief goes first, your body commits and your game opens up. When belief trails behind, hesitation slips in and your play tightens.

MORNING EDGE: SET THE INNER STORY

Before practice or competition, say, "I'm going to play like I believe in myself today." Keep your eyes up, stand tall, and speak with intention. Give your body the message before the pressure has a chance to write one for you.

FLIP THE SWITCH: ACTIONS FIRST

When doubt shows up, take one Return to Zero breath: Inhale through your nose for four seconds, then exhale through your mouth for six. Lift your chin, set your posture, and go fully into the next rep. Let your actions lead and your thoughts catch up.

CHAMPION'S WRAP: BELIEF IN ACTION

At the end of the day, name one moment when you played with conviction before you fully felt it. That is what belief looks like. You did not wait for confidence to arrive. You played in a way that helped create it.

DAY 72: BRING THE COMPETITIVE FIRE WITH YOU

"I'm super competitive. I hate to lose. I think that's been in me since I was a young girl."

Caitlin Clark

Some athletes wait for the game to wake something up in them. Others bring that something with them. Caitlin competes like it lives in her, because it does. That is why her edge shows up early, stays on, and holds its shape when the moment gets tight.

MORNING EDGE: WAKE UP YOUR EDGE

Before your first rep, decide what kind of fire you are bringing into the day. Set the tone with something small, because that is where identity starts to show itself. The day usually rises to the level of the edge you bring into it.

FLIP THE SWITCH: COMPETE FIRST

When your level drops, do not stand there waiting for your best self to return. Step into the next rep like a competitor, and let your behavior reignite your fire. Sometimes the fastest way to feel locked in again is to move like you already are.

CHAMPION'S WRAP: KEEP YOUR FIRE LIT

At the end of the day, ask yourself, "Did I bring my edge into the moments that mattered?" Your best days are rarely accidents. They are usually the result of bringing the same fire to the ordinary moment that you want in the big one.

DAY 73: BURN DOUBT FOR FUEL

"You have to keep showing up, even when it's hard, even when people doubt you. Especially then."
Caitlin Clark

Doubt shows up whenever you are reaching for something bigger. Sometimes it comes from other people, and sometimes it comes from your own mind. Either way, it says you are in the arena, stretching, risking, and going after something that matters. The edge belongs to the athlete who keeps showing up, keeps working, and keeps competing with purpose.

MORNING EDGE: TURN IT INTO FIRE

Think of one thing that has been questioned about you. Say, "I'll answer this with how I work today." Let that sharpen your focus, your pace, and your purpose from the first rep.

FLIP THE SWITCH: GO AGAIN WITH FORCE

When doubt shows up in the middle of the session, take one Return to Zero breath: Inhale through your nose for four seconds, then exhale through your mouth for six. Say, "Go again," and drive into the next rep with intent.

CHAMPION'S WRAP: YOU KEPT SHOWING UP

At the end of the day, think of one moment when doubt showed up and you stayed engaged anyway. That is how belief gets stronger. You build it by competing through the noise.

DAY 74: MENTAL TRAINING PARTNER

STEPHEN CURRY

"Be the best version of yourself in anything that you do.
You don't have to live anybody else's story."
Stephen Curry

Steph Curry was not handed the usual path to greatness. Coming out of high school, he was overlooked by major programs and only offered a walk-on spot at Virginia Tech, where his father had starred. He chose Davidson, bet on himself, and started building the game the world would eventually have to chase. That choice said a lot about him. He trusted his own path early.

What followed was not luck. Scouts said he was too small, too slight, and not built for the NBA. Steph answered by sharpening what was already his. He stretched his range, tightened his handle, learned to move constantly without the ball, and built a game that fit his body, his instincts, and his strengths. He did not try to look like the prototype. He became the prototype.

That is what makes Steph such a powerful training partner. His confidence comes from repetition, ownership, and the freedom that comes from knowing exactly who you are. He plays with joy, but that joy sits atop serious work. Every shot, every cut, and every burst of rhythm comes from hours of preparation.

This week, Steph is your mental training partner. He will show you how to trust your own lane, lean into what makes you different, and let your preparation speak when the pressure rises. Build your game your way. Then step out and let it fly.

DAY 75: COMMAND YOUR STATE

"Breathing is a skill. Being able to control your breathing for recovery, controlling your nerves . . . I've really tried to master that."

Stephen Curry

When Steph talked about the smallest details of basketball, he pointed to breathing. He sees it as a skill because it can be trained, sharpened, and used on purpose when the moment gets fast. Your breath is one of the quickest ways to recover, settle your nerves, and reset your focus when the game starts speeding up. Mastering it means knowing how to bring yourself back to center so your skill can show up when it counts.

MORNING EDGE: SET YOUR CENTER

Before your first rep, take one Return to Zero breath: Inhale through your nose for four seconds, then exhale through your mouth for six. Let your shoulders drop and your forehead soften. This is how you practice control before the game asks for it.

FLIP THE SWITCH: BLOW OUT THE JUNK

When the game speeds up or nerves rise, start with one sharp exhale through your mouth to blow out the junk—stress, tightness, and mental noise. Then take one Return to Zero breath. Let the longer exhale settle your body, bring you back to center, and prepare you for the next play.

CHAMPION'S WRAP: BACK TO CENTER

As the day winds down, take five Return to Zero breaths and let the day leave your body. Recovery is a skill, and every clean reset makes you better at coming back to yourself.

DAY 76: GREET THE MOMENT

"Thank you for the opportunity."
Stephen Curry

Right before a free throw, Steph uses a phrase that changes the whole feel of the moment. He does not treat pressure like a problem to solve. He treats it like an opportunity to welcome. "Thank you for the opportunity" turns stress into purpose and brings his mind back to the present. Gratitude steadies the breath, softens the body, and clears the way for skill to show up.

MORNING EDGE: OPEN WITH GRATITUDE

Before your first challenge today, pause and quietly say, "Thank you for the opportunity." Let those words settle your mind and set your tone. Start the day by welcoming what is in front of you.

FLIP THE SWITCH: WELCOME WHAT MATTERS

When the moment intensifies, take one Return to Zero breath. Then quietly say, "Thank you for the opportunity," and let the moment sharpen you instead of speeding you up.

CHAMPION'S WRAP: YOU WELCOMED IT

At the end of the day, think of one moment when the stakes rose and you met it with gratitude. That is how you train your mind to greet pressure like a competitor.

DAY 77: RESET FASTER THAN EVERYONE ELSE

"Next play mentality."
Stephen Curry

Steph's first college game at Davidson was rough. He had thirteen turnovers, and a lot of players would have let that spiral into a longer bad night. Instead, his coach gave him two simple words: "Next play." Steph took that lesson seriously, and it became one of the mental habits that shaped his career.

MORNING EDGE: OWN THE RESET

Before the day starts, decide this: mistakes will happen, and you will not carry them forward. Your job is to reset and reengage. Let go of anything that does not serve you today.

FLIP THE SWITCH: NEXT PLAY NOW

When your mind starts replaying an error, interrupt it. Say, "Next play now," and put your focus back on the next task in front of you. Reset your energy and attention, then move on.

CHAMPION'S WRAP: LET IT GO FAST

At the end of the day, think of one moment when you released a mistake and stayed present. That is how "next play" becomes automatic.

DAY 78: TAKE COMMAND OF THE DAY

"I always ask, 'What do I need to get out of the day?'"
Stephen Curry

A day without a purpose gets pulled in too many directions. Strong performers get clear before the noise starts. Steph begins by asking what the day is for, and that question gives the day a target. Once the target is clear, attention sharpens, choices get easier, and energy stops leaking into things that do not matter.

MORNING EDGE: NAME THE MISSION

Before the day gets moving, decide on one thing you want from today. Make it specific and useful. Say, "This is what today is for," and let that become your marching order.

FLIP THE SWITCH: RETURN TO THE MISSION

When your focus drifts, pause and ask, "Is this helping me accomplish today's mission?" If the answer is no, redirect right away and get back to what matters.

CHAMPION'S WRAP: MISSION ACCOMPLISHED

At the end of the day, think of one moment when you caught yourself drifting and brought your attention back with purpose. That is what it looks like to run your day instead of letting the day run you.

DAY 79: LEAD SO PEOPLE FEEL IT

"I've always been a lead-by-example type. My work ethic speaks for itself. I've had to develop my voice over the years. I'm not the loudest one in the room, but I've grown into that part of leadership."
Stephen Curry

Steph's quote shows that leadership is not one thing. It begins with how you work, how you carry yourself, and how consistently you show up. That is how trust gets built. Then, over time, leadership grows a voice. The strongest leaders do both. They live it first, then say what needs to be said.

MORNING EDGE: SET THE TONE EARLY

Lead with how you show up today. Prepare with care, work with purpose, and carry yourself in a way that makes people better just by being around you. Leadership starts before you say a word.

FLIP THE SWITCH: ADD YOUR VOICE

When the moment calls for it, speak clearly and keep it simple. One calm, useful message delivered at the right time can steady a group and raise the level of everyone around you.

CHAMPION'S WRAP: EXAMPLE AND VOICE

At the end of the day, think of one moment when your presence helped lead and one moment when your words helped lead. That is how leadership grows. It starts with your example and gets stronger when your voice joins it.

DAY 80: BEAT THE CLOCK

"There's no better time than now. You know what you've got to do, and you've got to show up and do it."
Stephen Curry

A lot of athletes spend too much time waiting for a better feeling, a cleaner moment, or a stronger surge of confidence before they begin. Champions treat now like their cue. They understand that hesitation drains power, while action builds momentum. The moment starts moving in your favor when you do.

MORNING EDGE: CATCH THE WINDOW

Before the day starts, identify the first moment that will ask something of you—effort, courage, focus, or follow-through. Tell yourself, "When the window opens, I go," and carry that mindset into your warm-up. Start the day ready to move on cue.

FLIP THE SWITCH: GO ON GREEN

When hesitation creeps in, steady your breath and say, "Now." Shift your focus to the first physical step you can take and take it right away. Action breaks the spell. Once your feet move, the rest of you can follow.

CHAMPION'S WRAP: YOU HIT GO

At the end of the day, think of one moment when you moved right into the task instead of hanging back. That is how momentum gets built. The day changed because you did.

DAY 81: MENTAL TRAINING PARTNER

MAYA MOORE

"You have to not only love the game; you have to love the training, the practice, and the competing. You have to love everything about it."

Maya Moore

Maya Moore set a standard that showed up in wins and in the way she prepared. At UConn, she helped drive a ninety-game win streak and two national titles. In Minnesota, she became the centerpiece of a dynasty that won four WNBA championships in eight seasons. She impacted the game in every way that mattered.

What made Maya so reliable was the work you didn't see. Extra skill sessions, film study that turned tendencies into instincts, and recovery handled with discipline every single day. She repeated the right habits until they became automatic. That is why her game held steady when the moment got big.

Maya competed with a team-first mindset that never wavered. Some nights called for scoring, others for defense, rebounding, or making the right play late in the clock. She stayed ready for all of it. The job stayed simple. Help the team win.

This week, Maya is your mental training partner. She will show you how to build trust through preparation, bring consistency to your game, and take pride in the parts that don't get attention. Do the work that travels. That is what shows up when it counts.

DAY 82: BEAT THE VOICE TO THE SPOT

"It's not necessarily about outworking the person across from me. It's outworking that voice inside of me that says, 'I'm too tired. I don't feel like doing it. I can settle.'"
Maya Moore

Every athlete hears that voice when it is time to go again. It speaks in calm, reasonable language and offers an easier road: You are tired, you have done enough, you can ease up. Maya understood that the real battle was often right there. She did not let that inner voice run the session. She answered it with action, because work has a way of clearing out doubt and putting you back in charge.

MORNING EDGE: WIN THE FIRST BATTLE

When you wake up feeling flat, tired, or scattered, treat that feeling like your first opponent. Say, "I'm moving," and do one small thing right away that gets you going. Momentum starts the moment your body does.

FLIP THE SWITCH: LET WORK TALK

When the voice starts making its case, stay out of the argument and go straight to action. Take one steady breath, settle your body, and give one clean rep, one strong play, or one committed effort. Action changes the conversation fast.

CHAMPION'S WRAP: YOU BEAT THE VOICE

At the end of the day, think of one moment when the voice told you to settle and you kept going anyway. That is where self-trust gets built. Your effort answered the question.

DAY 83: BRING THE LIGHT

"Always try to be a shining light, bringing life to every situation."
Maya Moore

Maya didn't fade when things got tough. She brought light. This isn't about being loud or fake-positive—it's about choosing not to be a shadow. Shadows retreat, complain, and wait for someone else to step up. Light shows up, stays present, and helps the group move forward. Maya understood that when the energy dropped, her responsibility was to lift it. That's leadership in action, and it's something anyone can practice.

MORNING EDGE: OWN YOUR LIGHT

Today, decide you won't be a shadow. Arrive alert, engaged, and ready to contribute something positive to the room—effort, encouragement, or calm. Light doesn't wait for permission; it shows up first.

FLIP THE SWITCH: SHIFT THE ROOM

When the mood dips, take one Return to Zero breath, stand tall, and reset the tone with your body language. Light travels fast when one person leads the way.

CHAMPION'S WRAP: LIGHT IMPACT

Before bed, ask yourself, "Where did I bring light today?" Those moments may seem small, but they matter. Teams remember them.

DAY 84: FALL IN LOVE WITH THE HIDDEN WORK

"After twenty years of competing for championships, I learned that so much of the work needed to create championship culture is actually hidden."
Maya Moore

Championship culture grows where almost nobody is looking. It is built in film study, recovery, honest conversations, extra discipline, and the choice to do things right behind closed doors. That work rarely gets applause in the moment, yet it shapes your habits, your character, and your edge. Over time, what stays hidden in the process starts showing up everywhere that counts.

MORNING EDGE: BUILD BEFORE IT SHOWS

Before the day gets loud, do one thing that moves you forward. Watch the extra film, get the recovery in, prepare with care, or handle one detail that makes you better. Start with a rep that nobody sees but you know matters.

FLIP THE SWITCH: TRUST THE INVISIBLE REPS

When the work feels quiet or thankless, remind yourself that this is where real growth gets built. Trust, confidence, and culture are formed here, long before anyone sees the results. The hidden work always shows up later.

CHAMPION'S WRAP: HIDDEN WORK LOGGED

At the end of the day, name one piece of work you did that nobody else noticed. Those are the reps that build something real. Championship culture grows in moments like that.

DAY 85: BE THE HELP

"My biggest desire when I played was to help my team in any way that they needed. I think they felt that from me."
Maya Moore

Maya played with a rare kind of usefulness. She stayed tuned in to what the team needed and moved there with purpose. Some moments called for defense, some for patience, some for a smart pass, and some for a steady presence. That mindset makes a team stronger fast. When your attention shifts from how you look to how you can help, trust starts to grow.

MORNING EDGE: CHOOSE YOUR HELP

Before the day starts, pick one way you will help a teammate today. Bring energy, communicate well, do the grunt work, or make the simple play that keeps things moving. Useful players make teams better in ways everyone can feel.

FLIP THE SWITCH: ASK THE TEAM QUESTION

When frustration hits, pause and ask, "What does my team need right now?" Let that answer guide your next move. That question has a way of pulling you out of yourself and back into what matters.

CHAMPION'S WRAP: YOU MADE THINGS BETTER

At the end of the day, think of one moment when you made someone else's job easier. That is the kind of impact teammates trust. That is what usefulness looks like.

DAY 86: BUILD THE TRUST THAT SETS YOU FREE

"One of the most profound aspects of team sports is seeing a group of individuals start to trust each other over time and truly play for each other."
Maya Moore

Maya understood that trust is one of the great forces in team sports. It grows over time through consistency, honesty, effort, and shared experience. When players know the person beside them is fully in, the game opens up. The ball moves better, communication gets cleaner, and people compete with more freedom. Trust changes how a team feels and how a team plays.

MORNING EDGE: DEPOSIT INTO THE TRUST

Show up ready, communicate clearly, and do the small things right. Trust grows through steady deposits, not grand speeches. Give your team something they can count on today.

FLIP THE SWITCH: STAY CONNECTED

When a teammate struggles, move toward them. A nod, a look, or a quick "I got you" can steady the moment. When a teammate does something well, let them feel that too. Strong teams stay connected through the whole ride.

CHAMPION'S WRAP: TRUST WAS BUILT TODAY

At the end of the day, think of one moment when you helped strengthen the bond between you and a teammate. That is how trust gets built. It grows through moments like that until a team starts playing for each other without even thinking about it.

DAY 87: FEED THE CULTURE YOU WANT

"Championship culture can be found not just in sports but in all aspects of life—in our homes, our schools, our neighborhoods."

Maya Moore

Culture is built in the small daily moments, especially in how people talk when things get hard. Words shape the room, direct attention, and influence how a team responds under pressure. Maya's point is that championship culture lives in everyday habits, attitudes, and choices. The best competitors bring language that raises the bar, sharpens focus, and moves the group forward.

MORNING EDGE: PROTECT THE CULTURE

Today, decide that complaining gets no airtime from you. If it does not help the team compete, improve, or lead, it does not deserve your voice. Feed the culture you want to build.

FLIP THE SWITCH: SHIFT THE CONVERSATION

When the talk turns negative, step in and redirect it. Ask, "What can we control right now?" or "What is the next play?" Leaders help the group find its footing again.

CHAMPION'S WRAP: YOU FED THE RIGHT CULTURE

At the end of the day, ask yourself, "What kind of culture did my words help create today?" Championship culture grows through moments like that. What you feed gets stronger.

DAY 88: CHOOSE WHAT DRIVES YOU

"You have to figure out what motivates you every day when you get up out of bed."
Maya Moore

Maya's point is that motivation begins with intention. Each day asks a new question: What is driving you today? Some days the answer is love for the game. Some days it is pride, loyalty, growth, or respect for the work you have already put in. Champions stay connected to effort because they choose a reason before the day starts pulling at them.

MORNING EDGE: NAME TODAY'S REASON

Before the day starts, say, "Today, I'm showing up for ______." Make it specific and make it real. Let that reason guide your effort, your attitude, and your follow-through.

FLIP THE SWITCH: COME BACK TO THE WHY

When your energy dips, pause and reconnect with the reason you chose. Say, "This is why," and step back into the work with purpose.

CHAMPION'S WRAP: REASON CARRIED THE DAY

At the end of the day, think of one moment when your reason helped carry you forward. That is how motivation becomes more dependable. You keep choosing it, and it keeps showing up for you.

DAY 89: WHAT CHAMPIONS ARE BUILT ON

"You do that and you overcome through love and dedication and trust. That's what makes champions champions."

Maya Moore

Maya is talking about the kind of strength that holds up over time. Love keeps you connected to the game and to the people around you. Dedication keeps you showing up for the small things that build greatness. Trust lets you stay steady when pressure rises and the moment gets big. Champions grow from that foundation.

MORNING EDGE: START FROM WHAT MATTERS

Before practice, remind yourself why you play. Pick one way today to show love for the game through your effort, your focus, or the way you help a teammate. Let that care shape how you show up.

FLIP THE SWITCH: STAND ON THE FOUNDATION

When pressure rises, come back to what you have built. Trust your work, trust your preparation, and trust the people beside you. Play from that foundation and let it steady you.

CHAMPION'S WRAP: WHAT HELD YOU UP?

At the end of the day, think about what carried you. Was it your love for the game, your dedication to the work, or your trust in what you had built? That foundation is what keeps champions steady.

DAY 90: FEEL THE POWER OF WE

"You don't have to be me or Sue or Syl or any of these greats to feel the joy of winning together."
Maya Moore (referring to Sue Bird and Sylvia Fowles)

Maya was talking about one of the best parts of sport: shared joy. You do not have to be the star to feel it. You get to feel it when you are part of a group that trusts each other, plays for each other, and rises together. That kind of connection changes everything. Pressure feels lighter, confidence spreads faster, and the win means more because everyone helped build it.

MORNING EDGE: ADD TO THE WE

Early in the day, do one small thing that helps a teammate or colleague. Encourage someone, communicate clearly, or make their job easier. Team joy grows when everyone adds something to it.

FLIP THE SWITCH: STAY CONNECTED UNDER PRESSURE

When things get tense, come back to your role and your connection to the group. Take one Return to Zero breath, trust the people around you, and do your part with purpose. Teams that stay connected think more clearly and recover more quickly.

CHAMPION'S WRAP: WHERE YOU FELT THE WE

At the end of the day, think of one moment when teamwork lifted the group. That feeling is part of the reward. Champions remember the bond as much as the result.

CHAMPION'S TAKEAWAYS: MADISON SQUARE GARDEN

March was pressure under lights. Madison Square Garden tested your ability to stay calm when the moment sped up and the noise got louder. You practiced emotional control, present focus, and rhythm—so your game could stay clean even when it felt personal.

Reflect:

- When did I stay steady when my emotions tried to take over?
- What did I do this month that made pressure feel more manageable?
- What do I trust more about myself under the lights now?

The Garden doesn't create champions. It reveals them. And you learned how to show up with calm, confidence, and control.

CHAPTER 4

APRIL: AUGUSTA NATIONAL

"Golf is a game that is played on a five-inch course, the distance between your ears."
Bobby Jones

Imagine standing on the first tee at Augusta National. The azaleas are in bloom, the air is still, and patrons line the fairway as if the course itself is holding its breath. You press the tee into the ground, set the ball, and take one last look at your target. Then everything gets quiet, and the question becomes simple. Do you trust your swing?

Augusta is more than a golf course. It is a place that exposes what is happening inside you. Every shot reveals what you trust when the pressure rises, what you do with nerves, and whether your mind stays with you when the stakes get real. This is where confidence becomes composure, and composure turns into execution.

This month is about mastering presence under pressure. You will train to breathe through nerves, trust your preparation, and lean on your habits when your heart rate climbs. The question is the same for every champion who has ever stood here. Can you stay free when the moment gets bigger?

Your guides this month are four champions who know that test well. Rory McIlroy learned how to trust his game again. Tiger Woods trained his mind so thoroughly that pressure became familiar. Annika Sörenstam freed herself with her ten-second rule. Scottie Scheffler shows what it looks like to stay steady through routine, faith, and full attention.

Augusta does not ask for perfect. It asks for trust. When the noise falls away and your name is called, can you let go and play the shot that is already there? That is the real major.

DAY 91: MENTAL TRAINING PARTNER
RORY MCILROY

"Our mind is way more powerful than really anything else. If you can utilize that the right way, it's inevitably going to help your game on the course."
Rory McIlroy

Rory McIlroy grew up in Holywood, Northern Ireland, swinging a club almost as soon as he could stand. By his early twenties, he was already a major champion, with a swing that made the game look effortless and a future that seemed unlimited.

But Augusta had other plans. Rory came painfully close at the Masters more than once, including the Sunday collapse in 2011 that stayed with him for years. Add in a decade-long stretch without a major, and every return to Augusta carried more weight. The career Grand Slam was waiting there, and the longer it took, the heavier it became.

That is why what Rory says the Masters taught him about life matters so much. His answer was simple and strong: "Just keep going," he said. "Just keep your head down and keep going. If you put the (reps) in and work on the right things, eventually, it'll come good for you." That is not just golf advice. That is life advice.

In 2025, Rory finally won the Masters and completed the career Grand Slam. Then, in 2026, he returned and won Augusta again. But even after the breakthrough, he realized something deeper: "I felt like the Grand Slam was the destination, and I realized it wasn't." The prize matters, but it is not where you live. The journey is.

That is the Rory you get this week. He will show you how to trust your rhythm, stay patient, and keep moving forward.

DAY 92: THIS SHOT ONLY

"Process over prize."

Rory McIlroy

Rory knows how quickly the mind can get ahead of itself. One great shot and suddenly you are thinking about the score, the finish, or what the day might become. The antidote is simple: let go of what already happened, let go of what might happen, and play this shot.

MORNING EDGE: START WITH ONE SHOT

Before your first rep, remind yourself that this shot does not need to carry the last one, the next one, or the whole round. Letting go means releasing that extra weight so you can give this shot your full attention. Then decide what matters for this shot—your tempo, your contact, or your commitment—and give your body one clear job.

FLIP THE SWITCH: BACK TO THIS SHOT

When your mind jumps ahead, that is the moment to reset. Take one Return to Zero breath—slow breath in, longer breath out—and let your body settle. Let go of the last shot, let go of the next one, and come back to this shot. Between shots, let your mind relax a little. Feel the breeze, take in your surroundings, and when it is time, get your eyes on the next target and bring everything back to this shot.

CHAMPION'S WRAP: THE RETURN IS THE REP

You are not trying to stay perfectly locked in all day. You are training to let go of the last shot and come back fully to the shot at hand. Think of one moment today when your mind drifted ahead and you brought it back to the shot at hand. That is how rounds stay together instead of starting to get away from you.

DAY 93: TRUST THE PLAYER YOU BROUGHT TODAY

"Stop trying so hard. Start trusting."
Dr. Bob Rotella (shared by Rory McIlroy)

Pressure has a way of making players want to tinker, force, and search for something extra. That is usually when the game starts getting crowded and tight. Rory's reminder is simple: Today's player is already here. You do not need to build a new swing on the first tee. You need to trust the one you brought and send it to the target.

MORNING EDGE: SIGN THE CONTRACT

Before you begin, make peace with the player you brought today. Say to yourself, "I compete with what I have today," and commit fully to the next target instead of wishing for a different version of you.

FLIP THE SWITCH: BE THE HUNTER, NOT THE MECHANIC

When you catch yourself trying to fix the swing in the middle of play, leave the toolbox alone. Take one Return to Zero breath, get your eyes on the target, and let the swing go chase something.

CHAMPION'S WRAP: THE PLAYER YOU BROUGHT

Think of one moment today when you stayed with your target and stopped trying to edit yourself mid-round. That is a big deal. That is the player you bring back tomorrow.

DAY 94: THE SCORECARD IS NOT A MIRROR

"My scores aren't me."
Rory McIlroy

A bad score can feel personal really fast. For athletes and other high performers, results have often been tied to pride, respect, and how they see themselves. That is why one rough day can start feeling bigger than it is. Rory's wisdom is that the number tells you how you played, not who you are. When you keep that line clear, you protect the person while still being honest about the performance.

MORNING EDGE: DRAW THE LINE

Before you begin, get clear on what belongs to the score and what belongs to you. The score can reflect your play today, but your standards, effort, and character still belong to you.

FLIP THE SWITCH: PROTECT THE PERSON

When the score starts pulling at your identity, stop it before it turns into a label. Take one Return to Zero breath and tell yourself, "I am always more than my score." Then get back to the next shot, the next choice, or the next response.

CHAMPION'S WRAP: SET THE BAG DOWN

At the end of the day, notice what you are still carrying from the round. It might be the score, a mistake, a bad stretch, or the story your mind is starting to tell about what it all means, so name it clearly and take one long exhale as if you are setting down a heavy golf bag. Keep the lesson you need for tomorrow, and leave the rest behind.

DAY 95: CARRY YOUR OWN ATMOSPHERE

"Home doesn't have to be a place. It can be a feeling and the people you surround yourself with."
Rory McIlroy

Travel, pressure, and unfamiliar settings can make even good performers feel a little off. A new bed, a different schedule, or a strange environment can quietly pull you away from your rhythm. Rory understands that what settles you is usually not something big. It is something familiar you can return to that reminds your body and mind, "I know this. I'm good here."

MORNING EDGE: PACK YOUR HOME BASE

Pick one thing you can bring with you anywhere and return to every day. It might be the same stretch, the same piece of gear, the same warm-up song, or a quick text to someone who steadies you, but make it simple enough that it travels well.

FLIP THE SWITCH: THIS IS STILL MY GAME

When things feel rushed, strange, or unfamiliar, take one Return to Zero breath and go back to your anchor. Remind yourself, "This is still my game," and let that familiar thing bring you back to your rhythm.

CHAMPION'S WRAP: BROUGHT YOUR WEATHER

Notice what helped you feel most like yourself today. Keep that close and use it again tomorrow. The goal is to stop needing the setting to feel right before you do.

DAY 96: DOUBLE DOWN ON YOUR EDGE

"You can't chase someone else's game."
Rory McIlroy

Rory learned this the hard way. The moment you start looking at someone else's strengths as the answer, your own game starts to get blurry. Your tempo changes, your decisions get less clear, and your attention starts drifting sideways instead of staying where your best golf lives. The goal is not to copy what works for someone else. The goal is to protect what works for you and bring more of that to the course.

MORNING EDGE: LOCK IN YOUR EDGE

Before the day starts, remind yourself what tends to travel with you when you play well. It may be your calm, your tempo, your trust, your toughness, or your creativity, but pick the quality that feels most like you and bring that version to the first shot.

FLIP THE SWITCH: COME BACK TO YOUR GAME

When comparison starts pulling your attention sideways, take one Return to Zero breath and bring your eyes and mind back to center. Ask yourself, "What does my game look like when I'm at my best?" Then go play from there.

CHAMPION'S WRAP: STAYED IN YOUR GAME

Think of one moment today when you trusted your style instead of reaching for somebody else's. Notice what that protected in you. Your rhythm, your confidence, and your timing tend to show up when you stay loyal to your own game.

DAY 97: BRING THE SWAGGER

"You know I need that cockiness, the self-belief, arrogance, swagger, whatever you want to call it, I need that on the golf course to bring the best out of myself."
Rory McIlroy

Rory is talking about something numerous athletes feel but do not always show. You can have the game and still act like you are asking permission to use it. That is when you get careful, tentative, and smaller than you need to be. Swagger is not about being bigger than other people. It is about being fully committed to your own talent.

MORNING EDGE: STOP PLAYING SMALL

Before the day starts, decide that you are not going to hide today. Stand tall, walk with intent, and let your actions show the belief you want your game to feel.

FLIP THE SWITCH: LET THE BODY GO FIRST

When doubt or flatness shows up, do not wait around for confidence to arrive. Lift your posture, get your eyes up, and move like the version of you that expects good things to happen.

CHAMPION'S WRAP: NO APOLOGY

Think of one moment today when you let your belief show instead of dialing yourself down. Notice what changed in your body, your choices, or your rhythm. That is the version worth bringing back tomorrow.

DAY 98: MENTAL TRAINING PARTNER

TIGER WOODS

"My mind has won me a lot of tournaments."
Tiger Woods

Tiger built one of the most dominant runs in sports on more than talent. He built it on a mind that stayed sharp, steady, and fierce when the stakes were highest. At Augusta National, he won five Masters titles across three different decades. The 2019 victory reminded everyone that his greatest weapon was never just his swing.

Tiger did not win because he felt comfortable. He won because he knew how to compete when the nerves hit, the pressure built, and the moment got heavy. He has spoken openly about his hands shaking on the first tee and feeling the same fear and adrenaline that every player feels. The difference was that he stayed with the shot and kept going right at it.

His mental game was trained every day. He relied on simple, repeatable habits that kept his mind from drifting and his body from rushing. He picked the target, committed to the shot, accepted the result, and moved on. His body language carried the same message. Calm, strong, and fully locked into the task.

That is what made Tiger so hard to beat. He kept bringing his mind back to the shot, the task, and the next chance to compete. This week, Tiger is your mental training partner. He will show you how to handle nerves, commit under pressure, and keep your mind working for you when the moment matters most.

DAY 99: THE TOUGHEST OPPONENT IS YOU

"The toughest competitor I've ever gone against? Myself."
Tiger Woods

Tiger was pointing to the battle that shows up inside every competitor. The hardest opponent is not always across from you. Sometimes it is the part of you that rushes, tightens up, doubts, or starts trying too hard. Those moments can pull you out of your game faster than anything else. Tiger's gift was not that he never felt them. It was that he recognized them quickly and got back to himself before they took over.

MORNING EDGE: CATCH YOURSELF EARLY

Before your first rep, pause and ask, "Am I fully here, or already somewhere else?" If your mind is drifting, bring it back before the day starts speeding up. The earlier you catch yourself, the easier it is to stay in command.

FLIP THE SWITCH: WIN THE MOMENT INSIDE

When rushing, frustration, or overthinking shows up, do not let it take the wheel. Tell yourself, "Back to me," then get fully into your next shot, breath, or decision. You do not have to win the whole day at once. You just have to win the moment in front of you.

CHAMPION'S WRAP: WON THE INNER BATTLE

At the end of the day, think of one moment when you caught yourself starting to slip and brought it back. That is a win worth noticing. The more often you do that, the stronger and steadier you become under pressure.

DAY 100: MAKE IT REAL BEFORE IT'S REAL

"I've been in this position before. I know how to do this. I've done it before."
Tiger Woods

Tiger did not wait for pressure to show up on Sunday. He built it into practice by creating must-make moments and telling himself, "This is the eighteenth hole at the U.S. Open. You have to hit the shot," then staying with the discomfort and committing anyway. By putting himself in demanding situations on purpose, pressure became familiar long before it ever mattered. That is one of the best ways to build trust in yourself under fire.

MORNING EDGE: REHEARSE THE MOMENT

Pick one rep today and make it feel real by seeing the situation clearly before you begin. Lock in with: "I've been here before," then step in and execute with full commitment.

FLIP THE SWITCH: SHRINK THE MOMENT

When pressure rises, do not wrestle with the whole outcome or the meaning of the moment. Come back to: "One target. Trust it," and give your full attention to one clear target, one simple cue, and one clean action.

CHAMPION'S WRAP: BANK THE MEMORY

At the end of the day, replay one rep or moment that you handled with composure and intent. Remind yourself, "That one counts," because every pressure rep you finish well becomes evidence you can borrow from later.

DAY 101: YOU'RE SWITCHED ON

"I'm nervous every time I tee it up. If you're not nervous, that means you don't care. It's just a matter of how you handle it."
Tiger Woods

Tiger expected the moment to bring energy with it. His heartbeat might quicken, his body might feel more alert, and the moment might feel a little sharper. He did not treat that as a problem. He treated it as part of getting ready to compete.

MORNING EDGE: EXPECT THE ENERGY

Before you begin, expect a little extra energy when it is time to compete. Read that feeling as a sign that you care, you are engaged, and you are ready to go.

FLIP THE SWITCH: PUT IT TO WORK

When that feeling shows up, do not waste energy fighting it. Get your eyes on the task, settle into your body, and put your attention on one thing you can do well right away.

CHAMPION'S WRAP: YOU STAYED WITH IT

Think of one moment today when you felt the nerves and stayed with the job anyway. That is how trust grows. You learn that you can compete with that feeling and still perform well.

DAY 102: LET THE PICTURE LEAD

"See the shot happen before you hit it."
Tiger Woods

Tiger did not leave the shot up for debate once he stepped in. He saw it first. He pictured the start line, the curve, the landing spot, and the kind of swing that would send it there. By the time he stood over the ball, the picture had already given the body its job.

MORNING EDGE: BUILD THE PICTURE

Before your first rep, take a moment to see the whole action clearly. Picture the line, the movement, and the finish, then step in and let your body follow what your mind has already shown it.

FLIP THE SWITCH: CLEAN UP THE PICTURE

When doubt starts clouding things, step back and rebuild the image. Give yourself a simple, clean picture of the next shot, then commit to bringing that one to life.

CHAMPION'S WRAP: THE PICTURE HELD

Think of one rep today where the picture was clear and the swing matched it. Replay it once more in your mind before the day ends. That is a good image to keep.

DAY 103: PROTECT YOUR STORY

"It's like reading a book with the TV on in the background. You know it's there, but you're so into the story you don't hear it."
Tiger Woods

When PGA Tour player Harold Varner III asked Tiger how he handled all the attention around him, Tiger said he heard everything. The crowds, the movement, the cameras, and the noise were all there, especially because so much of it was following him. None of that had to disappear for him to stay in command. He focused on his mission and kept his attention on what mattered most. At the Masters, people are always ready to tell you what the week means, what your game looks like, what this round could become, or what it says about your career. The challenge is to not let those outside narratives get inside your head and start shaping how you think, feel, or compete.

MORNING EDGE: CHOOSE THE MISSION

Before you begin, decide what matters most today and commit to staying with it. Do the job in front of you and do not let outside narratives hijack you.

FLIP THE SWITCH: BACK TO THE MISSION

When distractions pull at you, let them be there and bring your attention back to what you are here to do. Great focus is not about controlling the background. It is about returning to the mission and refusing to let anything outside you define the moment.

CHAMPION'S WRAP: PROTECTED YOUR STORY

Think of one moment today when things around you could have pulled your attention away and you stayed with what mattered anyway. That is how your focus gets stronger. You train yourself to protect your story even when the background presses in.

DAY 104: DON'T HEAD FOR THE PARKING LOT

"Days when you just don't have it, you don't pack it in. You give it everything you've got. You grind it out."
Tiger Woods

Some days the swing feels off from the start. The ball does weird things, the feel is missing, and your confidence starts acting like it has other plans. That is usually the moment when people begin checking out before the round is actually over. Tiger did not do that. He stayed with the day long enough to see what was still in it.

MORNING EDGE: STAY FOR ALL EIGHTEEN

Before you begin, decide that you are staying in the round no matter how the early part looks. Let the day unfold before you start telling yourself what kind of day it is.

FLIP THE SWITCH: STAY IN THE FIGHT CARD

When frustration shows up, do not start fast-forwarding to the end. Get back to the next shot, the next read, or the next decision, and play it like the round still has something good left in it.

CHAMPION'S WRAP: YOU STAYED ON THE COURSE

Think of one moment today when you could have drifted, coasted, or mentally checked out, but stayed with the job instead. That is how the habit is built. The more often you refuse to pack it in, the more natural it becomes to compete all the way to the finish.

DAY 105: MENTAL TRAINING PARTNER
ANNIKA SÖRENSTAM

"I've learned how to forget bad shots and move on . . . I'd be upset for about ten seconds, and then I'd move on to the next tee."
Annika Sörenstam

Annika built one of the most consistent and commanding careers in golf. She won seventy-two times on the LPGA Tour, claimed ten majors, and became the only woman ever to shoot fifty-nine in competition. Her edge was not just talent. It was precision, patience, and a mind that stayed clear under pressure.

Nothing captured that edge better than her ten-second rule. A bad shot got its moment, then she was done with it. She refused to let one swing linger long enough to steal the next one. That discipline kept her attention clean and her game moving forward.

Annika's connection to Augusta runs deep. She is a member at Augusta National and helped launch the Augusta National Women's Amateur, opening doors for the next generation. She also showed the golf world what courage under pressure looks like when she competed in a PGA Tour event in 2003 and striped her opening drive right down the middle.

This week, Annika is your mental training partner. She will teach you how to reset quickly, stay precise under pressure, and keep one bad shot from following you down the course. That is how consistency is built, one clear mind and one committed swing at a time.

DAY 106: HAVE A HOME BASE

"I never just show up and play. I always have a plan."

Annika Sörenstam

Annika never wanted her game floating around at the mercy of mood or momentum. She wanted something solid she could return to when the swing felt off, the nerves picked up, or the round started getting wild. That is what a plan gives you. It gives you a home base when the day starts moving fast.

MORNING EDGE: PICK YOUR HOME BASE

Before you begin, choose one simple default you can trust today. It might be your routine, your tempo, your target, or your attitude, but make it something solid enough to come back to when the round starts moving around.

FLIP THE SWITCH: BACK TO BASE

When something goes sideways, take one Return to Zero breath and come back to your default before you do anything else. Do not add more. Return to what steadies you, make one adjustment if needed, and go again.

CHAMPION'S WRAP: YOU CAME BACK HOME

Think of one moment today when you returned to what works instead of reaching for something extra. That is what good preparation does. It gives you a place to come back to when the day starts pulling you around.

DAY 107: CARRY IT WELL

"Pressure is a privilege. It means you've worked hard to get here."

Annika Sörenstam

Pressure usually shows up when something matters. Important moments are supposed to feel important. That feeling is part of what gives the game its energy, its edge, and its meaning. Annika learned that pressure did not need to be feared or fixed. It needed to be carried well.

MORNING EDGE: LET IT MATTER

When something important shows up today, let it feel important. Stay steady, breathe, and carry the weight without turning it into drama.

FLIP THE SWITCH: TAKE IT AS IT COMES

When a bad stretch hits, it can feel like the bottom just fell out and your head starts spinning. Take one Return to Zero breath and remind yourself, "Take it as it comes." Stay even-keel, steady your rhythm, and deal with the next shot instead of treating the whole day like it is gone.

CHAMPION'S WRAP: YOU CARRIED IT WELL

Look back on one moment today that mattered to you, especially if things got shaky for a stretch. Notice whether you stayed solid under the weight of it. That is a skill worth building.

DAY 108: STAY ON YOUR OWN FAIRWAY

"Focus on what you can do, not what others are doing."
Annika Sörenstam

Comparison can start with one glance on the range. Someone is striping it, attention starts shifting their way, and suddenly your eyes drift, your tempo changes, and your game starts to slip. Annika knew that trap. Her best golf came from staying locked into her own swing, her own targets, and her own rhythm.

MORNING EDGE: CLAIM YOUR FAIRWAY

Before you begin, decide what your fairway is today. It may be your tempo, your routine, your body language, or the way you respond after a mistake. Whatever it is, make that your lane and stay on it.

FLIP THE SWITCH: BRING IT BACK TO YOU

When your eyes start drifting to someone else's swing, score, or spotlight, catch it before it pulls your game off track. Take one Return to Zero breath, bring your gaze back to your target, and tell yourself, "My swing. My rhythm. My shot." Then step back into your own game and own it.

CHAMPION'S WRAP: FAIRWAY DISCIPLINE

Look back on one moment today when you kept your eyes and mind on your own game. That is how you protect your rhythm and stay true to what you do best.

DAY 109: WHAT'S THE PLAY?

"When the pressure is on, that's when I focus even more on the small details."
Annika Sörenstam

Pressure gets heavy when your attention starts going everywhere at once. The mind jumps ahead, starts chasing outcomes, and turns one shot into five different problems. Annika understood that the answer was to bring everything back to one clear decision. In moments like that, the best question is simple: What's the play?

MORNING EDGE: START WITH THE PLAY

Before you begin, decide what kind of detail helps you settle into your game. It may be your target, your tempo, your breath, or your setup, but know what brings you back to a clear play.

FLIP THE SWITCH: ASK THE BETTER QUESTION

When the moment starts feeling too big, stop feeding it with bigger thoughts. Take one Return to Zero breath and ask, "What's the play?" Then give all of your attention to that and nothing extra.

CHAMPION'S WRAP: STAYED WITH THE PLAY

Look back on one moment today when you got clear instead of scattered. That is how pressure becomes playable and you get back to your game.

DAY 110: FLY THE BUTTERFLIES

"Nerves show you care. The trick is to use them, not fight them."
Annika Sörenstam

Nerves are part of competing in moments that matter. Annika learned that the answer was not to get rid of them. It was to keep them from flying all over the place. A racing heart, quick breath, and extra energy can work for you when they are gathered and directed. The goal is not to feel nothing. The goal is to get the butterflies to fly in formation.

MORNING EDGE: LET THEM FLY TOGETHER

When nerves show up today, expect them and make room for them. Breathe slowly, loosen your body, and bring that energy into one clear place instead of letting it scatter.

FLIP THE SWITCH: LINE THEM UP

When you feel the flutter start bouncing everywhere, stop trying to get rid of it. Take one Return to Zero breath and give the energy a job by locking onto your routine, your tempo, or your target.

CHAMPION'S WRAP: BETTER FORMATION

Look back on one moment today when the butterflies showed up and you got them moving in the same direction. That is how nerves start working for you.

DAY 111: PLAY FOR MORE THAN YOURSELF

"Golf gave me a platform—now I want to give back."
Annika Sörenstam

Competing only for yourself can make the moment feel smaller and heavier at the same time. Every mistake feels personal, and every result starts to feel like a verdict. Annika understood that performance gets steadier when it is connected to something larger than ego. When you compete for a standard, for the people who helped you, or for the example you want to set, the moment gets clearer and your response gets stronger.

MORNING EDGE: REMEMBER WHAT YOU CARRY

Before you begin, take a moment to remember who or what you represent when you compete. Let that thought raise your standards and steady how you show up.

FLIP THE SWITCH: THE WHO RESET

When frustration starts pulling you inward, interrupt it with one clear question: "Who am I representing right now?" Take one Return to Zero breath, lift your eyes, and compete in a way that honors that answer.

CHAMPION'S WRAP: LEFT IT BETTER

Look back on one moment today when you made the space around you better. Maybe you raised the standard, encouraged someone, stayed composed, or handled a hard moment the right way. That is what it looks like to compete for more than yourself.

DAY 112: MENTAL TRAINING PARTNER

SCOTTIE SCHEFFLER

"I think it's always a battle to stay in the present. . . . I don't want to be at home thinking about my swing, and I don't want to be on the course thinking about being home."
Scottie Scheffler

Scottie Scheffler does not need flash to stand out. He lets his game do the talking. From Texas fairways to two Masters titles, a PGA Championship, Olympic gold, and the number one ranking, he has built one of the steadiest runs in golf. His edge comes from composure, discipline, and a mind that stays with the shot.

Scottie's calm can fool people. He is deeply competitive and loves the part most people try to skip—the work, the reps, the grind, and the fight it takes to stay in the mix. He is not just trying to win when things feel easy. He wants to be in the heat of it, hit the hard shots, and earn his way through the moments that demand patience, toughness, and belief.

He also understands how easily the mind can leave where the body is. You can be at home thinking about golf, or on the course thinking about being somewhere else. Either way, you lose the moment in front of you. Scottie knows that presence is not just the best way to play golf. It is the best way to enjoy life. When he is home, he wants to be home. When he is over the ball, he wants to be all the way there. That is why each shot gets his eyes, his breath, and his best attention.

That is what makes him so tough to beat. He keeps coming back to what is right in front of him and refuses to get ahead of himself. This week, Scottie is your mental training partner. He will show you how to stay present, trust your routine, and keep your mind where your game actually lives.

DAY 113: A COMMITTED MIND

"When I'm playing my best, I'm focused on the target.
I'm not thinking about swing mechanics."
Scottie Scheffler

Scottie keeps the game simple when it matters most. In practice, he can work on mechanics, positions, and feels. In competition, his job is different. He picks a clear target, lets his eyes settle there, and trusts the swing to respond. A golfer does not need a perfect mind, just a committed one.

MORNING EDGE: COMMIT BEFORE YOU SWING

Before your first rep, choose a clear target and let your eyes settle there. The goal is not to feel perfect. The goal is to be fully decided before you step in.

FLIP THE SWITCH: END THE NEGOTIATION

When you step into the shot still searching for the right feel, you are not fully committed yet. That is when doubt lingers, timing gets disrupted, and the motion loses its freedom. Take one Return to Zero breath and come back to the question that matters most: "What am I committed to right now?" Answer it clearly: "This target. This swing." Or, on the greens, "This line. This speed." Make the decision, step in, and let the body carry it out.

CHAMPION'S WRAP: FULLY COMMITTED

Think of one moment today when you made a clear decision and let it rip without second-guessing. Notice how it changed your rhythm, your trust, and your timing. That is what commitment feels like, and that is a feeling worth bringing back tomorrow.

DAY 114: STAY READY FOR THE TURN

"I try to be as mentally tough as possible. That's probably my greatest strength."
Scottie Scheffler

Anybody can handle one bad shot now and then. The real test is what you do when it turns into a rough stretch, a couple of bad holes, or a putt that lips out and acts like it has a personal issue with you. That is where some players start waiting for the next bad thing to happen. Tough players stay ready for the turn, because they know something good can show up just as fast.

MORNING EDGE: EXPECT THE BOUNCE BACK

Before the day starts, remind yourself that rough patches are part of the deal. Decide now that if one shows up, you will stay open, steady, and ready for the next good swing, good break, or good decision.

FLIP THE SWITCH: STAY IN BUSINESS

When things get messy, take one Return to Zero breath and tell yourself, "Still in business." Then get your eyes up and go play the next shot like something good is still available to you.

CHAMPION'S WRAP: YOU STAYED AVAILABLE

Think of one moment today when things were not going your way and you stayed in it anyway. Maybe you caught a good bounce, hit a clean shot, or simply gave yourself another chance. That is a huge part of mental toughness. Strong competitors stay open to good things happening.

DAY 115: BEST IS PLENTY

"All I can do is prepare and try to do my best."
Scottie Scheffler

Scottie competes with a truth that can save athletes a lot of trouble. You cannot magically give more than your best just because the moment is bigger, the score is closer, or you really, really want it. That is usually when people start swinging from their shoes, pressing, and asking today to be something other than what it is. The better move is simpler and smarter: Bring your best, quit shopping for extras, and go play.

MORNING EDGE: LET BEST BE PLENTY

You cannot do better than your best, but you can make a mess of things by trying to. Let that take some weight off right away, and compete with freedom instead of strain.

FLIP THE SWITCH: QUIT REACHING

When something slips, take one Return to Zero breath and stop reaching for a miracle. Get back to the best swing, choice, or response you can give right now, and let that be enough.

CHAMPION'S WRAP: NOTHING FANCY NEEDED

Think of one moment today when you stopped trying to do something extra and simply gave the moment your best. Notice how much cleaner the game felt when you trusted what you had. That is a good place to play from.

DAY 116: STAY IN POSITION

"Some weeks it just takes a little longer for things to click. You've got to stay patient and keep giving yourself chances."
Scottie Scheffler

Scottie understands that not every round clicks right away. Some days start a little off, and that is when players get impatient, start chasing, and try to force something that has not shown up yet. The best players resist that pull by staying patient, keeping themselves in position, and giving the round time to turn. If you compete long enough, some of the biggest moments of your career will go your way and some will break your heart. When you accept that both are part of the path, you stop making this moment bigger than it needs to be, and that is what helps you stay free inside it.

MORNING EDGE: KEEP YOURSELF IN IT

Today is not about forcing something to happen early. It is about staying in position, making solid decisions, and giving yourself chances to let the round come back to you.

FLIP THE SWITCH: DON'T CHASE IT

When you feel the urge to force something, pause and come back to the shot in front of you. Pick a target you trust, make a committed swing, and stay in the round instead of trying to jump ahead of it.

CHAMPION'S WRAP: STAYED IN POSITION

Think of one moment today when you stayed patient and kept yourself in it. Maybe nothing special happened right away, but you gave yourself another look, another swing, and another chance. That is how rounds begin to turn.

DAY 117: THE NEXT SHOT DOESN'T CARE

"I can't control the last swing, but I can control the next one."
Scottie Scheffler

The next shot is wonderfully unsentimental. It does not care what just happened, what you meant to do, or how unfair the last break felt. Scottie understands that every shot asks the same simple question: What are you bringing to me right now? Strong competitors answer that question quickly, because they know the game keeps moving and the next moment never waits for you to catch up emotionally.

MORNING EDGE: FRESH SHOT, FRESH MIND

Before the day starts, remind yourself that every rep, swing, and decision gets to be its own thing. Nothing carries over unless you drag it there.

FLIP THE SWITCH: ANSWER THE SHOT

When frustration hits, take one Return to Zero breath and let your hands soften. Put your eyes on where you want the ball to go and tell yourself, "This shot gets a fresh start." Then answer it with your full attention.

CHAMPION'S WRAP: KEPT IT FRESH

Think of one moment today when you left the last shot where it belonged and gave the next one a clean look. That is how momentum gets rebuilt. That is how rounds stay alive.

DAY 118: CHASE THE PURE STRIKE

"It does not get boring. Hitting a really well-struck golf shot close to the pin is an addictive feeling. That's what keeps everybody coming back."
Scottie Scheffler

Scores fade fast. A pure strike stays with you. The sound, the flight, and the feeling of everything matching up for a split second never really get old. Scottie understands that this is one of the deepest rewards in sport. When you stay connected to that feeling, the game gives you something the scoreboard never can.

MORNING EDGE: HUNT THE FEELING

Before you begin, bring to mind the sound and feel of one of your purest shots. Let that be part of what you are playing for today, not just the number that comes after it.

FLIP THE SWITCH: FIND THE CLICK

When frustration starts pulling you toward the score, step away from the math and back into the feel. Ask yourself, "What would a pure one feel like here?" and go chase that.

CHAMPION'S WRAP: THE PUREST ONE

At the end of the day, forget the whole card for a moment and replay the purest shot you hit. Hold on to the feeling, the sound, and the picture of it. That is one of the truest rewards the game has to offer.

DAY 119: DON'T LET THE GAP GET HEAVY

"If you're not trying to get better every day, you're falling behind."
Scottie Scheffler

Improvement is a lot more about maintenance than a makeover. The best players keep tightening the little things so the game never starts feeling heavy. Scottie understands that the danger is not one bad day. The danger is letting small slips pile up until you feel you have to force your way back. Staying on the rise is less about huge gains and more about never drifting so far that urgency takes over.

MORNING EDGE: FIND THE LOOSE SCREW

Ask yourself one simple question before you start: "What needs a small tightening today?" Pick one thing—a rushed transition, a lazy setup, a wandering mind—and give it your attention without making it a big production.

FLIP THE SWITCH: ADJUST, DON'T ARGUE

When something slips, skip the drama and skip the overhaul. Make one small correction, get back to work, and keep the day moving forward.

CHAMPION'S WRAP: KEEP THE GAP LIGHT

Name one small upgrade you made or one standard you kept from slipping today. That is how strong competitors stay ahead of the panic, protect their progress, and keep the game feeling playable.

DAY 120: KNOW WHO YOU ARE BEFORE YOU PLAY

"My faith and my family are what's most important to me . . . I don't think I'm anything special because some weeks I'm better at shooting a lower score than other guys are."
Scottie Scheffler

Golf can reveal a lot about you, but it does not define you. Scottie understands that the scorecard is a record of performance, not a measure of worth. When athletes tie their identity to the result, the game gets heavy, and the swing gets tight. When they remember who they are before they play, they compete with more freedom, more honesty, and a steadier heart.

MORNING EDGE: SET YOUR CENTER

Before the day begins, get clear on what matters most to you beyond the game. Start from there, so the round becomes something you do with purpose, not something you need in order to feel whole.

FLIP THE SWITCH: LEAVE YOUR NAME ALONE

When the score, the stakes, or other people's opinions start tugging at your identity, take one Return to Zero breath and strip the moment back down to the job. Tell yourself, "One shot. One job," and let your worth stay where it belongs.

CHAMPION'S WRAP: BIGGER THAN THE SCORECARD

At the end of the day, think of one moment that had nothing to do with the number you shot. Maybe it was the way you carried yourself, the way you responded, or the way you treated someone else. The round ends, but your character stays.

CHAMPION'S TAKEAWAYS: AUGUSTA NATIONAL

Augusta wasn't about forcing anything. It was about staying steady long enough for your game to show up.

You trained patience, trust, and follow-through. You practiced letting one shot end before the next began. You learned that good golf—and good performance—comes from clear decisions, solid routines, and moving on without drama. A divided mind drains both performance and joy. The more fully you can be where you are, the more freely you can play and the more deeply you can enjoy it.

Take a moment to reflect:

- What helped me stay patient instead of pressing?
- What routine or habit do I trust most right now?
- What would I tell myself before the first shot next time?

That Green Jacket isn't about perfection. It's proof you can stay composed, commit fully, and keep playing your game when it counts. Carry that forward.

CHAPTER 5

MAY: WRIGLEY FIELD

"Baseball is 90 percent mental. The other half is physical."
Yogi Berra

This month, your home base is Wrigley Field. It is not just another ballpark. Built in 1914, wrapped in ivy since 1937, and finally lit in 1988, Wrigley has a heartbeat of its own. When you step out onto the field, you can feel the weight of everyone who has ever walked on it. Here, even the field tests you. A routine fly ball can drift over the wall. A bullet in the gap can hang in the wind. Wrigley reminds you early that the game will not bend to your comfort level—what matters is your ability to handle tension.

And pressure? It's everywhere. The crowd doesn't sit back and observe. They live inside every pitch. They sense players trying to do too much. They taste hesitation. They don't need a scoreboard to know when you're squeezing the bat. That is why 2016 mattered so much. The Cubs didn't end a 108-year drought by sidestepping pressure. They settled into it, trusted each other, and stayed composed while the world held its breath.

Baseball continues to prove how mentally demanding the game really is. In 2025, Aaron Judge and Shohei Ohtani both repeated as MVPs—the first time in MLB history that both reigning MVPs won again in the same year. They didn't do that by accident. They did it through presence, discipline, and emotional control when the game tried to shake them.

This month, your mental training partners live by that standard. Ken

Ravizza taught athletes how to reset one pitch at a time. Joe Maddon teaches how to keep the game light without losing the standard. Aaron Judge shows how to carry New York's weight with steadiness. Shohei Ohtani shows how preparation and joy can coexist under the heaviest expectations.

Wrigley won't hand you anything. But if you breathe, focus, and trust your work, you'll learn how to make pressure feel like home.

DAY 121: MENTAL TRAINING PARTNER

DR. KEN RAVIZZA

"Be present, not perfect."
Ken Ravizza

Ken Ravizza did not coach from an office. He lived in dugouts, walked bullpens, and stood right in the middle of the mess with athletes who needed something real. He knew pressure would expose habits, emotions, and attention fast. His job was to help players steady themselves and compete like pros when the game got hard.

His message was simple and direct. Stop chasing perfect and get into this pitch, this breath, and this moment right here. In 2004, when Cal State Fullerton sat at 15–16, he brought a small plastic toy toilet into the clubhouse and told the team to flush the season and start fresh. They laughed, flushed it, and then went 32–6 on the way to winning the College World Series.

Ravizza understood that baseball always gives you something to handle. A bad call, a rough inning, a flat day, and a mind that wants to race all over the place are all part of the deal. That is why his one-liners stuck. "Flush it." "Control the controllables." "Feeling good is overrated." "Get 100 percent out of the day you're having."

This week, Ravizza is your mental training partner. He will teach you how to flush mistakes, breathe between pitches, and settle yourself when the game starts pulling you around. That is the real mental game. Respond well, pitch after pitch, no matter what just happened.

DAY 122: MAKE IT A GOOD CRAPPY DAY

"Hey . . . have a good crappy day."
Ken Ravizza

Some days feel smooth and electric, and some days feel like you showed up in concrete shoes. Your body is heavy, your timing is off, and the day gives you a little less than you hoped for. Ravizza loved that reality because it revealed something important. You do not need a perfect day to compete like a champion; you need the guts and skill to make a good one out of a crappy one.

MORNING EDGE: OWN THE DAY ANYWAY

If you wake up tired, tight, or off, do not turn it into a bigger story. Tell yourself, "It may be a crappy day, but I can still make it a good one." Then decide how you will compete with what you have.

FLIP THE SWITCH: COMPETE WITH WHAT'S THERE

When something goes sideways, take one Return to Zero breath and stop looking for perfect. Ask yourself, "What would a good crappy day look like right here?" Then do the next tough, smart, simple thing.

CHAMPION'S WRAP: MADE SOMETHING OF IT

At the end of the day, think of one moment when things were not ideal and you still found a way to compete well. That is how toughness grows. You stop needing a perfect day and start learning how to use the day you have.

DAY 123: CONTROL WHAT COUNTS

"You cannot control the umpire, the weather, or the crowd, but you can control your breath, your focus, your effort."
Ken Ravizza

Sport keeps throwing things at you that are out of your control. The call can go against you, the conditions can shift, and the moment can test your patience. Ravizza's point is that your power comes back the moment you return to what is yours. Your breath settles you, your focus directs you, and your effort keeps you moving the right way.

MORNING EDGE: OWN YOUR THREE

Start the day by naming your three anchors: breath, focus, and effort. Whatever shows up today, keep coming back to those three and let them set your standard.

FLIP THE SWITCH: BACK TO WHAT COUNTS

When a bad call, a mistake, or a distraction pulls your attention away, stop and take one Return to Zero breath. Then tell yourself, "Control what counts," and put your energy back into your breath, your focus, and your effort.

CHAMPION'S WRAP: STAYED WITH WHAT WAS YOURS

At the end of the day, think of one moment when you brought your mind back to what you could control. That is how composure is built, and it is one of the most reliable edges in sport.

DAY 124: FLUSH IT AND MOVE ON

"Use the mental toilet. Flush it and move on."
Ken Ravizza

Ravizza made this lesson unforgettable by bringing a small plastic toilet into the dugout. It was playful, visual, a little ridiculous, and completely effective. The point was simple. Mistakes, bad calls, rough innings, and frustrating comments do not belong in your head during the next pitch or play. If you keep carrying them, they start to take up space that belongs to focus, freedom, and the next opportunity. Champions flush them fast and get back to competing.

MORNING EDGE: BUILD YOUR FLUSH CUE

Before the day begins, decide how you are going to let things go. Choose a simple reset cue for anything that does not go your way—a mistake, a bad call, a negative comment, or an interaction that throws you off. It might be brushing your hands, tapping your leg, or saying, "Flush it." What matters is that it gives you a quick, clear way to stop carrying what does not belong in the next moment. Decide early that nothing lingers longer than it needs to.

FLIP THE SWITCH: FLUSH IT AND COMPETE

When something goes wrong, feels embarrassing, or gets under your skin, do not stand over it or carry it with you. Blow out the junk, take one Return to Zero breath, and use your cue: "Flush it." That one is gone, the next one is yours—get back to competing.

CHAMPION'S WRAP: LEFT IT THERE

Think of one moment today that could have stuck, but you let it go. You didn't carry it, replay it, or let it leak into what came next. That's how you keep one bad moment from becoming two.

DAY 125: SHOW UP ON TIME

"Be where you need to be when you need to be there."
Ken Ravizza

The only place you can compete is where you are right now. The past can teach you and the future can motivate you, but neither one can make the next play for you. Ken's point is simple and sharp. When the moment arrives, meet it with your full attention.

MORNING EDGE: FIND YOUR SPOT

Before the day begins, remind yourself that your job is not to be everywhere at once. Your job is to be fully where your feet are. Take one breath, feel the ground under you, and start from there.

FLIP THE SWITCH: RIGHT HERE

When your mind drifts to what just happened or what might happen next, bring it back fast. Take one Return to Zero breath, feel your feet, and tell yourself, "Right here." Then give the next play your full attention.

CHAMPION'S WRAP: YOU WERE THERE

As you close out the day, think of one moment when you were fully in it instead of mentally somewhere else. That is a real skill, and every time you come back to the moment, you make it easier to do again.

DAY 126: LET THE WORK SPEAK

"You've already done the work. Let it show up."
Ken Ravizza

Pressure can make athletes feel like they need to find something extra. That is when they start pressing, overthinking, and reaching for a fix instead of trusting what they have already built. Ken's point is simple. The work is done, the reps are in, and now it is time to let your game come through.

MORNING EDGE: START WITH TRUST

Before the day begins, remind yourself that preparation comes first and performance follows. Tell yourself, "The work is in me. My job is to let it come out." Then step into the day with trust instead of tension.

FLIP THE SWITCH: FREE IT UP

When you catch yourself forcing, fixing, or overtrying, stop right there. Take one Return to Zero breath, loosen your jaw, soften your hands, and tell yourself, "Less trying, more trusting." Then let your training take the next rep.

CHAMPION'S WRAP: IT SHOWED UP

As you close out the day, think of one moment when you trusted your training and let it work. That is not luck. That is what it looks like when preparation gets out on the field.

DAY 127: DREAMS NEED REPS

"This is not Disneyland. There's nothing magical about it."

Ken Ravizza

Ravizza said this because athletes often act like great performance should feel special before it happens. Competition is not Disneyland, where the lights are bright, the ride is smooth, and the magic is built into the ticket. Some days feel sharp, but most feel ordinary, awkward, or a little off. Dreams do come true, but usually because you handled enough ordinary days the right way.

MORNING EDGE: TRADE MAGIC FOR MASTERY

Start the day by choosing one habit you can trust when the mood is average and the spark is missing. Remind yourself that you do not need fairy dust today. You need your breath, your basics, and a willingness to go to work.

FLIP THE SWITCH: NO WAND, JUST WORK

When you catch yourself wishing the moment felt easier, smoother, or more exciting, stop waiting for the day to rescue you. Take one Return to Zero breath and ask, "What does good work look like right here?" Then do that and let the feeling come later.

CHAMPION'S WRAP: BUILD ON AN ORDINARY DAY

As you close out the day, think of one moment when nothing felt especially magical and you still showed up well. That is how big dreams are built. Not through fairy tales, but through the way you handle regular days.

DAY 128: MENTAL TRAINING PARTNER
JOE MADDON

"Don't ever let the pressure exceed the pleasure."
Joe Maddon

Joe Maddon believed players perform best when they are prepared, loose, and free to be themselves. He learned the game from every angle—catcher, scout, coach, and manager—and that shaped how he led. He knew a 162-game season tests more than skill. It tests your mindset, your energy, and your ability to keep showing up.

Maddon built clubhouses with life in them. He welcomed personality, humor, and individuality because he understood that tight players lock up and flat teams fade. At the same time, he expected professionalism, attention to detail, and real commitment to the work. His teams played free because they were prepared, and they were prepared because the standard was clear.

Maddon respected pressure and kept it in its place. He wanted players to enjoy the game, trust their work, and keep it from feeling heavier than it needed to. His famous line, "Try not to suck," carried more truth than sarcasm. Keep it simple, stay loose, and compete.

This week, train with Maddon's mindset. Bring structure to your preparation and freedom to your performance. Protect your joy, trust your routine, and let your personality show up. When the moment builds, settle in and play your game.

DAY 129: EARN YOUR RESPECT

"Respect ninety . . . run hard for ninety feet, and the respect will come back to you."
Joe Maddon

Respect 90 starts with a baseball truth. It means running hard to first base, all ninety feet, every time, whether the ball is crushed, chopped, or hit right at someone. Maddon used that idea to teach a larger lesson. Full effort on your part builds self-respect, sharpens identity, and keeps your standard higher than your mood.

MORNING EDGE: RESPECT THE 90

Before the day begins, choose one area where you will give your full effort, no matter how you feel. Tell yourself, "My standard does not depend on my mood." Then go honor it.

FLIP THE SWITCH: FINISH IT RIGHT

When you feel yourself easing up, drifting, or cutting a corner, catch it fast. Take one breath, remind yourself, "Respect the standard," and finish the rep, the play, or the task the right way.

CHAMPION'S WRAP: EARN YOUR RESPECT

At the end of the day, think of one moment when you gave full effort even though it would have been easier not to. That is how self-respect is built, and it is one of the strongest foundations in the mental game.

DAY 130: PLAY WITH FREEDOM

"I don't want anyone to ever go out there afraid to make a physical mistake, because that will lead to a mental mistake."
Joe Maddon

Maddon understood that playing not to mess up is its own mistake. A physical mistake is part of sport, but fear of that mistake can make you hesitate, steer, and second-guess. That is the mental mistake he is talking about. When you stop trusting your training and start trying to be too careful, your game loses its speed, rhythm, and edge.

MORNING EDGE: CHOOSE COMMITMENT

Start the day by reminding yourself that you are here to compete, not to protect. Pick one cue that helps you stay aggressive and committed, then bring that into your work today.

FLIP THE SWITCH: TRUST IT AND GO

When you feel yourself holding back, stop trying to guide the moment. Take one Return to Zero breath, tell yourself, "Commit," and make the next move with speed and conviction.

CHAMPION'S WRAP: THAT WAS YOUR GAME

At the end of the day, think of one moment when you trusted your training and let yourself go. That is the version of you that performs best, and every rep like that makes it easier to find again.

DAY 131: THIS PITCH ONLY

"The process is fearless."
Joe Maddon

Fear usually shows up when your mind gets ahead of the play. It starts chasing results, meaning, and everything that might happen next. The process brings you right back to the one job in front of you. That is why it frees you up to compete.

MORNING EDGE: HONOR THE PROCESS

Start the day by giving your full attention to the habits, cues, and choices that actually lead to success. You do not need to anticipate victory today; you need to take care of the steps that make it possible.

FLIP THE SWITCH: SHRINK THE MOMENT

When your mind starts chasing results, bring it back to size. Ask yourself, "What is the pitch right now?" Then do that one thing with full attention and let the rest wait.

CHAMPION'S WRAP: WON THE NOW

Think of one moment when you came back to your job instead of getting lost in the outcome. That is how fearless performance is built, one present-tense choice at a time.

DAY 132: DO NOT ADD TO THE MESS

"When things go badly, be a grown-up."
Joe Maddon

Anybody can look good when things are going well. The real test comes when the call goes against you, the play breaks down, or your game feels off. That is where maturity shows up. A pro settles the moment, keeps the inning from getting out of hand, and goes back to work.

MORNING EDGE: CHOOSE THE GROWN-UP MOVE

Before the day begins, ask yourself, "What is the grown-up move for me today?" It may be something you need to face, a conversation you need to have, or a habit you need to stop. Decide now that when the moment gets hard, you will steady yourself and handle what needs to be handled.

FLIP THE SWITCH: CLEAN UP YOUR SIDE

When the moment gets messy, do not add emotion, blame, or negative body language. Take one Return to Zero breath, unclench your jaw, drop your shoulders, and ask, "What is the next right move?" Then do that and let the rest wait.

CHAMPION'S WRAP: HELD IT TOGETHER

Think of one moment when you handled yourself well instead of letting the moment pull you down. That is how trust is built, and it is how you become someone who can be counted on when things go sideways.

DAY 133: MAKE IT FEEL LIKE FRIDAY NIGHT

"Every day is Friday night."
Joe Maddon

Great performers bring their own life to the day. Maddon wanted his players to show up with Friday night juice, even in the middle of a long season. Your state shapes your game, so energy, presence, and edge are part of the job. The best competitors know how to flip that switch on purpose.

MORNING EDGE: SET THE VIBE

Before the day begins, choose one thing that lifts your energy, such as your music, your clothes, your posture, or the way you walk into the room. Do not just show up today. Arrive like something good is about to happen.

FLIP THE SWITCH: BRING IT ON PURPOSE

When the day starts to feel flat, do not wait for energy to find you. Take one steady breath and carry yourself like it matters. Ask yourself, "How would I move right now if this were Friday night?" Then act like it.

CHAMPION'S WRAP: YOU SET THE TONE

At the end of the day, think of one moment when you lifted the energy instead of letting the day drag you down. That is a real skill, and the more you practice it, the more natural it becomes.

DAY 134: WEAR THE BULLSEYE

"Embrace the target."
Joe Maddon

The bullseye appears when you become the standard. Expectations rise because people see something worth chasing. The best competitors wear that target with pride and keep taking their cuts. They stay on the front foot and make the other side deal with them.

MORNING EDGE: STEP INTO THE TARGET

Name one expectation you feel today. Meet it head-on and say, "This is what I earned." Start from strength, not avoidance.

FLIP THE SWITCH: HUNT THE MOMENT

When pressure shows up, take one Return to Zero breath and say, "Hunt the moment." Then move toward the play, not away from it. The hunted team waits. The standard attacks.

CHAMPION'S WRAP: OWN THE BULLSEYE

Tonight, notice the moment when you leaned into the pressure instead of shrinking from it. That's what it looks like to compete from strength.

DAY 135: MENTAL TRAINING PARTNER

AARON JUDGE

"The mental game is what separates the good players from the great players."

Aaron Judge

Judge was built for baseball: 6'7", 280 pounds, all power and presence. But what truly separates him isn't his size; it's his mindset. From the time he joined the Yankees, Judge learned that the most challenging part of the game isn't hitting hundred-mile-per-hour fastballs. It's staying calm when the stadium shakes.

He didn't come in as an instant superstar. In 2016, he hit .179 and struck out forty-two times in eighty-four at-bats. Most would have folded. Judge studied, adjusted, and came back to hit fifty-two home runs the following year, win Rookie of the Year, and become the face of the franchise. That turnaround came from mastering his head as much as his swing.

He learned to crush a mistake by squeezing a handful of dirt and throwing it away. He built a routine that brought him right back to the present. He cleared his mind, trusted his breath, set his eyes, and owned the moment.

Judge leads the Yankees as captain the same way he leads himself. He is calm, steady, and in command. He carries himself like a man who belongs, and his presence does the talking.

This week, Judge is your mental training partner. You will train to think, breathe, and carry yourself like a captain on the biggest stage. Stay calm when the pressure rises, strong in your presence, and steady whatever the scoreboard says.

DAY 136: CRUSH IT AND MOVE ON

"For me, all my negative thoughts . . . I just kind of sit there and crush it up, and once I'm done doing that, I just kind of toss it aside."
Aaron Judge

Judge has a simple way of dealing with a bad moment. He gives it a shape, crushes it, and gets rid of it. That sends a message to his mind and body that the play is over. The best competitors keep the reset quick so they can get right back to the next chance.

MORNING EDGE: LEAVE IT BEHIND

Think of one mistake, frustration, or piece of baggage you do not need today. Write it down or grab a small object to stand for it, then crush it, crumple it, or toss it away. Start the day with a clean mind and free hands.

FLIP THE SWITCH: RESET FAST

When frustration hits, do not argue with it or carry it. Brush your hands, exhale hard, and tell yourself, "That one is gone." Then get right back to the next play.

CHAMPION'S WRAP: BACK TO THE NEXT ONE

At the end of the day, think of one moment when you let something go quickly instead of dragging it forward. That is how presence returns and confidence stays alive.

DAY 137: START LIKE IT'S OPENING DAY

"I just take it one day at a time, and try to forget about what I did the day before. I go out there like every day is Opening Day."
Aaron Judge

Judge treats every day like Opening Day because today asks for a fresh start. Yesterday can leave you too comfortable or too tight if you let it hang around. Great performers show up fresh, hungry, and ready to earn it again. That is how consistency gets built over a long season.

MORNING EDGE: ARRIVE NEW

Before the day begins, remind yourself that you do not get credit for yesterday and you do not have to carry it either. Tell yourself, "New day. Earn it again." Then step into today with fresh energy and full intent.

FLIP THE SWITCH: THIS DAY, THIS PLAY

When your mind drifts back to yesterday, whether it was good or bad, take one Return to Zero breath and bring it back to what is in front of you. Tell yourself, "This day. This play." Then compete from there.

CHAMPION'S WRAP: READY AGAIN TOMORROW

At the end of the day, think of one moment when you came back to the present instead of carrying yesterday with you. That is how pros stay ready, day after day.

DAY 138: THIS STARTS WITH ME

"Champions take responsibility and never back down."
Aaron Judge

Champions do not waste time ducking, blaming, or explaining away the moment. They step toward it. Taking responsibility puts you back in charge of your response and keeps you from backing down when it counts.

MORNING EDGE: STEP TOWARD IT

Pick one part of your day where you need to lead instead of react. Decide now that if something gets hard, you will meet it head-on rather than avoid it.

FLIP THE SWITCH: OWN YOUR RESPONSE

When frustration rises, pause and take one Return to Zero breath. Say, "This starts with me," and ask, "What is my move here?" Then make the strongest next move you can.

CHAMPION'S WRAP: NO BACKING DOWN

At the end of the day, think of one moment when you stayed with the challenge instead of pulling away from it. That is what responsibility looks like under pressure.

DAY 139: HELP THE TEAM WIN

"My main focus is, 'What can I do today to help the team win the ballgame.'"
Aaron Judge

When a team is off, the game gives everyone a choice. You can get wrapped up in your own frustration, or you can get useful. The best teammates look for what the group needs most and bring it. That mindset sharpens your role and gives the team something steady to follow.

MORNING EDGE: BE USEFUL EARLY

Before the day begins, ask yourself, "How can I help the team today?" Choose one clear way to do it through your effort, your communication, or your presence. Start there.

FLIP THE SWITCH: MAKE A TEAM MOVE

When frustration hits, take one Return to Zero breath and get your attention off yourself. Ask, "What helps us most right now?" Then do that, even if it is small and even if no one notices.

CHAMPION'S WRAP: EARNED TRUST

At the end of the day, think of one moment when you helped settle, lift, or strengthen the group. Teams improve when players bring value rather than waiting for better conditions.

DAY 140: BATTLE

"Sometimes you've got to tip your cap when they're painting stuff on the corner. But you can't give up, got to keep battling and make some adjustments."
Aaron Judge

At the highest level, hard is part of the deal because the other side can play too. Some pitches are nasty, some breaks go against you, and some moments demand more than your first answer. The edge is staying in the fight, respecting the challenge, and making the next adjustment. That is what battle looks like.

MORNING EDGE: RESPECT THE CHALLENGE

Think of one challenge you are likely to face today. Acknowledge it honestly and remind yourself that hard does not mean wrong. Then decide how you want to respond when the moment gets tight.

FLIP THE SWITCH: BATTLE AND ADJUST

When things are not going your way, take one Return to Zero breath and settle yourself. Tell yourself, "Tip your cap, then battle." Stay engaged, make the next smart adjustment, and keep competing.

CHAMPION'S WRAP: STAYED IN IT

At the end of the day, think of one moment when you stayed with the challenge instead of getting frustrated by it. That is what it looks like to compete like a pro.

DAY 141: SIGNED UP FOR THIS

"The ups and downs, that's baseball life. That's what I live for, play for."

Aaron Judge

You do not get the dream without the ride that comes with it. Judge knows the highs, the slumps, the cheers, and the frustration all belong to the same life. Some days give you results, and some days give you edge. When you remember that you signed up for all of it, you stop wasting energy fighting the ride and start playing the game.

MORNING EDGE: TAKE THE FULL DEAL

Start the day by reminding yourself that you did not choose a smooth path. You chose a meaningful one. Say, "I signed up for all of it," and let that steady you before the day begins.

FLIP THE SWITCH: THIS COMES WITH IT

When the day gets hard, do not treat it like something has gone wrong. Take one Return to Zero breath and tell yourself, "This comes with it." Then stay with the moment and keep competing.

CHAMPION'S WRAP: STILL IN THE RIDE

At the end of the day, think of one moment you handled without getting thrown by the ups or the downs. That is part of earning the life you chose.

DAY 142: MENTAL TRAINING PARTNER

SHOHEI OHTANI

"I still consider myself far from a complete player, with so many things I must work on."
Shohei Ohtani

Ohtani is a dual threat with a single mind. He grew up in Oshu, Japan, the son of athletic parents, learning early on that humility keeps you grounded when talent wants to take off. As a teenager, he could throw a baseball at ninety-nine miles per hour, yet he still cleaned toilets with his high school teammates. That wasn't punishment. That was perspective.

He built himself through honest work and steady improvement. He was Rookie of the Year in 2018, then navigated injuries, setbacks, and rebuilds, turning each comeback into a lesson in patience and purpose. In 2021, he made history as an All-Star pitcher and hitter. He joined the Los Angeles Dodgers in 2023. In 2024, despite not pitching, he delivered a historic 50–50 season and helped lead LA to a World Series title. The Dodgers won it again the following year.

Ohtani doesn't say much. He studies, adjusts, and gets back to work. He loves the game enough to keep evolving, and that's the secret—stay in love with the work.

This week, train like Ohtani and bring every part of your game together. Turn pressure into purpose, trust your preparation, and build real progress one step at a time. Play with joy, serve the team, and compete with a clear, steady mind.

DAY 143: STAY TEACHABLE

"I didn't think I was good. Before high school, I didn't participate in many tournaments, so I assumed there must be many players better than me."
Shohei Ohtani

Ohtani stayed open, hungry, and ready to grow because he believed there was always more to learn. That is the power of a student mindset. It keeps you sharp and it keeps you moving. When you stay teachable, you keep improving.

MORNING EDGE: LEAVE ROOM TO LEARN

Start the day by asking, "What can I get better at today?" You do not need to prove yourself before you begin. You just need to stay open enough to learn.

FLIP THE SWITCH: LET IT HELP YOU

When feedback, correction, or a hard moment shows up, resist the urge to get defensive. Tell yourself, "This can help me," and look for the lesson instead of protecting your pride.

CHAMPION'S WRAP: USE WHAT YOU LEARN

At the end of the day, name one thing you learned and one way you used it. Growth does not come from collecting insight. It comes from applying it.

DAY 144: TRUST THE STEPS

"Naturally, I just want to progress and get better, so I do have a vision of just getting better and many, many steps. So, that's what I'm trying to do on a daily basis."
Shohei Ohtani

Ohtani talks like someone who trusts the process of getting better. He sees improvement as many small steps stacked with purpose and consistency. That mindset keeps him patient, steady, and honest. When you respect the next step, progress becomes something you build every day.

MORNING EDGE: TAKE THE NEXT STEP

Start the day by asking, "What is the next step for me today?" Keep it simple and specific. Then give that step your full attention.

FLIP THE SWITCH: DO NOT SKIP STEPS

When frustration or impatience shows up, remind yourself that growth still counts when it is quiet. Tell yourself, "This step matters," and do the next right thing well.

CHAMPION'S WRAP: YOU BUILT ONE MORE STEP

At the end of the day, name one step you took that made you better. Greatness is often built more quietly than people think, one honest step at a time.

DAY 145: CARRY WHAT YOU EARNED

"It's actually an honor to feel the pressure, because that means there are a lot of expectations, and I just change that to something that's more of a positive."

Shohei Ohtani

Pressure changes when you read it as a sign instead of a threat. Expectations usually rise because your game, growth, and reliability have risen first. The weight is not random. It is something you earned.

MORNING EDGE: STAND UP TO IT

Start the day by reminding yourself that expectations often follow growth. Tell yourself, "I earned the chance to carry this." Let that thought make you stand taller, not tighter.

FLIP THE SWITCH: CARRY IT WELL

When pressure hits, take one Return to Zero breath and settle yourself. Tell yourself, "This weight was earned." Then make the next strong, simple play.

CHAMPION'S WRAP: COUNTED ON

At the end of the day, think of one moment when something was asked of you and you met it well. That is what earned expectations look like in real life.

DAY 146: DO NOT LIMIT IT

"I think it's wasteful to limit myself without any reason."
Shohei Ohtani

Ohtani does not step into the day with a ceiling over his head. A lot of athletes cut themselves short with doubt, caution, and a picture that is far too small for what is really there. Great visualization clears the sky and lets your full game come forward. The goal is to see it clearly, trust it fully, and compete with nothing held back.

MORNING EDGE: SEE YOUR FULL GAME

Before the day begins, take a calm breath and picture yourself moving the way you want to move today. See yourself loose, clear, aggressive, and in rhythm. Let that picture remind you that you do not need to hold back before anything has even happened.

FLIP THE SWITCH: REMOVE THE BRAKE

When doubt or hesitation shows up, pause and ask yourself, "What unnecessary limit am I putting on myself right now?" Then tell yourself, "Take the brake off," and make the next move with freedom and intent.

CHAMPION'S WRAP: FEED THAT VERSION

Before bed, replay one moment when you moved with freedom, trusted your game, or let yourself compete more fully. That version of you is real, and the more often you return to it, the stronger and more natural it becomes.

DAY 147: USE THE THOUGHT

"I have negative thoughts. I remember the bad things more vividly than the good ones. Therefore, when I see my weakness, I strongly feel that I want to fix it."
Shohei Ohtani

A negative thought can either drain your energy or sharpen your focus. The difference comes from what you do with it next. The best performers turn that thought into useful information. They make the adjustment and get right back to work.

MORNING EDGE: TAKE THE HINT

Think of one weakness, mistake, or thought that has been bothering you lately. Ask yourself what it is pointing to and what small fix would help. Then go to work on that instead of just thinking about it again.

FLIP THE SWITCH: TURN IT INTO WORK

When a negative thought shows up, do not wrestle with it or let it run the day. Tell yourself, "Use it." Then make one clear adjustment and get back to the next rep, play, or task.

CHAMPION'S WRAP: MADE IT USEFUL

At the end of the day, think of one moment when you turned a bothersome thought into a better action. That is how real improvement happens. You stop fearing the thought and start using it.

DAY 148: DON'T LOCK IT IN

"I feel like I was more talented as a hitter growing up, and it was hard for me to pitch, actually. So I feel like I'm more of a hitter who learned how to pitch more than a pitcher learning how to hit."
Shohei Ohtani

Early strengths can feel like a definition, and early struggles can feel like a limit. Both can start shaping how you see yourself if you let them. The best performers keep their identity open and keep building. They give themselves room to become more.

MORNING EDGE: DROP THE LABEL

Think of one label that has been shrinking you. It might be something like "I'm not built for that," or "That has never been my thing." Replace it with "I can learn this," and start the day with more room to grow.

FLIP THE SWITCH: DO NOT DECIDE TOO SOON

When you catch yourself thinking, "That is just not me," pause and stop yourself there. Tell yourself, "Maybe not yet," and take the next rep, the next swing, or the next step. Let the work say what is possible.

CHAMPION'S WRAP: LEFT ROOM TO GROW

At the end of the day, think of one moment when you did not let an old label run the show. That is how growth stays alive. You stop locking yourself in and keep becoming more.

DAY 149: LOOK ACROSS, NOT UP

"Let's stop admiring Team USA. If you admire them, you can't surpass them. We came here to surpass them, to reach the top. For one day, let's throw away our admiration for them and just think about winning."

Shohei Ohtani

Ohtani knew the first battle was mental. The moment you admire an opponent too much, you give away ground before the contest even begins. Respect keeps you sharp, but awe makes you hesitate and play small. Great competitors do not look up at the other side. They look across, trust their game, and compete.

MORNING EDGE: BRING THEM TO EYE LEVEL

Think of one person, team, or stage you have been giving too much power. Remind yourself that they feel pressure, make mistakes, and have to execute too. Respect them, but meet them at eye level.

FLIP THE SWITCH: SAME FIELD

When intimidation creeps in, take one Return to Zero breath and settle yourself. Tell yourself, "Same field. Same game." Then lock back into your strengths and compete your way.

CHAMPION'S WRAP: STAYED IN YOUR GAME

At the end of the day, think of one moment when you stayed true to your standard instead of reacting to someone else's reputation. That is how you compete as an equal.

DAY 150: BE THE STANDARD

"There's a really good vibe in the clubhouse right now, all the new guys seem like they're really great guys. I'm excited to play with this team."
Shohei Ohtani

The environment matters because it shapes what starts to feel normal. Every day, the people around you influence the standard, the energy, and the level of belief in the room. Even in the big leagues, not every voice lifts the standard. The best players stay connected without letting other people's doubt, drift, or complacency become their own.

MORNING EDGE: PROTECT THE STANDARD

Before you step into the day, decide what kind of energy, focus, and belief you want to carry with you. Lock in with "Stay true to the standard," and remember that not everybody around you will think, work, or dream at your level.

FLIP THE SWITCH: RISE ABOVE THE DRIFT

When the room feels flat, negative, or uninspired, take one Return to Zero breath and refuse to let it set your emotional temperature. Come back to "Rise above the drift," and keep showing up with the effort, body language, and intent that match your goals.

CHAMPION'S WRAP: I HELD MY ALTITUDE

Think of one moment when you stayed true to yourself instead of letting other people's moods, limits, or resistance pull you off course. Lock it in with "I held my altitude," because that is how real standards are kept, on the field and away from it.

DAY 151: GIVE IT YOUR BEST

"Many fans tell me that they came all the way from Japan to see me. That's the real blessing, so I want to show them my best."

Shohei Ohtani

The moment carries a different energy when you see it as something to honor. Support, belief, and the chance to compete can pull you out of tension and into purpose. Gratitude gives your effort meaning and your presence life. It helps you step in with freedom and give your best.

MORNING EDGE: REMEMBER WHO SHOWS UP

Before the day begins, think of one person who believes in you, supports you, or loves watching you compete. Let that remind you that today is not just another obligation. It is a chance to give something good back.

FLIP THE SWITCH: GIVE THEM YOUR BEST

When tension or frustration shows up, take one good breath and lift your chin. Tell yourself, "This is a privilege, so give it your best." Then compete with energy, purpose, and respect for the moment.

CHAMPION'S WRAP: PLAYED WITH PURPOSE

At the end of the day, think of one moment when gratitude helped you compete better. That is the power of perspective. It turns pressure into purpose.

CHAMPION'S TAKEAWAYS: WRIGLEY FIELD

Wrigley taught you what toughness really looks like. It is not something you either have or do not have. It is how you respond when the game speeds up, the feel disappears, or things start going against you.

This month, you trained how to come back after mistakes, compete when your best stuff was not there, and stay solid for the people around you when the room got tight. You practiced owning what was still yours to control, including your breath, your focus, your effort, and your presence. That is what holds up when the inning gets messy and the moment matters most.

As you step out of the clubhouse, ask yourself:

- What's my most reliable reset after a mistake?
- How do I want to look and act after things go wrong?
- What standard did I hold even when I didn't feel like it?

This month was about how you responded, not whether the day was perfect. Carry that forward.

CHAPTER 6

JUNE: KONA

"The body will quit a hundred times before the mind does. Teach the mind to finish the race."
Ironman proverb

Kona is not the postcard version of Hawaii. It is heat rising off black lava, wind slamming across the Queen K, salt in your eyes, and a course that keeps asking harder questions the longer you stay out there. Since 1981, the Ironman World Championship has lived on the Big Island, and it has become one of the toughest proving grounds in sport. Out here, comfort has no say.

The race is built to strip you down to what is real. A 2.4-mile ocean swim, a 112-mile bike through crosswinds and open heat, and then a marathon when your body is already begging for mercy. Kona does not care what you have done before. It cares what you do when the day gets long, the rhythm gets shaky, and the voice in your head starts bargaining for relief. The question is always the same. Will you keep going?

That is the question for this month too. June is your Kona in real life. You will practice staying steady when your breathing shortens, your legs feel heavy, and your mind starts negotiating for an easier way. You will learn how to answer discomfort with rhythm, composure, and continued execution. That is the skill. Keep moving well when quitting would be easier.

Your training partners know this terrain. Chrissie Wellington stayed calm and purposeful even as her body screamed. Mark Allen learned patience and restraint when the race got savage. Daniela Ryf got sharper when the fun ran out. Jan Frodeno brought a professional mindset that stayed steady in every condition. This month, treat every rep like a mile on the Queen K. Do the basics well when it gets hard, and keep going anyway.

DAY 152: MENTAL TRAINING PARTNER

CHRISSIE WELLINGTON

"When things are tough, you get tougher."

Chrissie Wellington

Chrissie Wellington did not come up through the usual pipeline of elite sport. She studied geography, worked in international development, and spent her twenties serving a bigger mission than racing. Then the triathlon found her and asked for everything she had. She answered fast, turned professional, and shocked the sport by winning the Ironman World Championship in Kona in 2007.

She went on to win four world titles and never lost an Ironman-distance race. What made Chrissie so special was not raw power alone. It was the way she met suffering when the race got long, hot, and brutal. She had a way of staying composed when other people started unraveling.

One of her great weapons was a smile. When the lava fields were baking, her legs were screaming, and the race was asking hard questions, she smiled anyway. That iron grin was not for show. It relaxed her body, steadied her breathing, and reminded her that she was still in command.

This week, Chrissie is your mental training partner. She will show you how to stay steady in the hurt, how to use your mind when the body starts complaining, and how to keep your spirit strong deep into the race. When the burn hits, lift your head, steady your breath, and bring back the iron grin.

DAY 153: STACK THE ROCK

"Some sessions are stars, and some sessions are stones, but in the end, they are all rocks. and we build upon them."
Chrissie Wellington

Not every session feels great, and that is part of the deal. Some days you feel sharp, and some days you feel heavy, flat, or out of rhythm, but every session still gives you something to build on. You are creating something bigger than one workout, one mood, or one result. Even the hard days add to the foundation when you stay with the work.

MORNING EDGE: LAY ONE MORE STONE

Choose one task you will finish today no matter how you feel. Let discipline make the first deposit.

FLIP THE SWITCH: BUILD ANYWAY

When training feels flat, stop waiting for the day to feel special. Stay steady, do the work in front of you, and add another rock to the stack.

CHAMPION'S WRAP: ADD TO THE FOUNDATION

Before bed, name the hardest moment you handled well today. That is another layer of strength you can stand on.

DAY 154: SMILE AT THE STORM

"Just seize every opportunity you have, embrace every experience. Make a mark, for all the right reasons."
Chrissie Wellington

Chrissie understood that you do not get to choose the conditions, only your response to them. Her grin in the middle of deep pain was not fake confidence. It was a signal to her body and mind that she was still composed, still present, and still ready for the fight. Sometimes the smallest physical cue can help you regain command when the moment gets loud.

MORNING EDGE: SET THE SIGNAL

Before the day begins, take one slow breath and soften your face with a slight iron grin. Make it subtle, just enough to say, "I choose how I show up today." Your nervous system listens, and that small signal can steady you before the day speeds up.

FLIP THE SWITCH: BRING BACK THE GRIN

When training gets tense or messy, relax your jaw and bring the grin back. That tiny reset can loosen tension, clean up your rhythm, and help you stay locked in on the moment.

CHAMPION'S WRAP: THE CALM ADVANTAGE

Think of one moment today when things got tense and you stayed composed anyway. That was your iron grin doing its job.

DAY 155: STRONG THE RIGHT WAY

"I'm a warrior and a fighter. I race fair and I race clean."
Chrissie Wellington

To Chrissie, being a warrior was never about looking intense or acting tough. It was about competing the right way when pressure showed up. Her strength came from clarity, discipline, and loyalty to her standard. When fatigue rose, the body tightened, and the race pushed back, she stayed true to who she was.

MORNING EDGE: LOCK IN YOUR STANDARD

Begin the day with one Return to Zero breath: Inhale through your nose for four seconds, then exhale slowly through your mouth for six. The long exhale settles your body and lowers urgency. Then tell yourself, "Today, I hold my standard," and let that guide your pace, choices, and attitude.

FLIP THE SWITCH: BE THE CALM FIGHTER

When your body tightens, your breathing shortens, or you start forcing instead of flowing, return to one Return to Zero breath. Settle first, then tell yourself, "Stay steady," and give the next rep what it deserves.

CHAMPION'S WRAP: REAL STRENGTH SHOWS HERE

Think of one moment today when you stayed true to your standard instead of reacting. That is strength done right.

DAY 156: CREATE A PLACE OF POWER

"Develop a mind bank of positive images and thoughts: family, friends, previous successes, favorite places, a big plate of chips."
Chrissie Wellington

When things get hard, your mind goes somewhere. If you do not guide it, it often runs toward doubt, panic, or mental clutter that pulls you off your game. Chrissie trained her mind to head somewhere better. She built a small bank of images and memories she could access fast, ones that settled her body, cleared her head, and helped her stay composed when pressure hit.

MORNING EDGE: PICK YOUR POWER PLACE

Begin with one Return to Zero breath: Inhale through your nose for four seconds, then exhale slowly through your mouth for six. Choose one image that calms you and one memory that reminds you that you have handled hard moments before. That is your place.

FLIP THE SWITCH: GO TO STRENGTH

When tension or doubt hits, take one Return to Zero breath. Return to one image from your list and let it steady you before you act.

CHAMPION'S WRAP: TRAIN THE RETURN

Before bed, note one moment today when pressure showed up and you guided your mind somewhere useful instead of reacting. That is preparation you can trust.

DAY 157: FIND THE WINNING GEAR

"But life is a lot more balanced and varied now. My competitive nature has softened, and my drive and determination are channeled into different pursuits."
Chrissie Wellington

Chrissie understood that drive is powerful, but it works best when it is directed well. Every serious performer has more than one gear. There are moments to press, attack, and push the pace, and there are moments to settle, stay smooth, and trust your rhythm. It is not enough to be driven. You also have to know how to channel it.

MORNING EDGE: START IN THE RIGHT GEAR

Before the day gets moving, ask yourself what this day calls for from you. More push? More patience? More edge? More control? Start there on purpose instead of letting the mood of the moment decide for you.

FLIP THE SWITCH: MATCH THE MOMENT

When you feel yourself getting too rushed or too passive, make the adjustment. If the moment needs more urgency, step in stronger. If it needs more control, slow yourself down and clean things up. Winning often comes down to matching your gear to the moment.

CHAMPION'S WRAP: YOU MADE THE SHIFT

Think of one moment today when you adjusted well instead of staying stuck in the wrong gear. That is how you stay in command of your drive and use it to your advantage.

DAY 158: HOLD TO WHAT GROUNDS YOU

"Friends and family are the thread that runs throughout our lives, no matter where those lives take us."
Chrissie Wellington

When fatigue and doubt start creeping in, thinking harder about results rarely helps. What steadies you is remembering who matters, what matters, and why the effort is worth it. That kind of connection gives you something solid to hold when the grind starts pulling at your focus and resolve. Support does not make champions soft. It helps keep them steady, strong, and moving forward.

MORNING EDGE: CHOOSE YOUR ROCK

Begin with one Return to Zero breath. Choose one person who grounds you, then picture their face or quietly say their name. Decide that this connection stands for steadiness, strength, and perspective.

FLIP THE SWITCH: RETURN TO WHAT HOLDS YOU

When you start to drift, bring that person to mind and take a deep, cleansing breath. Let the connection settle you, then lock back in on the next right thing.

CHAMPION'S WRAP: DRAW STRENGTH FROM THE BOND

Before bed, send a short thank-you or take a moment to acknowledge how that connection helped carry you today. That is how support becomes a real source of strength.

DAY 159: MENTAL TRAINING PARTNER
MARK ALLEN

"The beauty of sport is that it forces you into situations where you must challenge yourself. My best race is the one that hurt the most."
Mark Allen

Mark Allen grew up in Glendale, California, swam at the University of California, San Diego, and eventually found his way to triathlon. He had the engine right away, but Kona demanded something deeper. In his first six tries at the Ironman World Championship, the island kept exposing him. Heat, wind, pain, and doubt all took their turn.

Most athletes would have had enough. Allen stayed with it. In 1989, after years of coming up short, he ran shoulder to shoulder with Dave Scott for twenty-three miles through the lava fields in what became known as the Iron War. Then he made his move, won his first Ironman World Championship, and finally broke through in the race that had tested him more than any other.

That breakthrough came from more than fitness. Allen learned how to quiet the noise, stay patient, and trust what he had built. He stopped letting ego push the pace and started letting purpose guide the effort. That shift helped turn him into the calmest mind in the sport and carried him to six Kona titles and more than twenty straight Ironman victories.

This week, Allen is your mental training partner. He will show you how to stay patient in the fire, trust your training when the race starts asking hard questions, and keep your mind steady when your body is hurting. When the day gets painful, stay with it. That is where growth begins.

DAY 160: CHOOSE THE DREAM

"As soon as your dream becomes stronger than your doubts
and fears, your dream begins to manifest."
Mark Allen

Doubt does not vanish just because you want it gone, and fear does not stop showing up just because the moment matters. The deeper skill is learning what gets your attention and what does not. Champions do not spend all day wrestling with fear. They keep pointing their mind, body, and effort toward what matters most. Under pressure, especially when you are tired, tested, or uncomfortable, your mind tends to follow the direction you give it.

MORNING EDGE: POINT YOURSELF FORWARD

Start the day by naming what you are moving toward. Picture the effort, standard, or behavior you want to embody. Tell yourself, "This is the direction I choose today," and let that become your mental compass.

FLIP THE SWITCH: MOVE TOWARD WHAT MATTERS

When doubt shows up, take one Return to Zero breath and redirect your attention to the dream. Then take one action that lines up with it right away. Forward action strengthens belief.

CHAMPION'S WRAP: FOLLOWED THE RIGHT SIGNAL

Before bed, identify one moment when you aimed yourself toward the dream instead of drifting toward hesitation. That is how commitment gets stronger.

DAY 161: COMPETE WITH PURPOSE

"What's my purpose?"
Mark Allen

Purpose matters most when the work gets hard. It is easy to feel connected to your why when things are flowing and your body feels good. The real test comes when pressure rises, discomfort builds, or comparison starts pulling at your attention. In those moments, purpose becomes more than an idea. It becomes a decision about how you will compete when the moment tries to take something from you.

MORNING EDGE: DECIDE HOW YOU COMPETE

Set your purpose for today as a clear competitive decision. Say, "Today, I compete with composure," or "I stay disciplined when the moment speeds up," or "Steady, then strike." Pick one line that fits you, write it down, and carry it with you.

FLIP THE SWITCH: LET PURPOSE LEAD

When frustration, doubt, or pressure hits, go back to your line and repeat it exactly. Then take the next action that matches it. Purpose gets powerful when it moves from words into behavior.

CHAMPION'S WRAP: YOU STAYED TRUE UNDER PRESSURE

Before bed, identify one moment when you competed in line with your purpose even when it would have been easier to drift. That is what power looks like under pressure. That is how purpose stops being talk and starts becoming part of you.

DAY 162: STAY WITH THE EFFORT

"The magnitude of the satisfaction that a triathlete experiences upon crossing a finish line is directly proportional to the amount of suffering he has overcome to get there."
Mark Allen

The best part of a hard effort is knowing you earned it. A lot of athletes feel discomfort and start treating it as a sign to back off. But discomfort is often just part of doing something that matters. The key is learning to stay with the effort without getting too caught up in how it feels.

MORNING EDGE: EXPECT THE WORK

Before training, remind yourself that hard effort is part of the deal. Tell yourself, "When it gets hard, I stay with it." Decide that you will keep working with good body language and a steady mind.

FLIP THE SWITCH: STAY IN MOTION

When fatigue hits, do not make a big deal out of it. Settle your breathing, keep your rhythm, and use one simple cue like "Stay with it," or "Keep working." Bring your attention back to the job and keep going.

CHAMPION'S WRAP: YOU EARNED THAT

At the end of the day, note one moment when you stayed with the effort instead of pulling away from it. That is where real satisfaction comes from.

DAY 163: RESPOND WELL

"Trying to control the entire journey is impossible."
Mark Allen

You cannot control everything once the day begins. Something will feel off, the plan may change, or the moment may ask more of you than you expected. A lot of athletes waste energy fighting that reality. The better move is to stay steady and respond well to what is actually in front of you.

MORNING EDGE: PREPARE, THEN LET GO

Start the day by reminding yourself that you do not need to control every part of it. Your job is to prepare well, stay present, and be ready for whatever shows up. Tell yourself, "I'll meet the day well."

FLIP THE SWITCH: FIND THE NEXT GOOD MOVE

When something unexpected happens, pause for a second and settle yourself. Ask, "What's the next good move?" Then do that and stay with it.

CHAMPION'S WRAP: YOU MET THE MOMENT

Before bed, note one moment when the day asked you to adjust and you did. You stayed present, made a good move, and kept competing. That is what it means to trust yourself in real time.

DAY 164: AIM WHAT YOU'VE GOT

"You have everything you need. A miraculous body, a phenomenal brain, and a vast, powerful subconscious mind. Now it's just a matter of focusing them in the right direction."

Mark Allen

You already have what you need to perform well. Power leaks when attention scatters. Performance usually breaks down not because something is missing, but because attention gets scattered. The skill is bringing your energy, thoughts, and effort into one clear direction when it matters most. When everything points in the same direction, execution becomes simpler and stronger.

MORNING EDGE: SET THE AIM

Before the day gets noisy, decide where your energy is going. Pick one thing that matters most and aim your attention, effort, and attitude at it

FLIP THE SWITCH: NARROW THE LENS

When your focus starts to scatter, bring it back to one clear thing. Pick one target, task, or cue and lock in on it. Say, "Right here," and give that one action your full intention.

CHAMPION'S WRAP: CHECK THE AIM

Before bed, note one moment when you aimed your effort well today. Even one clear moment matters. That's how consistency is built.

DAY 165: SPEED UNDER COMMAND

"There is a fine line between fast and stupid."
Mark Allen

Athletes get in trouble when they confuse intensity with control. Adrenaline can make you feel sharp when you are actually getting reckless. Going hard only helps if you can still think clearly and stay in command of yourself. The real skill is knowing where that line is and having the discipline to stay on the right side of it.

MORNING EDGE: FIND YOUR WINNING PACE

Decide what smart effort looks like today. Know the pace or intensity that sharpens you, and know the point where control starts to slip.

FLIP THE SWITCH: STAY FAST, STAY SMART

When adrenaline spikes, ask yourself, "Fast or stupid?" If control is fading, steady your rhythm and regain command.

CHAMPION'S WRAP: WIN THE LINE

Note one moment today when you noticed the line and stayed on the right side of it. That kind of awareness is an elite skill.

DAY 166: MENTAL TRAINING PARTNER

DANIELA RYF

"At some point, it's not fun anymore. That's when it starts to count."

Daniela Ryf

Daniela Ryf turned endurance into her playground and then into her kingdom. Born in Solothurn, Switzerland, she raced as a junior, represented her country at the 2008 Beijing Olympics, and then found her true home in long-course triathlon. Once she got there, she started piling up titles in one of the hardest sports on earth. Five Ironman World Championships in Kona and five Ironman 70.3 World Championships tell the story.

They called her the Angry Bird, and the nickname fit. When the effort rose and the race got serious, something fierce came alive in her. She trained in cold Swiss lakes, mountain passes, and headwinds that could break your rhythm and your mood. By the time she got to Kona, the suffering did not surprise her. The Angry Bird had already been there.

What made Ryf so formidable was the way she handled the hard part. When the race stopped being fun, she got cleaner, tougher, and more precise. Fatigue did not send her searching for comfort. It told her the race had finally reached the place where champions separate.

This week, Ryf is your mental training partner. She will show you how to stay composed when the body pushes back and how to compete with precision when the fun runs out. That is when it starts to count. Bring out your own Angry Bird and keep going.

DAY 167: PROTECT YOUR HEADSPACE

"You can't do great results if your head is not in a good place."
Daniela Ryf

A good headspace doesn't happen by accident. It comes from where you place your attention and how you carry yourself under stress. When your head is in a good place, decisions stay simple and effort stays directed. When it slips, performance gets rushed, forced, or distracted.

MORNING EDGE: DEFINE IT IN ACTION

Before the day starts, decide what a good headspace looks like in behavior. Pick two actions that show your head is where it needs to be, like lifting your eyes and bringing your attention back to the task when it starts to wander.

FLIP THE SWITCH: FIX THE BEHAVIOR

When you feel sped up, distracted, or off-center, don't overthink it. Ask, "What does this moment need from me?" It might be one steady breath, better posture, or your full attention on the next task. Then do that immediately.

CHAMPION'S WRAP: KNOW THE RESET

Before bed, note one moment when you got yourself back on track today. That matters. It means you know how to reset. Let the rest of the day go and get some sleep.

DAY 168: SIGN THE WALL IN THE PAIN CAVE

"In training, I go to places I don't like, so on race day, I've already been there."

Daniela Ryf

Ryf trained herself to know hard before race day asked for it. She went toward the tough parts in practice so they would feel familiar later. That gave her a big advantage when the race started to bite. Hard gets easier to handle when it feels like somewhere you already know. When pain shows up, panic fades faster if you have already been there on purpose.

MORNING EDGE: ENTER ON PURPOSE

Pick one part of today that you usually avoid because it is uncomfortable, tedious, or demanding. Go there on purpose and stay there a little longer than your comfort zone wants. Say, "I know this place," and do the work like someone who is learning how to operate where others back off.

FLIP THE SWITCH: SIGN THE WALL

When fatigue, resistance, or doubt shows up, do not act like you landed somewhere unfamiliar. Say, "Leave your autograph in the pain cave." Then settle in, trust your rhythm, and keep moving like someone who belongs there.

CHAMPION'S WRAP: YOUR NAME'S ON THE WALL

Think of one hard moment today when you stayed composed and kept working instead of flinching or backing off. That is how the pain cave becomes familiar territory. The more often you go there on purpose, the more your mind learns, "I've been here before, and I know how to move through it."

DAY 169: SOLVE THE DAY

"Success doesn't mean winning everything, but making the best of every situation."
Daniela Ryf

Some days feel smooth, and some days make you figure things out. The weather shifts, the body feels off, the rhythm takes longer to find, and the plan needs adjusting. Strong competitors treat those days like puzzles, not problems. They stay steady, keep solving, and make the best of what is there.

MORNING EDGE: READ THE PUZZLE

Think of one part of today that may ask for an adjustment. Picture yourself meeting it with patience, clear eyes, and a problem-solving mindset. Say, "Let's solve the day." Then step in ready to work with what shows up.

FLIP THE SWITCH: SOLVE WHAT'S IN FRONT OF YOU

When the day feels off, stop wishing for a different one. Ask, "What is this moment asking for?" Then make the next smart adjustment and keep moving.

CHAMPION'S WRAP: FOUND THE PIECE

Think of one moment today when the day felt tricky and you figured part of it out. Maybe you adjusted your pace, changed your mindset, or stayed patient until something clicked. That is how tough days get handled. You keep finding pieces and putting the day together.

DAY 170: DON'T MAKE IT A BIG DEAL

"I've learned to deal with pressure by not making it special."
Daniela Ryf

Pressure gets heavier when you start treating it like a major event. You feel something in your body, then your mind starts adding drama, danger, and meaning. That is when simple things get hard. Strong competitors feel the pressure and keep the job the same. They do not turn one hard moment into a whole movie.

MORNING EDGE: SAME JOB

Before the day gets going, remind yourself that pressure does not change your assignment. Pick one basic you trust, like your breathing, rhythm, or body language, and make that your home base. Say, "Same job, same me." Then carry that into your first action.

FLIP THE SWITCH: CUT THE MOVIE

When you catch yourself speeding up or making the moment feel huge, stop feeding it. Say, "Do less drama, and more job." Then soften your face, settle your breathing, and handle the next thing in front of you.

CHAMPION'S WRAP: DIDN'T ADD DRAMA

Think of one moment today when pressure showed up and you kept it simple. You handled what was there without turning it into something bigger.

DAY 171: PLAY BEYOND THE APPLAUSE

"People love you when you win. But you can't need that."
Daniela Ryf

Winning brings attention, praise, and approval. Those things can feel good, but they are never steady enough to build your game on. The best competitors enjoy the applause without chasing it. When you stop needing the reaction, you can give your full attention to the way you want to compete.

MORNING EDGE: BRING YOUR OWN SPARK

Before you start, decide what kind of competitor you want to be today. Maybe you want to be steady, sharp, fearless, or fully committed. Say, "I bring that with me." Then step into the day and show it.

FLIP THE SWITCH: STAY ON YOUR SIGNAL

When you feel yourself looking for a reaction or worrying about how it looks, bring it back inside. Say, "Stay on my signal," and lock back into your effort, your rhythm, and your next move.

CHAMPION'S WRAP: NO AUDIENCE NEEDED

Think of one moment today when you played free, without needing anything back. That is your game at its best. That is something you can take anywhere.

DAY 172: RESET AND COMPETE

"I've had races that broke me. But you can always go again."
Daniela Ryf

Bad days hurt because the investment was real. The work, time, and belief all mattered, even if the result didn't show it. Ryf felt the disappointment without letting it follow her into the next moment. Champions don't pretend mistakes don't matter, but they don't carry them longer than they help.

MORNING EDGE: MAKE THE PACT

Decide this before the day starts: nothing gets more than one moment of attention. If something goes wrong, you acknowledge it, make the adjustment, and keep moving.

FLIP THE SWITCH: CLOSE THE FILE

When a mistake occurs, acknowledge it once, then mentally close the file and shift your attention to the next action.

CHAMPION'S WRAP: RESET WELL

Before bed, note one moment you moved on quickly instead of replaying it. That ability to reset is what keeps performance steady over time.

DAY 173: MENTAL TRAINING PARTNER
JAN FRODENO

"Success is not determined by what you do once, but by what you do every day."
Jan Frodeno

Jan Frodeno built one of the most complete careers in triathlon that the sport has ever seen. He won Olympic gold in Beijing in 2008, then moved to long-course racing and became a dominant force in Kona. Three Ironman World Championship titles and two Ironman 70.3 World Championships followed. Across every format, he kept raising the level.

He was born in Cologne, Germany, and spent part of his childhood in South Africa, where swimming gave him his first engine. Triathlon came next, and he quickly rose through the German national team to the top of the Olympic podium. When he shifted to long-course racing, he did more than make the transition. He became the standard. He raised the bar and earned the nickname Frodissimo for his poise and command under pressure.

What made Frodeno so reliable was how seriously he treated the daily work. Sleep, nutrition, recovery, and focus all counted, and he handled them with care and consistency. When injury hit, including a major sacral issue, he stayed patient and rebuilt step by step. He trusted the process and kept showing up.

This week, Frodeno is your mental training partner. He will show you how to build your edge through daily habits and steady discipline. Do the work, respect the details, and bring the same standard every day. That is how greatness gets built.

DAY 174: ACT LIKE A PRO

"Success is not measured solely by results but by the resilience of the mind."
Jan Frodeno

Frodeno isn't a champion just because he is talented. Plenty of athletes have talent. What makes Frodeno exceptional is that he showed up day after day. Long before his success, he adhered to professional habits and maintained his standards, whether anyone was watching or not.

MORNING EDGE: SET THE STANDARD

Ask yourself one simple question: "What's one professional thing I can do today?" Choose something concrete—preparation, focus, recovery, or follow-through—and do it the right way, even if no one notices.

FLIP THE SWITCH: DO IT RIGHT

When you feel tempted to coast or cut a corner, take one Return to Zero breath: Inhale for four, exhale for six. If you're training, let that breath stretch across a few steps, strokes, or pedal turns. Then ask, "What's the right way to do this rep?" and do that.

CHAMPION'S WRAP: THAT'S A PRO MOVE

Name one moment today when you chose the professional response over the easy one. That's how habits turn into identity.

DAY 175: STAY ORGANIZED UNDER STRESS

"Find comfort in discomfort, for that is where growth begins."

Jan Frodeno

Discomfort is part of the deal in any serious pursuit. The moment gets big when your body tightens, your rhythm changes, and your mind starts acting like something has gone wrong. Strong competitors stay organized when it gets uncomfortable. They keep their posture, their breathing, and their effort working together. That is how they stay in control while others start to leak energy.

MORNING EDGE: DECIDE YOUR LOOK

Before you begin, picture the moment when discomfort shows up today. See yourself staying tall, breathing steady, and moving with patience instead of rush. Say, "When it gets hard, I stay organized." Then bring that into your first action.

FLIP THE SWITCH: HOLD YOUR SHAPE

When the feeling hits, check your posture, your breathing, and your pace. Loosen what does not need to work so hard, stay with your rhythm, and keep moving like yourself.

CHAMPION'S WRAP: STRONG THROUGH IT

Think of one moment today when discomfort showed up and you handled it well. That is how trust gets built under pressure.

DAY 176: KEEP YOUR MIND ON THE JOB

"A focused mind is the most powerful asset in any challenge."
Jan Frodeno

Your attention is always aiming at something. Under pressure, it can lock onto fear, comparison, or outcomes and pull you away from what actually helps. A strong competitor keeps bringing it back to the work that matters most. That return is a skill, and it gets stronger every time you use it.

MORNING EDGE: PICK THE HANDLE

Before you start, choose one cue you can grab when the day gets noisy. It might be your breathing, your posture, your tempo, your first move, or the next simple decision. Say, "This is where I come back." Then carry that into your first action.

FLIP THE SWITCH: BACK TO THE JOB

When your mind jumps ahead or sideways, catch it and bring it home. Say, "Back to the job," and put your full attention on what needs to be done right now.

CHAMPION'S WRAP: WON THE RETURN

Think of one moment today when your mind drifted and you brought it back on purpose. That is a real win. Pressure always tests attention, and this is how you train it to hold.

DAY 177: COMPETE WITH HEART

"Passion is the fuel that ignites the fire within."
Jan Frodeno

Passion gives effort life. Caring deeply brings energy, sharpens commitment, and pulls more out of you. Strong emotion can move straight into focus, rhythm, and drive when you know how to carry it well. The goal is to compete with your whole heart and let that fire work for you.

MORNING EDGE: LIGHT THE FIRE

Before you begin, think about why this matters to you today. Feel that reason land in your chest, then bring it into your body language, your breathing, and the way you step in. Say, "My fire helps me." Then go compete with life in you.

FLIP THE SWITCH: TURN FIRE INTO FORCE

When emotion rises, ask, "Where does this help me most right now?" Then pour it into something simple and physical like stronger posture, better tempo, sharper focus, or full commitment to the next action.

CHAMPION'S WRAP: FIRE UNDER CONTROL

Think of one moment today when you cared deeply and stayed composed. That is a powerful combination. The fire was there, and you used it well.

DAY 178: DON'T BITE

"Fear is just a temporary illusion that keeps you from achieving greatness."
Jan Frodeno

Fear does not always look dramatic. A lot of times it shows up as a sudden urge to force something, chase something, fix something, or prove something right now. That is how it pulls athletes off their plan. The bait might be another athlete's move, a bad split, a wave of doubt, or the feeling that you need to make something happen. Great competitors feel the urge and stay with their race anyway. They do not let a temporary feeling make a permanent decision.

MORNING EDGE: SPOT THE BAIT

Before you begin, name the thing most likely to pull you off your plan today. It might be another athlete surging, a shaky start, fatigue, or the feeling that you need to prove yourself early. Picture that moment clearly and see yourself letting it pass without grabbing it. Say, "See the bait. Stay with my race." Then bring that discipline into your first action.

FLIP THE SWITCH: LET IT PASS

When the urge hits, pause for one beat and feel your feet. Say, "Don't bite." Then come right back to your pace, your rhythm, and your next job. The urge can be loud without getting a vote.

CHAMPION'S WRAP: BEAT THE BAIT

Think of one moment today when you felt pulled to react and stayed with your plan instead. That is a huge win. The more often you beat the bait, the more dangerous and dependable you become.

DAY 179: DO THE DARK WORK

"Champions are made in the dark, when no one is watching."
Jan Frodeno

The dark work isn't dramatic. It's the long stretch where nothing feels special, and no one is paying attention. Training feels ordinary, lonely, or forgettable, and there's no spark to lean on. Everyone reaches these moments, but not everyone stays with the work when the only thing present is effort.

MORNING EDGE: COMMIT TO THE QUIET

Start the day knowing it might feel flat or unremarkable. Decide in advance that if the energy isn't there, you'll rely on habits and execution instead of motivation.

FLIP THE SWITCH: STAY WORKING

When boredom or fatigue shows up, don't look for a lift. Narrow your focus to doing the work you planned, at the quality you planned, and keep going until the task is done.

CHAMPION'S WRAP: COUNT IT

Name one moment today you kept working when it would've been easy to drift or check out. That work doesn't get applause, but it's the work that adds up.

DAY 180: EARN THE NOD OF THE GODS

"You can't control the wind, but you can control your reaction to it."
Jan Frodeno

Picture the sports gods looking down and adding something extra to the day. A little more wind. A little more heat. A little more resistance right when you were hoping things would settle in. They do not do that to break you. They do it to see who embraces the challenge and who gets thrown by it. When the day asks for more, do you welcome that, or do you resist it?

MORNING EDGE: EXPECT THEIR TEST

Start the day knowing it may ask for more than you planned to give. The rhythm may be off, the situation may get messy, or the effort may feel heavier than it should. Tell yourself, "Bring it."

FLIP THE SWITCH: ANSWER LIKE A COMPETITOR

When the day asks for more, do not flinch, complain, or drift. Settle your breathing, lift your eyes, and let a slight smile loosen you up for a second. Tell yourself, "This is my kind of day," then meet the challenge with strong body language and steady effort.

CHAMPION'S WRAP: EARN THEIR NOD

Think of one moment today when the day asked for more and you rose to meet it. That was your response to the sports gods. Give them a quiet wink and think, "Mark that one down for me."

DAY 181: LET YOUR GAME OUT

"On race day, the work is done. All that's left is to give everything you have."
Jan Frodeno

Frodeno is saying race day is not for tinkering, searching, or trying to become someone new. It is for uncaging everything you built. The work is already in your legs, lungs, mind, and muscle memory. You do not need more effort in the wrong places. You need the freedom to let your trained self all the way out.

MORNING EDGE: OPEN THE GATE

Before the noise starts climbing on you, take a breath and picture yourself opening the gate and letting your real game run. Say, "Bring it out." Then step into the day as if nothing in you needs to stay hidden.

FLIP THE SWITCH: LET IT RUN

When nerves, doubt, or hesitation show up, stop hovering over the moment. Feel your feet, find your rhythm, and tell yourself, "Let it run." Freedom does not come from waiting for certainty. It comes from full commitment.

CHAMPION'S WRAP: NOTHING LEFT IN THE CAGE

Ask yourself one question tonight: "Did I let my game out today?" If you did, that is something real to be proud of, no matter what the scoreboard said. One of the best feelings in sport is knowing you competed with nothing held back and nothing left in the cage.

CHAMPION'S TAKEAWAYS: KONA

Kona took away shortcuts and comfort and forced you to manage yourself through heat, distance, and long stretches of effort. You learned that endurance isn't about being tough at the start, but about staying steady when the body complains and the mind starts looking for exits. The real win here was how you handled yourself when things got uncomfortable. You practiced settling instead of panicking, staying present instead of drifting, and continuing to compete even when the effort felt heavy.

As you step away from Kona, ask yourself:

- When did I stay composed instead of getting dramatic?
- How did I bring myself back when discomfort showed up?
- What did this arena teach me about my ability to stay in it?

That's Kona. You didn't just get through it. You became harder to break.

CHAPTER 7

JULY: CIRCUIT DE MONACO

"I've always believed that you should never, ever give up, and you should always keep fighting even when there's only the slightest chance."
Michael Schumacher

Monaco is not just a race. It is one of the purest pressure tests in sport. Since 1929, the best drivers in the world have flown through a narrow street circuit where one small mistake can end everything. Speed matters here, but control matters more. The margin is tiny, and the mind has to stay sharp.

This month, your mental training partners are Max Verstappen, Lewis Hamilton, Ayrton Senna, and Alain Prost. Verstappen brings full commitment when the opening appears. Hamilton shows what calm looks like when expectation is everywhere. Senna represents focus so complete that the lap becomes its own world. Prost brings judgment, patience, and the discipline to stay just under the limit when that is the smartest place to live.

From the outside, Monaco looks smooth and glamorous. Inside the cockpit, it is heat, vibration, narrow walls, and decisions that have to come fast and clean. There is no room to drift. Every lap demands precision, composure, and the ability to recover instantly when something goes slightly off.

This month is your mental track. You will train how to hold your line when space gets tight, manage your pace when fatigue rises, and reset quickly after mistakes. You will learn how to stay clear when the margin gets thin and the pressure gets real. You do not master Monaco in one lap. You meet the moment, recover fast, and do it again tomorrow.

DAY 182: MENTAL TRAINING PARTNER

MAX VERSTAPPEN

"I always try to get the best result out of it. I'm not there to just sit second or sit third. I'm a winner, and I want to win every single race, and I will always go for it."

Max Verstappen

Max Verstappen competes in Formula One for Red Bull Racing and has built one of the fiercest runs the sport has seen. He won four straight World Drivers' Championships and more than sixty Grands Prix by racing with total conviction. He grew up around speed. His father raced in Formula One, his mother was an elite kart racer, and pressure was part of the environment from the start.

By seventeen, Verstappen was already on the Formula One grid. One year later, he became the youngest Grand Prix winner in history. What separates him is not just talent or reflexes. It is the clarity he brings to competition. He shows up knowing exactly how he wants to race, regardless of the weather, the field, or what happened last weekend.

When Verstappen says he always goes for it, he is talking about commitment. Once the lights go out, hesitation has no place in the car. He trusts his preparation, makes the decision, and lives with it at full speed. That is what allows him to stay decisive when the margins are tiny and the pressure is huge.

This week, Verstappen is your mental training partner. He will show you how to compete with commitment, make clear decisions under pressure, and stay aggressive without getting reckless. Trust your preparation, go fully into the moment, and keep moving with intent.

DAY 183: LEAVE THE CAR AT THE TRACK

"For me, what works very well is when I go back home, I don't think about Formula 1. If I thought about Formula 1 every single day, I'd burn out."
Max Verstappen

Elite performers do not compete every minute of the day. They know when it is time to lock in and when it's time to shut it down. Verstappen understands that intensity works best when it has a beginning and an end. Stepping away is not a break from excellence. It is part of how excellence is sustained.

MORNING EDGE: TURN IT ON

When it is time to work, be all the way there. Settle into the task in front of you, narrow your focus, and compete with full attention instead of halfway energy.

FLIP THE SWITCH: KNOW WHEN TO UNPLUG

When the work is over, make it over on purpose. Take off the gear, close the laptop, leave the field, or change rooms, and let that physical action signal to your mind that the session is done.

CHAMPION'S WRAP: OFF MEANS OFF

When it is not time to compete, your mind does not need to analyze or replay. Let your mind move to normal life. Eat, rest, talk with people you care about, or do something enjoyable.

DAY 184: TURN THE NEXT CORNER

"If you keep replaying the mistake, you'll miss the next corner. I reset instantly."
Max Verstappen

Mistakes happen fast, and what follows matters just as much. Many athletes make one error and then lose the next moment because their mind stays tied to the last one. Verstappen understands that performance lives in the corner you are in now. The goal is to return to the present so quickly that the next moment stays clean and fully yours.

MORNING EDGE: DECIDE THE RECOVERY

Before the day begins, remind yourself that mistakes are part of competing. Decide in advance that when one happens, you will not waste time judging it, explaining it, or carrying it. Your job is to get back to the present faster than everyone else.

FLIP THE SWITCH: NEXT CORNER

When a mistake happens, cut it loose with one sharp exhale. Get your eyes up, say, "Next corner," and put your full attention on the very next decision.

CHAMPION'S WRAP: RECOVERY SPEED

At the end of the day, do not count how many mistakes you made. Notice how quickly you came back from them. That speed of reset is one of the clearest signs of a high-level competitor.

DAY 185: HOLD YOUR STANDARD

"When I get in the car, it's me against myself."
Max Verstappen

The scoreboard gives you information, but it does not give you your job. Verstappen understands that once the race begins, his best attention belongs on his own driving, decisions, and response to the moment. That is what keeps him steady under pressure and sharp when things get tight. The strongest competitors measure themselves first by their standard, then by the result.

MORNING EDGE: SET TODAY'S STANDARD

Before you begin, decide what good competing looks like today. Pick one clear standard you can control, such as staying composed after mistakes, communicating clearly, or sticking to your routine when things get uncomfortable.

FLIP THE SWITCH: RETURN TO YOUR STANDARD

When frustration, fatigue, or comparison pulls your attention out, bring it back in-house. Take one Return to Zero breath, ask yourself, "What is my standard right here?" and do the next thing the right way.

CHAMPION'S WRAP: THE STANDARD HELD

At the end of the day, ask yourself whether you competed in a way that matched your standard. Notice one moment when you chose discipline, clarity, or composure over reacting to the scoreboard. That is how strong days stack up and strong competitors are built.

DAY 186: SAME JOB, BIGGER STAGE

"As a driver, it is important to focus on yourself and believe in yourself, and there shouldn't be a reason why. When you are in F1, and there is more attention, you change your approach."
Max Verstappen

Big moments can make athletes feel like they need to become someone else. More attention can tempt you to press, speed up, or put on a show. Verstappen understands that the stage may get bigger, but the job stays the same. The athletes who perform best are the ones who keep trusting the approach that got them there.

MORNING EDGE: CHOOSE YOUR APPROACH

Before the day begins, decide how you want to compete. Choose one quality to lead with, such as calmness, patience, or commitment, and stay with it when the pressure rises.

FLIP THE SWITCH: SHRINK THE WORLD

When the moment starts to feel too big, make your world smaller. Take one Return to Zero breath, bring your eyes to what is right in front of you, and lock back into the next part of the job.

CHAMPION'S WRAP: YOU STAYED WITH YOUR GAME

Ask yourself whether you stayed with your approach today. Notice one moment when the noise rose but your process stayed steady. Big stages reward athletes who keep doing their work their way.

DAY 187: CLOSE THE LAB AND COMPETE

"Don't think too much."
Max Verstappen

Thinking has its place, and so does trust. Great performers study, prepare, and plan before the moment arrives. Once it is time to perform, all of that work has to change hands. You cannot drive the car and build the engine at the same time.

MORNING EDGE: CHOOSE THE MODE

At the start of the day, remind yourself that preparation time and competition time ask for different versions of you. Think clearly when it is time to prepare, then close the lab and let your training take over when it is time to go.

FLIP THE SWITCH: HAND OFF THE KEYS

When you catch yourself thinking in the middle of a performance, stop trying to coach the moment. Take one Return to Zero breath, put your eyes on the target, and hand the keys to your training.

CHAMPION'S WRAP: THE KEYS CHANGED HANDS

Ask yourself whether you let your preparation carry the load today. Notice one moment when you stopped thinking and started trusting. Knowing when to hand the keys to your training is part of competing well.

DAY 188: TRUST THE TRAINED FEEL

"I want to rely on my gut feeling. Isn't that what made great race drivers in the end?"
Max Verstappen

What athletes call gut feeling is usually trained recognition. It comes from doing the work well enough, long enough, that your body starts to know the pattern on sight and on feel. Verstappen understands that this kind of feel is one of the fastest tools in performance. When pressure rises, the mind can get late, but trained feel keeps you on time.

MORNING EDGE: FIND THE CLICK

Before you begin, picture one clean rep and notice what it feels like in your body when everything is connected. Take a breath, find that internal click, and let your first rep come from that feeling instead of from thought.

FLIP THE SWITCH: BACK TO THE SIGNAL

When things start to feel clunky, skip the mental video room and go back to sensation. Slow your breath, feel your feet, your hands, or your rhythm, and let one clean physical cue lead you back to center.

CHAMPION'S WRAP: SAVE THE FEELING

At the end of the day, replay your smoothest moment and notice exactly how it felt. That feeling is a signal, not a fluke. Save it, trust it, and carry it with you into tomorrow.

DAY 189: MENTAL TRAINING PARTNER

LEWIS HAMILTON

"I've learned that the calmest driver is often the fastest."
Lewis Hamilton

Lewis Hamilton built his greatness on speed you can see and calm you can feel. In a sport where decisions happen fast, and mistakes get punished fast, he learned how to stay composed when the pressure spikes and the margins get razor thin. That steadiness shows up in his timing, his choices, and the way he keeps the car alive when others start forcing it. He does not just race fast. He races clear.

What makes Hamilton so special is that his calm is working all the time. It helps him read conditions, feel grip, and stay smooth when the race starts getting chaotic. When others get jumpy, he stays connected to rhythm, control, and execution. That is why calm is never soft. It is one of the sharpest weapons in sport.

Hamilton proves that calm is not the opposite of intensity. It is intensity with command. It keeps your skill available when the moment gets big and helps your best training show up when it counts. That is how pressure turns from something heavy into something useful.

This week, Hamilton is your mental training partner. He will show you how to steady yourself before you move, trust your rhythm when fatigue hits, and stay patient without backing off. Calm does not slow you down. Calm lets you use everything you have.

DAY 190: WIN AT THE RIGHT PACE

"You don't win the race in the first corner. You win it through patience, awareness, and execution."

Lewis Hamilton

A lot of athletes want to make something happen too soon. They rush to separate, force the action, and spend energy before the moment has asked for it. Hamilton understands that early impatience often creates late problems. The goal is not to win the first corner. The goal is to stay composed enough for your skill, timing, and judgment to keep showing up all the way through.

MORNING EDGE: PICK YOUR PACE

Start the day by identifying one place where you tend to hurry, press, or get ahead of yourself. Decide now that you will stay patient there, trust your rhythm, and let the moment unfold before you make your move.

FLIP THE SWITCH: CHECK THE ENGINE

When urgency starts trying to drive for you, pause for one steady breath and ask, "Am I in control of the pace, or am I getting pulled by the moment?" Then settle your body, return to your rhythm, and keep moving at a speed you can trust.

CHAMPION'S WRAP: FINISH STRONGER

Look back on one moment today when patience helped you perform better. Where did you resist the urge to rush, stay with your rhythm, and give yourself a better chance to finish well? That is how smart competitors gain ground.

DAY 191: EXHALE TO WIN

"When you're under pressure, you don't need to explode. You need to exhale."
Lewis Hamilton

Pressure usually shows up in the body before it shows up anywhere else. Your breathing shortens, your shoulders rise, and your timing speeds up. Hamilton understood that the first win in a pressure moment is physical. The person who breathes the best, thinks the best.

MORNING EDGE: CHOOSE YOUR FIRST MOVE

Before the day begins, decide that your first response to pressure will be physical, not emotional. When the heat rises, lengthen your exhale, let your shoulders drop, and give your body the signal that you are still in control.

FLIP THE SWITCH: COOL THE ENGINE

When stress spikes, breathe in for four seconds and out for six seconds, with your full focus on emptying your lungs slowly and completely. Let the exhale cool the engine, loosen your jaw, and bring you back to the clear, composed version of yourself that knows what to do next.

CHAMPION'S WRAP: COOL UNDER FIRE

Look back on one moment today when you exhaled instead of exploding. That is what control looks like when the heat is on. That is how competitors stay sharp when the moment gets hot.

DAY 192: STOP DRIVING WITH THE BRAKE ON

"The battle is always with yourself. You can't drive well if you're fighting inside."

Lewis Hamilton

Many performance problems begin before the body even moves. Frustration, doubt, and impatience create tension long before they show up in your mechanics. When you are fighting yourself inside, part of your energy is going to the task and part of it is going to the fight. The fastest way to speed up is to stop slowing yourself down.

MORNING EDGE: NOTICE THE BRAKE

Before the day begins, notice where your mind tends to create drag. Then make the decision that when that voice shows up, you will not wrestle with it. You will get back to the job and let calm execution take the lead.

FLIP THE SWITCH: NEUTRAL FIRST

When you feel yourself tightening up inside, do not argue with the noise. Breathe in for four seconds and out for six seconds, then tell yourself, "Brake off. Eyes up." Get to neutral first, and let the next clear action pull you forward.

CHAMPION'S WRAP: BRAKE OFF

Think of one moment today when you stopped fighting yourself and got back to execution. Where did you feel the inner noise without letting it drive? That is what it looks like to lead the mind and free up the body.

DAY 193: LET YOUR ACTIONS TALK

"I don't need to prove I'm the best by shouting it. I just try to live it."
Lewis Hamilton

The strongest competitors do not waste energy trying to look strong. They stay connected to themselves, steady in their body, and locked in on what matters. Hamilton's kind of confidence is quiet because it is grounded. When pressure rises, composure, presence, and clean action say more than any display ever could.

MORNING EDGE: LEAD WITHOUT NOISE

Start the day by setting your body the way you want your mind to perform. Stand tall, breathe more slowly, and carry yourself with calm control rather than restless energy.

FLIP THE SWITCH: DROP THE SHOW

When you feel the urge to prove something, strip the moment back down to the job. Relax your face, loosen your shoulders, and move in a way that says, "I'm here to do the work, not perform for the crowd."

CHAMPION'S WRAP: CALM WITH TEETH

Look back on one moment today when you stayed composed and let your actions speak for you. That is the kind of confidence people feel before they can even explain it.

DAY 194: LET IT FLOW

"You can't force a result. You flow with the process, and let the result unfold."
Lewis Hamilton

Pressure has a way of making people try too hard. They squeeze, rush, and reach for the outcome as if they can drag it closer by force. That usually breaks timing, clouds feel, and pulls the athlete out of the rhythm they trained for. Hamilton's edge is knowing that the goal is not to make it happen, but to let what has been built come through cleanly.

MORNING EDGE: PREPARE, THEN RELEASE

Choose one thing to prepare with full care and attention today. Then leave it alone and trust that, when the moment comes, your job is not to force it but to let it work.

FLIP THE SWITCH: UNCLENCH THE MOMENT

When you feel yourself squeezing for the outcome, widen your eyes a bit and loosen your jaw, as if you're giving the moment more room. Let your hands, face, and breathing say the same thing: "Easy speed," then go do the job without trying to overpower it.

CHAMPION'S WRAP: LOOSE AND LETHAL

Look back on one moment today when you stayed loose instead of pushing. That is where timing returns, feel comes alive, and your best work starts to show itself.

DAY 195: WIN AS ONE

"We win and lose together."
Lewis Hamilton

In Formula One, the driver is the one people see, but the result belongs to far more than the driver. A race can turn on a clean pit stop, a smart adjustment, or one small mistake somewhere else in the chain. Hamilton understands that performance is never just personal when others help build it, guide it, and sustain it. The strongest competitors know how to do their part at a high level while staying deeply connected to the people around them.

MORNING EDGE: KNOW YOUR LINK

Start the day clear on your role and how it helps the whole group move. Do your job in a way that makes life easier, sharper, and stronger for the people counting on you.

FLIP THE SWITCH: STRENGTHEN THE CHAIN

When frustration hits, do not drift into blame or self-protection. Get back to the next useful action, communicate clearly, and become the kind of teammate the moment needs.

CHAMPION'S WRAP: STRONG LINKS

Look back on one moment today when you helped the team hold together, move better, or respond well. Then name one place where better connection, clarity, or trust could have made everyone stronger.

DAY 196: MENTAL TRAINING PARTNER

AYRTON SENNA

"I was in a different dimension. It was like I was driving by instinct, in a tunnel, far beyond my conscious understanding."

Ayrton Senna

When Ayrton Senna was locked in, hesitation disappeared and instinct took over. Everything narrowed to the line, the grip, and the next decision. That kind of focus made him one of the most electrifying competitors Formula One has ever seen.

Born in São Paulo, Brazil, Senna showed that edge early in karting, where fearless precision and deep concentration became part of his style. When he arrived in Formula One in 1984, people saw right away that he could read the conditions, trust his instincts, and commit fully in moments when others backed off. He did not just drive fast. He drove with total conviction.

Senna won three World Championships and forty-one Grands Prix, but Monaco is where his legend burned brightest. He won there six times, including five in a row, and his 1988 qualifying lap remains one of the greatest drives in the history of the sport. He later said he had gone beyond conscious understanding. He was no longer thinking his way around the track. He was simply in it.

This week, Senna is your mental training partner. He will show you what it means to trust your instincts, stay fully committed, and compete without holding back. Bring your focus fully into the moment. That is where instinct comes alive.

DAY 197: TAKE THE GAP

"If you no longer go for a gap that exists, you're no longer a racing driver."
Ayrton Senna

Openings do not stay open for long. They appear, ask a question, and disappear. Senna understood that the gap was not just something to notice. It was something to trust. The longer you wait for certainty, the more likely you are to miss the very chance you were hoping for.

MORNING EDGE: BE READY TO GO

Start the day with this mindset: "I am not here to watch opportunities pass." "When the opening is there, I trust myself enough to take it." "Today, I will act with clarity instead of waiting for perfect certainty." Then identify one situation where you usually hesitate and decide in advance that, when the moment comes, you will move.

FLIP THE SWITCH: CUT THE DELAY

When you see the opening and feel hesitation start to creep in, use your Return to Zero breath, inhale for four and exhale for six. Clear the noise, lock onto what is there, and commit before overthinking can close the gap.

CHAMPION'S WRAP: YOU DROVE IT

At the end of the day, name one moment when you acted on an opening instead of letting it pass. Where did you close the distance between seeing it and doing it? That is how instinct sharpens.

DAY 198: COMMAND THE MOMENT

"On a given day, a mind can go further than the body."
Ayrton Senna

Pressure does not just test the body. It tests who stays clear when discomfort, fatigue, and doubt start getting loud. Senna understood that the mind can either magnify the strain or organize the response. When your thoughts get scattered, your performance usually follows. When your mind gets simple, direct, and locked on the next job, you can keep going far beyond what the moment first seems to allow.

MORNING EDGE: DEFINE YOUR COMMAND

Start the day with this mindset: "When pressure rises, I get clear." "When fatigue speaks, I stay with the task." "My mind gives the next instruction." Then choose one cue you can return to when things get hard, such as "Drive," "Up," "Quick hands," or "One more."

FLIP THE SWITCH: ISSUE THE COMMAND

When strain hits, do not argue with it and do not study it. Drop your shoulders, lift your eyes, and give yourself one short command that sends you back into action.

CHAMPION'S WRAP: MIND OVER NOISE

At the end of the day, name one moment when you stayed clear while your body or emotions were getting loud. Where did you simplify, refocus, and keep executing anyway? That is how real mental strength gets built.

DAY 199: OWN THIS LAP

"There's no past, no future. Only the lap."
Ayrton Senna

Great performers get in trouble when they carry too much into the moment. The past brings frustration, the future brings pressure, and both pull attention away from what can actually be done right now. Senna understood that performance only lives in the present piece of the race. His mind stayed with the grip, the line, and the next decision, which is why he could drive with such feel, freedom, and precision.

MORNING EDGE: START CLEAN

Start the day with this mindset: "I do not carry yesterday into today." "I do not race the end from the beginning." "My job is to own the lap I am in." Then put your full attention on the first rep, the first task, or the first decision in front of you and meet it with clear eyes.

FLIP THE SWITCH: SNAP BACK TO THE GRIP

When your mind drifts to what has already happened or what might happen next, blink once, as if taking a snapshot of the moment in front of you. Lock onto one precise detail, tell yourself, "This lap," and go right back to work.

CHAMPION'S WRAP: ALL HERE

At the end of the day, name one moment when you caught your mind drifting and brought it all the way back. Where did being fully here help your timing, decision-making, or poise? That is where your best performance lives.

DAY 200: COMPETE TO WIN

"When you are fitted in a racing car and you race to win, second or third place is not enough."

Ayrton Senna

At some point, you have to decide how you are going to compete. Senna did not drive hoping things would work out. He drove with clear intent to go forward, create pressure, and race for the top spot. That mindset matters because the moment you start protecting, you stop performing as freely and decisively as you can. Winning begins with the courage to compete on the front foot.

MORNING EDGE: SET YOUR INTENT

Start the day with this mindset: "I am not here to hold on." "I am here to go after what matters." "Today I compete with purpose, not caution." Then identify one place where you have been a little too careful and decide to meet it with stronger intent.

FLIP THE SWITCH: GET BACK ON THE FRONT FOOT

When you feel yourself slipping into protection mode, lift your posture, look up, and move toward the next opening with intent. Do not manage the moment. Step into it and make it answer to you.

CHAMPION'S WRAP: YOU WENT FORWARD

At the end of the day, name one moment when you could have played it safe but chose to stay aggressive, clear, and purposeful. That is what it feels like to compete to win. That is how a champion's mindset gets built.

DAY 201: RESPECT THE WORK

"I have no idols. I admire work, dedication, and competence."
Ayrton Senna

Admiring greatness is easy. Building it takes something different. Senna understood that putting people on a pedestal does not move you closer to their level. What moves you forward is respecting the work, the discipline, and the skill that made their performance possible.

MORNING EDGE: CHOOSE THE STANDARD

Start the day with this mindset: "I do not chase inspiration. I build skill." "I do not worship results. I respect the reps." "Today, I will give my best attention to what actually makes me better." Then choose one skill, rep, or task that deserves full effort and do it with care, precision, and pride.

FLIP THE SWITCH: STUDY THE RECIPE

When comparison or intimidation creeps in, stop staring at the finished product. Break greatness back down into parts. Ask yourself, "What is the actual work here?" Then return to one specific thing you can practice, sharpen, or do well right now.

CHAMPION'S WRAP: ADMIRE LESS, BUILD MORE

At the end of the day, ask yourself whether your effort matched the standard you admire. Where did you choose real work over image, discipline over hype, and competence over wishing? That is how high standards become part of who you are.

DAY 202: MAKE THE WEATHER YOUR EDGE

"You cannot overtake fifteen cars in sunny weather, but you can when it's raining."

Ayrton Senna

Perfect conditions rarely separate the field. Tough conditions do. When things get uncomfortable, chaotic, or unpredictable, most people tighten up and hope to get through it. Senna understood that hard conditions create openings for the competitor who stays composed, adapts quickly, and keeps moving forward.

MORNING EDGE: WELCOME THE WEATHER

Start the day with this mindset: "Hard conditions help me separate." "When things get messy, I get sharp." "Today, I will use the weather instead of waiting for it to pass." Then identify one challenge you are likely to face and decide now that it will be a place to compete better, not back off.

FLIP THE SWITCH: HUNT THE OPENING

When conditions get slippery, use one Return to Zero breath and settle your body before the moment can speed you up. Then narrow your focus, trust your cue, and move forward while others hesitate.

CHAMPION'S WRAP: YOU PASSED PEOPLE IN THE RAIN

At the end of the day, look back at the hardest moment you faced. Did you shrink with the conditions, or did you use them to sharpen your focus, trust your training, and move ahead? That answer tells you a lot about who you become when the weather turns.

DAY 203: MENTAL TRAINING PARTNER
ALAIN PROST

"I always say that my ideal is to get pole with the minimum effort, and to win the race at the slowest speed possible."
Alain Prost

Alain Prost did not race to impress people. He raced to win. Nicknamed "The Professor," he built one of the smartest careers Formula One has ever seen, winning four World Championships by staying clear, controlled, and brutally efficient. While others tried to overpower the race, Prost kept solving it.

He came up in an era when Formula One punished mistakes hard and fast. Prost understood that speed alone was never enough. He drove with patience, mechanical feel, and a long view that let him protect the car, manage the race, and stay in position when others burned too much too early. He knew you cannot win on Sunday if you have already lost the car on Saturday.

What made Prost so dangerous was his restraint. He did not need to live on the edge every second to be at his best. He stayed just under the limit, where thinking stayed clean, reactions stayed sharp, and decisions stayed smart. That was not caution. That was mastery under pressure.

This week, Prost is your mental training partner. He will show you how patience can be a weapon, how composure can create an edge, and how the smartest pace is often the winning one. Stay clear, stay under control, and let discipline carry you deep into the race.

DAY 204: TRUST THE CALL

"You were not in control. You had no visibility: Maybe there was a car in front of you, maybe not."

Alain Prost

Pressure gets hardest when you want certainty and cannot get it. You want to know what is coming, how it will turn out, and whether the move in front of you is the right one. Prost competed in conditions where the view was clouded and the margin was razor thin, yet he still trusted himself enough to make the call. That is the deeper lesson. Elite performers do not wait around for perfect clarity. They read what they can, trust what they know, and choose with conviction.

MORNING EDGE: OWN YOUR THRESHOLD

Start the day with this mindset: "I do not need perfect clarity to make a strong decision." "I trust my eyes, my instincts, and my preparation." "If the line is there, I take it. If it is not, I pivot."

FLIP THE SWITCH: KILL THE GRAY ZONE

When things feel unclear, do not get stuck hovering between options. Settle your breathing, clear the noise, and make the cleanest call you can with the information you have. Left, right, or stop. A clear decision frees you to compete.

CHAMPION'S WRAP: YOU SET THE TERMS

At the end of the day, name one moment when you stopped waiting for certainty and trusted your judgment. Where did you decide cleanly, own the choice, and move without hesitation? That is how authority grows under pressure.

DAY 205: STAY SMOOTH UNDER PRESSURE

"Sometimes I think I could have got some better results if I had a different mentality, if I could have pushed hard and attacked. But then I would have had a good chance of making a mistake."
Alain Prost

Pressure makes people think they need to push harder, force more, and squeeze results out of the moment. Prost understood that this is often when performance starts to break down. The harder you strain, the easier it is to lose rhythm, tighten up, and make mistakes you would not make at your best. His edge was not caution. It was the discipline to stay smooth, clear, and in control when others got frantic.

MORNING EDGE: PRECISION OVER POWER

Start the day with this reminder: "I do not need to redline to perform well." "I stay smooth, sharp, and under control." "Today, I trust precise effort over rushed effort."

FLIP THE SWITCH: RETURN TO SMOOTH

When you feel yourself starting to force it, use your Return to Zero breath: Inhale for four, exhale for six. Let that longer exhale settle your body, clear the excess tension, and bring you back to a smooth, controlled rhythm.

CHAMPION'S WRAP: THE EFFICIENCY CHECK

At the end of the day, name one moment when you stayed composed instead of forcing the issue. Where did you get a better result by staying fluid, patient, and disciplined? That is what high-level control looks like under pressure.

DAY 206: OWN THE TEMPO

"I remember in the first part of the race I was sixth and I could have gone quicker, but I had to go slow. It was one of the most difficult things I have ever done."
Alain Prost

Pressure makes most athletes speed up. The moment gets big, the field gets frantic, and suddenly rushing feels like the right answer. Prost understood that this is exactly when discipline matters most. He knew that changing the pace on purpose could protect his timing, sharpen his decisions, and put him in a position to finish strong.

MORNING EDGE: SET THE TEMPO

Start the day with this mindset: "I do not let the moment rush me." "I set the pace that serves the goal." "Today, I move with control, clarity, and purpose." Then identify one part of your day where staying patient and composed will give you an edge.

FLIP THE SWITCH: SLOW DOWN TO SEE MORE

When the moment starts speeding up, use your Return to Zero breath: Inhale for four, exhale for six. Let the longer exhale settle your body, loosen the rush in your mind, and bring you back to your pace instead of the moment's pace.

CHAMPION'S WRAP: THE TEMPO CHECK

At the end of the day, ask yourself, "Where did I hold my pace when things around me wanted to speed me up?" Notice what that protected. It may have been your timing, your judgment, your energy, or your poise. That is how control becomes repeatable.

DAY 207: BUILD A PACE YOU CAN TRUST

"When I test, I never go right to the limit. Only because when you are below the limit, you can go at the same speed all day, and that's the only way you can be absolutely sure about what you are testing."
Alain Prost

Most people think excellence means pushing right to the edge. Prost understood that living on the edge makes it harder to stay clear, steady, and repeatable. When you press too hard, you lose feel, judgment, and control. The goal is not to find a speed you can hit once. The goal is to build a pace you can trust again and again when it matters most.

MORNING EDGE: HUNT THE SIGNAL

Start the day with this mindset: "I am not chasing a miracle today." "I am building a level I can trust." "If I can repeat it, I can own it." Then aim for a standard of effort that keeps you sharp, steady, and fully connected to what you are doing.

FLIP THE SWITCH: CLEAR THE STATIC

When you feel yourself getting scattered, tight, or overamped, it's a sign that noise is taking over. Ease back just enough to clear the static, soften your eyes, loosen your grip, and return to the pace where you can feel your mechanics, trust your rhythm, and compete with clarity.

CHAMPION'S WRAP: THE RELIABILITY CHECK

At the end of the day, name one moment when you chose repeatability over redlining. Where did you stay steady enough to trust yourself, read the moment clearly, and keep delivering? That is how championships are built. Not from one perfect flash, but from a standard that holds.

DAY 208: PROTECT YOUR EDGE

"I don't like to go over curbs, because I don't want to be hard on the car."
Alain Prost

Performance is not just about how hard you push. It is also about what you protect along the way. Prost understood that damage does not always show up right away. What feels small in the moment can take something out of you later, which is why disciplined performers take care of the machine that makes winning possible.

MORNING EDGE: GUARD THE SYSTEM

Start the day with this mindset: "My body, mind, and energy are tools for performance." "I do not waste them on careless effort." "Today, I protect what I will need when it counts." Then notice one area where being more precise, patient, or disciplined will help you stay stronger through the full day.

FLIP THE SWITCH: STAY CLEAN

When you feel yourself rushing, forcing, or cutting a corner, recognize that as wear going into the system. Take one slow breath, relax your jaw, soften your grip or posture, and choose the cleanest path instead of the hardest one.

CHAMPION'S WRAP: THE INTEGRITY CHECK

Name one moment when you chose precision over wear and tear. Where did you protect your body, your focus, or your energy instead of burning through it? That is how great performers stay sharp, steady, and ready for the moments that matter most.

DAY 209: FINISH WITH SOMETHING LEFT

"Another big part of my success is that I hated not to finish a race."

Alain Prost

Prost knew you cannot win if you do not finish. But he also understood something deeper: Finishing is not about flooring it the whole way. It is about managing the race with intelligence, restraint, and discipline. He became known as "The Professor" because he did not waste energy chasing every flashy moment. He stayed composed, protected his fuel, and made sure he still had what he needed when the race was there to be won.

MORNING EDGE: PROTECT YOUR FUEL

Start the day with this mindset: "I do not waste energy on what does not matter." "I stay steady, sharp, and under control." "I save my best for when it counts most."

FLIP THE SWITCH: SETTLE, THEN SUSTAIN

When things get hard, resist the urge to force it. Take one steady breath and ask yourself, "Do I need more effort here, or better pacing?" Sometimes the winning move is to dial it back just enough to stay clean, composed, and fully in the race.

CHAMPION'S WRAP: THE PROFESSOR'S QUESTION

At the end of the day, look back on one moment when you chose precision over pace. Where did you stay patient, manage your energy well, and keep yourself in a strong position to finish? That is how trust is built. That is how races, days, and seasons are won.

DAY 210: BE BRAVE ENOUGH TO WAIT

"I'm brave to say that I won't take this sort of risk."
Alain Prost

Most people think courage means pushing harder, attacking sooner, or forcing the issue. Under pressure, that mindset can make a reckless move feel like a brave one. Prost understood that real courage is not about proving you are fearless in the moment. It is about having the discipline to hold back, trust your judgment, and wait for a move that truly serves the outcome.

MORNING EDGE: REDEFINE COURAGE

Start the day with this mindset: "I do not confuse impulse with bravery." "I stay disciplined when others rush." "I play for the result, not the moment." Then identify one area today where patience, restraint, or better timing will give you a real edge.

FLIP THE SWITCH: AUDIT THE RISK

When you feel the urge to force a move, pause and ask, "Is this helping the outcome, or feeding my ego?" Use your Return to Zero breath, inhale for four and exhale for six, then settle your jaw, hold your line, and wait for the opening that is actually there.

CHAMPION'S WRAP: THE COURAGE OF NO

At the end of the day, name one false opportunity you turned down. Where did you have the discipline to pass on a bad risk, stay patient, and protect the bigger outcome? That is courage with judgment. That is how strong competitors stay in the hunt.

DAY 211: PLAY THE LONG GAME

"So, in fact, the only thing you can judge in this sport is the long term. You can judge a career or a season, but not one race."
Alain Prost

Pressure has a way of shrinking your view. One bad race, one bad rep, or one bad day can start to feel bigger than it really is. Prost understood that performance only tells the truth over time. The athletes who grow, last, and win at a high level are the ones who stay steady enough to let the larger pattern reveal itself.

MORNING EDGE: ZOOM OUT AND STAY WITH IT

Start the day with this mindset: "Today is one data point, not the whole story." "I do not judge myself by one moment." "My job is to give today a strong sample of my process." Then lock back into the habits, standards, and mindset that matter most over time.

FLIP THE SWITCH: CLOSE THE FILE

When one rep, one result, or one mistake starts pulling you into a spiral, pause and refuse to turn a moment into a meaning. Take one steady breath, close the file on that play, and get back to the work before you with clear eyes and a long memory.

CHAMPION'S WRAP: CHECK THE TREND

At the end of the day, do not ask, "Was I perfect today?" Ask, "Is my process moving in the right direction?" Name one moment when you refused to let a rough stretch define the whole day. That is how mature performers stay grounded while the bigger picture takes shape.

DAY 212: SMOOTH IS FAST

"When I look fast, I'm not smooth, and I am going slowly. And when I look slow, I am smooth and going fast."

Alain Prost

Rushing feels fast, but it usually slows you down. Prost knew real speed comes from rhythm, timing, and control. When you are smooth, everything starts working together. Your body stays connected, your mind stays clear, and your performance carries more speed with less waste.

MORNING EDGE: FIND YOUR RHYTHM

Start the day with this thought: "Smooth is sharp." Then bring that feeling into your first reps, tasks, or decisions. Move in a way that feels clean, connected, and under control. That is the rhythm you want with you when the pressure climbs.

FLIP THE SWITCH: BACK TO SMOOTH

Take one Return to Zero breath: Inhale for four, exhale for six. Let your jaw loosen, your hands relax, and your eyes settle. Then get back to the tempo where your timing, mechanics, and instincts can work together.

CHAMPION'S WRAP: LET RHYTHM LEAD

At the end of the day, name one moment when staying smooth made you better. Where did rhythm create speed? Where did control sharpen your edge? Remember that feeling. That is what speed feels like when it is under control.

CHAMPION'S TAKEAWAYS: CIRCUIT DE MONACO

Monaco trained your ability to stay composed when space is tight and consequences are immediate. You practiced competing with full commitment, resetting quickly after mistakes, and staying present under pressure. You also strengthened an elite skill: knowing when to push and when to settle, so your mind stays clear when it counts. The deeper lesson was learning to trust your own way of competing under pressure.

As you step off this track, reflect:

- Where did I stay composed and committed when the moment got tight?
- What reset worked best for me, and when did I use it?
- What do I trust more about how I compete under pressure than I did before?

Carry forward your ability to stay composed, reset fast, and trust your approach when pressure hits. That is how control travels with you.

CHAPTER 8

AUGUST: WEMBLEY STADIUM

"The only time you run out of chances is when you stop taking them."
David Beckham

Wembley is not just another stadium. It is a place where history, pressure, and possibility all hit at once. You feel it walking up Olympic Way, with the arch above you and the stage opening wider with every step. It is big, exposed, and built for moments that ask for courage.

First opened in 1923 and rebuilt in 2007, Wembley has hosted some of the biggest matches in soccer history. History does not sit quietly here. The question is whether you can stay yourself inside it.

That is what this chapter is about. When the stage grows, the best athletes do not rush to prove something. They trust their instincts, hold their tempo, and let preparation come alive. They stay clear enough to take their chance when it appears. Wembley rewards courage that is calm and confidence that is ready.

This month, you will train with Lionel Messi, Carli Lloyd, Cristiano Ronaldo, and Marta Vieira da Silva. Each brings a different kind of edge, but all four know how to meet a big moment without losing themselves. Wembley teaches that mastery is alive, poised, and ready to strike. When your moment comes, take it.

DAY 213: MENTAL TRAINING PARTNER

LIONEL MESSI

"Everything I did, I did for football, to achieve my dream."

Lionel Messi

Messi built one of the greatest careers in sport without needing to make a show of it. His game has always spoken with the ball at his feet, in the timing of a pass, the tight touch in traffic, and the calm he brings to the biggest moments. For more than two decades, he has shown that greatness can be quiet and still leave the whole world stunned. His edge is mastery, repeated under pressure.

Born in Rosario, Argentina, Messi faced a growth hormone deficiency as a boy and needed treatment his family could not easily afford. At thirteen, Barcelona offered him that chance and famously sealed the agreement on a napkin. From there, he grew into the club's all-time leading scorer, won a record eight Ballon d'Or awards, and led Argentina to the Copa América in 2021 and the World Cup in 2022. The dream was enormous, and he kept growing into it.

What separates Messi is how he stays calm amid the chaos. Defenders close, the crowd swells, the stakes rise, and he still looks like he has more time than everyone else. That kind of poise comes from trust, feel, and endless repetition. He lets the game come to him, then changes it with one touch, one cut, or one brilliant decision.

This week, Messi is your mental training partner. He will show you how to stay composed, trust your preparation, and let your game breathe under pressure. Train with discipline, play with joy, and keep your attention on the task right in front of you. That is where freedom starts.

DAY 214: STAY CURIOUS

"The day you think there is no improvement to be made is a sad one for any player."
Lionel Messi

Messi is saying there is always something to find. The best keep looking, even when things are going well. They stay open, they stay interested, and they keep their game alive. Curiosity is what keeps progress moving and the work feeling fresh.

MORNING EDGE: HUNT FOR THE EDGE

Before practice or competition, pick one small thing you want to sharpen today. It could be your timing, your breathing, your body language, or the way you reset after a mistake. Say, "Let's see what I can find today." Bring that mindset into your first action.

FLIP THE SWITCH: TINKER, AND GO

When something feels off, go to RTZ: In for four and out for six. Then ask, "What is one small thing that would make this better?" Make the adjustment and get right back into it. Great performers stay curious longer than other people stay frustrated.

CHAMPION'S WRAP: FOUND SOMETHING

Look back on the day and name one thing you discovered about your game, your mindset, or your rhythm. Maybe it was a better cue, a calmer response, or a small change that helped things click. That is a good day.

DAY 215: ANSWER THE DREAM

"You have to fight to reach your dream. You have to sacrifice and work hard for it."
Lionel Messi

Messi is saying a dream asks something of you every day. It calls for work, sacrifice, patience, and heart. Big goals are reached by the people who keep answering that call with their actions. The dream grows stronger each time you show up and give it what it needs.

MORNING EDGE: HEAR THE CALL

Before you begin, ask yourself, "What does the dream need from me today?" Maybe it needs focus. Maybe it needs discipline. Maybe it needs one more hard thing from you. Then say, "I will answer with my actions." Carry that into your first action.

FLIP THE SWITCH: PAY THE PRICE

When the work gets heavy, go to RTZ. Take one Return to Zero breath and remind yourself, "This is part of the dream." Then step back in with purpose. Hard days are part of the cost.

CHAMPION'S WRAP: PAID IN FULL

Look back on the day and name one thing you gave your dream. Maybe it was your focus, your effort, or the way you kept going when it would have been easy to back off. Every day you answer the dream like that, you make it more real.

DAY 216: TRUST YOUR GAME

"I do what comes to me at that moment. Instinct. It has always been that way."

Lionel Messi

Messi can trust his instincts because he trained them until they became part of him. There is a time to study, correct, and think your way through the details. There is also a time to stop coaching and start playing. Train it clean so you can trust it later.

MORNING EDGE: TRAIN IT CLEAN

Before training, decide that your job is to give each rep your full attention. Do it cleanly, finish it fully, and save the analysis for breaks or after the session. Keep this in mind: "Train it clean so you can trust it later."

FLIP THE SWITCH: LET IT GO

When you feel yourself tightening up or trying to guide every movement, stop coaching in the middle of the play. Get your eyes on the target and bring this cue to the front: "I've trained this. Let it go." Then, react with the skills you already have.

CHAMPION'S WRAP: YOUR REAL GAME CAME OUT

At the end of the day, think of one moment when you stopped interfering and let your game come through. That is what it looks like when training starts turning into instinct.

DAY 217: LEARN FAST, MOVE ON

"When you lose, you get up. You make mistakes, and you learn. And then you become a better player."
Lionel Messi

Mistakes are part of growth, but only if you handle them the right way. Most athletes either overreact emotionally or try to pretend nothing happened, and both approaches miss the point. The best competitors take a quick lesson and then let the moment go. They learn without lingering and move on without dragging the mistake into the next play.

MORNING EDGE: MISSES WELCOME

Before you start, remind yourself that mistakes are information, not emergencies. Decide that today you'll take the lesson and then return to your normal rhythm instead of replaying or rushing.

FLIP THE SWITCH: FIX IT, FORGET IT

When you make a mistake, pause just long enough to ask, "What's the adjustment?" Make that correction, then tell yourself, "Next one, best one," and reengage at your usual pace rather than trying to force a response.

CHAMPION'S WRAP: BETTER, NOT BITTER

Think of one moment today when you learned from a mistake and didn't carry it forward. That's control of your response—and that's how improvement sticks.

DAY 218: FIND THE KID AGAIN

"My motivation comes from playing the game I love. If I wasn't paid to be a professional footballer, I would willingly play for nothing."
Lionel Messi

Messi is talking about the part of the game that existed before pressure, money, and expectations showed up. He is reminding you that love of the sport is not soft. It is a real source of energy. When you lose touch with that, the game can start to feel heavy even when you are doing well. When you find it again, you move with more freedom, more life, and more of yourself.

MORNING EDGE: TAP THE SPARK

Before practice or competition, think of one part of your sport that used to light you up right away. Maybe it was the feel of the ball, the rhythm of movement, the challenge, the speed, or the simple fun of it. Picture that version of you for a second. Then say, "Bring that into today."

FLIP THE SWITCH: BACK TO PLAYING

When the day starts to feel tight, heavy, or overly serious, go to RTZ. Take one Return to Zero breath and ask yourself, "What would this look like if I were just playing?" Then loosen your grip, trust your training, and bring some life back into the next action.

CHAMPION'S WRAP: WHERE IT CAME ALIVE

Look back on the day and find one moment when the sport felt fun, clean, or alive again. Hold onto that moment and what brought it out of you. That feeling is not random. It is a clue.

DAY 219: BUILT OVER TIME

"I start early and I stay late, day after day, year after year. It took me 17 years and 114 days to become an overnight success."
Lionel Messi

Messi is pointing to something most people forget. What looks sudden is usually the result of years of work no one saw. Long before the praise, the breakthrough, or the headlines, he was already building the player those moments would require. He kept showing up, kept training, and kept trusting that steady work would have its time.

MORNING EDGE: BUILD THE PLAYER

Start the day with one clear thought: "I'm building the player my dream requires." Then go to work on what matters most. Do today's work well, even if today gives you nothing back.

FLIP THE SWITCH: STAY WITH THE BUILD

When impatience shows up, bring your attention back to the work in front of you. You do not need a big moment right now. You need another strong rep, another solid decision, and another day handled well.

CHAMPION'S WRAP: IT ADDED UP TODAY

Think of one small thing you did well today that will matter later. Maybe nobody noticed it. Maybe the results haven't shown it yet. It still counts, and it is still part of what you are becoming.

DAY 220: MENTAL TRAINING PARTNER

CARLI LLOYD

"I'm a go-getter. I'm someone who wants to constantly find ways to make myself better. To do that, I have to get out of my comfort zone."
Carli Lloyd

Carli Lloyd built her career on drive, discipline, and a standard that did not blink. She grew up in South Jersey, starred at Rutgers, and turned herself into one of the fiercest competitors the game has seen. Long before the biggest goals, there was extra work, extra reps, and a mindset that kept reaching for more. She trained like the moment was coming.

When the moment came, she met it. Lloyd won Olympic gold in 2008 and 2012, then delivered one of the most electric performances in soccer history in the 2015 World Cup Final. She scored a hat trick in the first sixteen minutes, including a goal from midfield that stunned the world. Across 316 international appearances and 134 goals, she became the player coaches trusted when everything was on the line.

What separated Lloyd was the way she built belief. She visualized the moments she wanted, then trained until those moments felt familiar. She kept her habits sharp, her preparation serious, and her focus steady regardless of mood. That is why she could step into huge moments looking ready for them.

This week, Lloyd is your mental training partner. She will show you how to raise your standard, get out of your comfort zone, and turn repetition into trust. Bring intent to the work, stay hungry, and train like your moment is coming.

DAY 221: PAY THE PRICE TODAY

"Work hard at everything you do. Never give up. Never quit. Many people have talent, but without the hard work, you won't get anywhere."

Carli Lloyd

Lloyd did not treat greatness like something you buy once and keep forever. She treated it like something you pay for again and again. Talent can open the door, but it cannot carry you through the days when your energy is low, your mood is off, or the work feels repetitive. That is where the real separating happens. This is the part where talent runs out and earning begins.

MORNING EDGE: SPOT THE EXIT

Start the day by asking yourself, "Where am I most likely to want to coast, cut corners, or check out today?" Then decide in advance what the stronger move will be when that moment shows up.

FLIP THE SWITCH: THIS IS THE PRICE

When you hit the part of the day where your brain starts looking for the exit, do not act surprised. Tell yourself, "This is the price of entry," and give your best to the next few minutes, the next rep, or the next task. If you do not have your A game today, give a full B game with discipline.

CHAMPION'S WRAP: PAID UP TODAY

As you close out the day, name one moment when you stayed with the work instead of slipping into what was easy. That is how standards are built, and it is how goals stay alive from one day to the next.

DAY 222: TRAIN WHAT COSTS YOU

"Fitness, defending, the mental stuff—those were all weaknesses of mine. And I turned those into strengths."
Carli Lloyd

Lloyd paid close attention to the areas that kept costing her. She did not avoid them, complain about them, or hope they would somehow disappear. She treated them like instructions and built her work around them. That same principle applies to your game, your habits, your recovery, your nutrition, and anything else that quietly pulls your level down.

MORNING EDGE: ATTACK ONE, RESIST ONE

Start the day by naming one behavior to attack and one behavior to resist. Attack what makes you better, such as extra work on a weakness, better fuel, or better recovery, and resist what keeps costing you, such as junk food, sloppy habits, mindless scrolling, or putting off the hard part.

FLIP THE SWITCH: THIS IS THE WORK

When you feel yourself drifting toward what is easy or familiar, catch it quickly. Tell yourself, "This is the work," then make the stronger choice, whether that means staying with the drill, putting the phone down, eating like a pro, or getting your mind back where it belongs.

CHAMPION'S WRAP: CLOSE THE GAP

As you close out the day, name one place where you chose growth over comfort. That is how weaknesses lose ground and strengths get built.

DAY 223: BUILD THE COMEBACK

"It's always hard to deal with injuries mentally, but I like to think about it as a new beginning. I can't change what happened, so the focus needs to go toward healing and coming back stronger than before."

Carli Lloyd

Lloyd did not waste the setback by arguing with it. She accepted that the injury was real, but she refused to let it be the end of the story. That is the mental shift that matters most. A setback can break your rhythm, but it can also become the place where you rebuild your body, your patience, your habits, and your edge.

MORNING EDGE: START THE REBUILD

Name one part of your life or game that this setback is asking you to strengthen. Stop asking why it happened and start asking what you can build because it happened.

FLIP THE SWITCH: DO THE NEXT USEFUL THING

When frustration, fear, or self-doubt starts creeping in, bring it back to action. Tell yourself, "Build the return," then do the next thing that helps you heal, recover, or get stronger.

CHAMPION'S WRAP: PROGRESS NOTED

As you close out the day, name one thing you did that helped your comeback, even in a small way. That is how strong returns are built, one honest brick at a time.

DAY 224: LET SUCCESS PULL YOU

"Any professional athlete will tell you that the mind is everything. For me, there is no shame in saying that I visualize and I meditate, because it really works."
Carli Lloyd

The mind moves toward the pictures you give it. When you see yourself strong, sharp, and composed, you start building familiarity with that version of you before the moment arrives. Visualization adds fuel, and meditation helps you stay clear enough to carry that image into real life. The future suddenly feels closer, brighter, and more within reach. What you rehearse with belief starts to feel more possible.

MORNING EDGE: SEE IT FIRST

Before the day gets moving, take a few seconds to picture one moment going exactly how you want it to go. See your posture, your rhythm, your expression, and the way you want to move through it. Make the picture vivid enough that your mind wants to go there.

FLIP THE SWITCH: STEP INTO THE PICTURE

When the moment arrives, bring back the image you already created. Let it guide your body, your tempo, and your attention. Move like you have already seen yourself do this well.

CHAMPION'S WRAP: END WITH THE HIGHLIGHT

At the end of the day, replay one moment you handled well and enjoy seeing it again. Let that image sink in and leave a good trace behind. That is how belief grows and success starts to feel more natural.

DAY 225: WIN THE STATE

"At the end of the day, you can be physically strong, you can have all the tools out there, but if your mental state isn't good enough, you can't bring yourself to bigger and better things."
Carli Lloyd

Lloyd understood that talent is only as useful as the state of mind behind it. Your skills do not vanish under pressure, but your mind can cut you off from them when you get tight, scattered, or stuck in your own head. That is why mental state comes first. When your mind is working with you instead of against you, your training has a chance to show up.

MORNING EDGE: SET THE STATE

Before the day gets moving, ask yourself, "What state helps me perform at my best?" Pick two or three words, such as calm, clear, and aggressive, and carry them with you on purpose.

FLIP THE SWITCH: GET BACK ON YOUR SIDE

When your mind starts racing or pulling you away from the moment, do not fight it or feed it. Take one good breath and tell yourself, "Get back on my side." Then bring your attention back to your body, your breath, and the next thing you need to do well.

CHAMPION'S WRAP: FINISHED IN A BETTER PLACE

As you close out the day, think of one moment when you shifted your state instead of letting it run you. That is real mental strength. It is not about having a perfect mind, but knowing how to come back to a better one.

DAY 226: FALL IN LOVE WITH THE MIDDLE

"You don't want to get too wrapped up in that final destination. You want to enjoy the journey, enjoy the process, and just take it one step at a time."

Carli Lloyd

The mind loves the big finish. It wants the medal, the applause, and the part where everything suddenly makes sense, but it can get weirdly impatient with the boring little steps that actually get you there. The truth is, most great performances are built in the middle, not at the end. When you stop acting like the middle is just something to survive, the work gets lighter and a lot more alive.

MORNING EDGE: CHOOSE THE PART YOU'LL LOVE

Before the day gets moving, choose one part of the work you are going to fully enjoy. It might be your rhythm, the feel of strong movement, the snap of clean execution, or the quiet satisfaction of doing something hard well. Let that part pull you into the day.

FLIP THE SWITCH: STAY WITH THIS STEP

When your mind jumps ahead to outcomes, timelines, or how far you still have to go, bring it back down. Tell yourself, "This step," and reconnect to what is right in front of you. Great days are built by fully owning the piece you are in.

CHAMPION'S WRAP: YOU WERE HERE FOR IT

At the end of the day, think of one moment when you were fully in the work instead of trying to get through it. Notice what changed when you stopped chasing the finish line and gave yourself to the step. That is where the journey becomes alive.

DAY 227: MENTAL TRAINING PARTNER
CRISTIANO RONALDO

"I see myself as the best footballer in the world. If you don't believe you are the best, then you will never achieve all that you are capable of."
Cristiano Ronaldo

Cristiano Ronaldo built his career on a huge belief in who he could become. That belief was never just talk. It gave shape to his training, sharpened his response to adversity, and pushed him to keep raising the bar long after most players would have been satisfied. He saw greatness clearly, then went to work on it every day.

He grew up on the island of Madeira and left home at twelve to join Sporting CP. Far from family and still just a kid, he carried a powerful picture of the player he intended to become. That picture kept pulling him forward. It drove the habits, the discipline, and the daily standards that took him from Sporting to Manchester United, Real Madrid, Juventus, and beyond.

The numbers are staggering. Five Ballon d'Or awards, five Champions League titles, and more than eight hundred career goals. But the deeper lesson is how he used belief. Praise never made him comfortable, criticism never knocked him off course, and the work kept coming whether it was a final or an ordinary training day.

This week, Ronaldo is your mental training partner. He will push you to get clear on the athlete you are becoming and bring your habits up to that level. See it big, train with purpose, and let your standards reflect the player you believe you can be.

DAY 228: WORK HARD, THEN LEAVE THE STADIUM

"Talent without working hard is nothing."
Cristiano Ronaldo

Ronaldo did not build greatness by training halfway. He attacked his work, then knew how to leave it there. That second skill matters more than most athletes realize. A lot of performers finish practice physically but keep competing in their head for the rest of the day. Real recovery begins when you stop carrying the arena with you.

MORNING EDGE: EMPTY THE TANK AT THE RIGHT TIME

Go after your work today with purpose. Be sharp, demanding, and fully there while it is time to work. Give the session your fire, then earn the right to turn the flame down when it is over.

FLIP THE SWITCH: CLOCK OUT CLEAN

When the work is done, make the exit real. Change the channel on purpose by stepping into something simple and human, such as music in the car, a good meal, sunlight on a walk, or laughter with someone you love. Great performers know how to stop carrying the arena into every room they enter.

CHAMPION'S WRAP: PUT THE SWORD AWAY

Tonight, notice whether your mind is still gripping the day. If it is, picture yourself setting the gear down, turning out the lights, and leaving the field where it belongs. Recovery begins the moment you stop dragging effort into hours meant for repair.

DAY 229: MAKE THE NOISE YOUR EDGE

"Your love makes me strong. Your hate makes me unstoppable."
Cristiano Ronaldo

If you put yourself out there, people will have something to say. Some will cheer you, some will doubt you, and some will watch just to see what happens next. Ronaldo understood that outside noise only has power when you hand it the controls. Support can lift you, criticism can sharpen you, and both can become fuel when you decide what they mean. The goal is not to block it out, but to use it and keep moving.

MORNING EDGE: OWN THE MEANING

Decide how you will handle opinions today. Let support steady you and let criticism sharpen you, but keep your direction clear. Your job is not to manage reactions. Your job is to compete.

FLIP THE SWITCH: CONVERT THE NOISE

When your attention drifts to what others might think, feel the pull and then redirect it. Picture the noise hitting you and converting into energy that drives your next action. Lock back into the task and move with purpose.

CHAMPION'S WRAP: MAKE IT YOUR EDGE

Take a minute tonight and replay one moment when you used the noise to compete better. Notice how you stayed in control of the meaning instead of reacting to it. That is how you make noise your edge.

DAY 230: PROBLEMS ARE THE TRAINING

"When everything is good, I don't think you grow up fantastically. I think maybe you need a few problems to grow up."
Cristiano Ronaldo

Ronaldo did not become who he became because life stayed easy. He grew through pressure, challenges, and the kinds of problems that force you to adapt quickly. Smooth days can build rhythm, but hard days build range. They make you think better, respond better, and carry yourself better when things get messy. Problems are not a break from the training. Problems are the training.

MORNING EDGE: EXPECT THE REP

Go into the day knowing something may test you. It might be annoying, unfair, inconvenient, or just plain hard. See it early, and decide that when it shows up, you will treat it like part of the workout. That mindset keeps you ready instead of rattled.

FLIP THE SWITCH: THIS IS THE WORK

When something goes sideways, do not waste the moment wishing it were easier. Tell yourself, "This is the work," and meet the problem in front of you. Solve what you can, settle what you can't, and keep moving. That is how toughness gets built in real time.

CHAMPION'S WRAP: STRONGER WITH PROBLEMS

Before bed, think of one problem you handled better than the old version of you would have handled it. Notice what was stronger in your response—your patience, your focus, your poise, or your effort. That is growth you can trust, because it showed up under pressure.

DAY 231: SET YOUR OWN PACE

"I know I'm a good professional. I know that no one's harder on me than myself and that's never going to change, under any circumstances."
Cristiano Ronaldo

Ronaldo is not talking about perfection here. He is talking about ownership. He does not need someone else to tell him when he is sharp, flat, locked in, or drifting. He can feel the difference, and he takes responsibility for correcting it. That is one of the deepest mental game skills in sport. The strongest standard is the one you carry and enforce yourself.

MORNING EDGE: SET THE LINE

Before you begin, decide what your level looks like today. Make it specific and visible, like sharp feet, full effort, strong posture, clean follow-through, or real presence. Start the day by drawing the line clearly so you can recognize it when you are on it.

FLIP THE SWITCH: CATCH THE DRIFT

When you feel yourself getting loose, casual, distracted, or halfway in, catch it early. Say, "Raise it," or "Back to my level," and make the correction on the next rep. The goal is not to be perfect. The goal is to notice the drop fast and respond before it spreads.

CHAMPION'S WRAP: HOLD YOUR OWN STANDARD

At the end of the day, ask yourself whether you held your standard when nobody was pushing you. Notice where you stayed true to it and where you let the line slide. That answer is useful because it shows you whether your standard is real or just something you talk about.

DAY 232: MAKE EXCELLENCE FEEL NORMAL

"You can. You can. Cross the barrier, same as always. For you, it is normal to score."
Cristiano Ronaldo

Before a penalty kick, Ronaldo does something brilliant. He does not talk to himself like a man standing in a once-in-a-lifetime moment. He talks to himself like a man returning to familiar ground. "Same as always" pulls the moment out of the spotlight and puts it back into rhythm. "For you, it is normal to score" reminds him that pressure does not change who he is or what he does. Making the big moment feel like home is one of the greatest skills in the mental game.

MORNING EDGE: CHOOSE YOUR NORMAL

Pick one quality you want to make feel normal today, such as staying composed, committing fully, or finishing with authority. Treat it like part of your game, not something you are hoping to find. Step into the day like this is just what you do.

FLIP THE SWITCH: SAME AS ALWAYS

When the pressure tries to make the moment feel bigger, bring it back down to size. Use a line like "Same as always," "I know this moment," or "This is in my game." Then trust one clear action and let the rep be the rep.

CHAMPION'S WRAP: PRESSURE MADE ORDINARY

At the end of the day, replay one moment when you kept something important feeling simple. Notice how your body, mind, or rhythm settled when you treated the moment like familiar work. That is how pressure loses some of its bite.

DAY 233: TEACH ME SOMETHING

"If you think you're perfect already, then you never will be."
Cristiano Ronaldo

Ronaldo is not talking about insecurity here. He is talking about staying open enough to keep rising. The best athletes do not waste energy defending the version of themselves they already are. They stay teachable, adjustable, and hard to outgrow. Ego wants to be right, but confidence wants to get better. That difference changes everything.

MORNING EDGE: LEARN, NOT PROVE

Start the day with one simple thought: "Teach me something." Let that mindset travel with you into training, competition, and conversation. Athletes improve faster when they stop performing for approval and start looking for the lesson.

FLIP THE SWITCH: STAY OPEN, STAY SHARP

When feedback comes, resist the urge to explain yourself too quickly. Listen for what is useful, honest, and actionable. Take what helps, leave what doesn't, and keep moving without closing up.

CHAMPION'S WRAP: GROWTH STILL OPEN

At the end of the day, think of one moment when you stayed open instead of getting defensive. Notice what that allowed you to see, hear, or improve. That is how growth stays alive, even when you are already good.

DAY 234: MENTAL TRAINING PARTNER

MARTA VIEIRA DA SILVA

"Believe in yourself. Believe in your instinct. And you'll find out just why God has given you this talent."

Marta Vieira da Silva

Marta grew up in a small town in Brazil where girls were not expected to play football, and she played anyway. She learned the game in the streets, often barefoot, taking on anyone who would step in and compete. Even then, she played with joy, daring, and a deep belief that her gift could take her somewhere. At fourteen, she left home and carried that belief with her.

That belief helped carry her to the top of world football. Marta won six FIFA World Player of the Year awards and became Brazil's all-time leading scorer. She was the first player, man or woman, to score in five World Cups and five Olympic Games. Her greatness came from honoring her talent again and again through training, courage, and relentless work.

What makes Marta so powerful is not just what she can do with the ball. It is the way she treats her talent like something worth developing and protecting. She plays with freedom, but she also respects the work that freedom demands. For her, belief is alive in the habits, the preparation, and the way she keeps showing up.

This week, Marta is your mental training partner. She will remind you to trust your gift, play with instinct, and back your talent up with real work. Bring belief to the day, then honor it with how you train. That is how a gift grows into something special.

DAY 235: YOU'VE DONE THE WORK

"Believe in yourself and trust yourself."

Marta Vieira da Silva

Self-belief rises when you remember what is already yours. You have put in the hours, carried the hard days, learned from the misses, and kept growing. Your training is in you now. Your experience is in you now. Your strength is in you now. Trust turns all of that into freedom. When you trust yourself, you move with more rhythm, play with more courage, and let your best come through.

MORNING EDGE: TRUST WHAT'S THERE

Before you begin, ask yourself, "What is already in me?" Think of your work, your growth, and the moments you rose before. Let that remind you who you are. Step into today with that feeling.

FLIP THE SWITCH: LET YOURSELF PLAY

When it is time to go, keep your mind simple and your body free. Choose one clear anchor—tempo, target, or feel—and compete from there. Trust gives your talent somewhere to go.

CHAMPION'S WRAP: THE FINAL REP

Think of one moment today when you stopped overthinking and let yourself play. Hold onto that feeling for a few seconds. That's what belief feels like when it's alive.

DAY 236: TAKE CARE TO COMPETE

"It's wanting more. It's training more. It's taking care of yourself more. It's being ready to play ninety plus thirty minutes."
Marta Vieira da Silva

Wanting more shows up in how you train, recover, and handle the end of the day. The athletes who truly want it prepare to finish strong, not just start fast. They also know when to shut it down so they can come back ready tomorrow. That's how wanting becomes real.

MORNING EDGE: PREPARE TO LAST

Before training, ask yourself, "What will help me still be sharp at the end?" Make one choice today that supports that, whether it's focus, effort, or pacing.

FLIP THE SWITCH: STAY WITH IT

When fatigue or boredom hits, remind yourself, "This is where it counts," and give one steady, committed rep.

CHAMPION'S WRAP: LET THE DAY GO

At the end of the day, name one thing you did well, then mentally release the rest. Turning it off on purpose is how you show you want it again tomorrow.

DAY 237: DO THE HARD PART FIRST

"Cry in the beginning so you can smile in the end."
Marta Vieira da Silva

The way you start the day shapes how the rest of it feels. When you handle the toughest task first, everything after it feels more manageable. You stop dragging things with you. You move more lightly because the big task is already done. That's how strong finishes are built.

MORNING EDGE: START WITH THE HARD THING

Before the day gets busy, identify the one task you're most tempted to delay. Do that first, even if it's uncomfortable.

FLIP THE SWITCH: STAY WITH THE WORK

When the effort feels heavy, tell yourself, "This is the work I chose," and stay steady through the rep.

CHAMPION'S WRAP: NOTICE THE PAYOFF

At the end of the day, notice one moment that felt easier because you handled the hard part early. That's how discipline turns into freedom.

DAY 238: WHEN IT GETS HEAVY

"Never give up, and be confident in what you do. There may be tough times, but the difficulties you face will make you more determined to achieve your objectives and to win against all the odds."
Marta Vieira da Silva

Some days feel heavy for no clear reason. Your body is there, but everything takes more effort than it should. These are the days that test what your confidence is actually built on—not how fired up you feel, but how steady you stay.

MORNING EDGE: SAY THE LINE

Start the day with one thought: "I've got this in me." That means you trust your preparation, your toughness, and your ability to handle the work even when it's uncomfortable.

FLIP THE SWITCH: NARROW THE FOCUS

When things tighten up, stop looking at the whole day. Choose the next simple task and do it cleanly. Staying present is how confidence survives hard moments.

CHAMPION'S WRAP: WHAT STAYED SOLID

Before bed, recall one moment when it got heavy but you didn't bail. That's the kind of confidence that carries over.

DAY 239: EARN THE SMILE

"We all have obstacles. The feeling of satisfaction comes from overcoming something."
Marta Vieira da Silva

The best kind of satisfaction comes from meeting the day well. It comes from knowing something in front of you asked for effort, discipline, or courage, and you gave it what it required. Every day brings a test. It might be fatigue, distraction, a hard conversation, a tough rep, or the part of you that wants the easy way out. You do not need a huge win to feel good about your day. One honest win over something that challenged your standard is enough. That is how satisfaction is earned.

MORNING EDGE: NAME TODAY'S TEST

Ask yourself, "What is most likely to test me today?" Keep it simple and tell the truth. That is the moment that deserves your best.

FLIP THE SWITCH: HANDLE IT WELL

When that moment comes, meet it with intent. Stay present, stay steady, and do the next right thing. A lot of self-respect is built in moments like this.

CHAMPION'S WRAP: SLEEP EASY

Think of one thing you handled well today. That is the kind of win that helps you sleep easy.

DAY 240: THE GROUND YOU'VE EARNED

"It's about challenging yourself, about believing in you, in your talent, in your feet."
Marta Vieira da Silva

Belief grows from experience. You've trained tired, competed when uncomfortable, and finished sessions that asked for more than you wanted to give. Those days shaped your base. When pressure shows up, stand on what you've already built.

MORNING EDGE: FIND YOUR BASE

Before you start, name one hard thing you've already handled in your sport. Let that be the ground you stand on today.

FLIP THE SWITCH: TRUST THE BODY

When the moment starts to feel bigger and your body reacts by tightening up, bring attention to your feet, your rhythm, or your next simple action. Let your body lead the moment.

CHAMPION'S WRAP: SOLID GROUND

Before bed, recall one moment today when you stayed steady and kept going. That's earned belief you can use again tomorrow.

DAY 241: BE FIRST

"When I started playing, I didn't have a role model."
Marta Vieira da Silva

Marta grew up without seeing someone who looked like her or came from where she came from succeed at the highest level. There was no clear example to follow and no proof handed to her in advance. Instead of waiting for permission or representation, she chose to move anyway. Sometimes the reason you cannot find the role model you need is because you are meant to become it.

MORNING EDGE: LEAD BY EXAMPLE

Show up today like someone out there needs to see how it's done. Compete in a way that quietly proves this path is possible.

FLIP THE SWITCH: TAKE THE FIRST STEP

When you catch yourself thinking, "No one's done this before," treat it as a signal to move. Being first is not a flaw. It is an opportunity.

CHAMPION'S WRAP: RAISE THE STANDARD

Ask yourself, "If someone trained the way I did today, would that make them better?" That answer tells you exactly where your standard is.

DAY 242: OUTGROW YOUR LIMITS

"The only limits in life are the ones we place upon ourselves."
Marta Vieira da Silva

Think about all the things you once believed you could not do until you did them anyway. That is your real résumé. You have already outgrown versions of yourself that once felt permanent. Champions are not driven by approval or comparison but by curiosity about what they are capable of next. The real work is not proving others wrong but continuing to outgrow the limits you once accepted.

MORNING EDGE: TEST YOUR CEILING

Start the day with one question: "What if I'm better than I think?" Then compete today in a way that gives you a clear answer.

FLIP THE SWITCH: TREAT DOUBT AS A SIGNAL

When doubt shows up, do not back off. Lean in and take it as a dare to find out what is actually possible.

CHAMPION'S WRAP: NOTICE THE GROWTH

Before you shut it down tonight, name one moment where you handled something better than you would have in the past. That is a clear sign you are still expanding.

DAY 243: GREATNESS IS IN YOU

"We are all capable of greatness, if only we believe in ourselves."
Marta Vieira da Silva

You are capable of greatness because greatness is not reserved for a select few. It comes from qualities you already have—attention, courage, effort, discipline, honesty, love of the game, the ability to stay with hard things, and the willingness to rise when it matters. Greatness is built out of ordinary things done at a high level.

MORNING EDGE: BRING YOUR BEST

Start the day by choosing the qualities you want to bring forward. Bring your attention. Bring your effort. Bring your courage. Greatness starts when you bring the best of yourself into the moment.

FLIP THE SWITCH: RAISE THE STANDARD

As the moment grows, bring more intention to the basics. Sharpen your focus, stay with the rep, and do simple things with care. Greatness shows up when ordinary things are done with uncommon quality.

CHAMPION'S WRAP: SEE YOUR GREATNESS

Think of one moment today when you brought your best into it. That is what greatness looks like in real time.

CHAMPION'S TAKEAWAYS: WEMBLEY

Wembley was your month in the spotlight: big stage, big expectations, and nowhere to hide. You learned how pressure feels in your body and how belief shows up in real time, not as hype but as steadiness. You discovered that mistakes do not define you, but your response does. Over and over, you stayed composed, reset faster, and trusted what you had built.

Belief and bounce-back proved to be the same skill. When something went wrong, you did not disappear. You stayed present, stayed connected, and kept playing. That is how confidence becomes durable instead of fragile.

As you step off the pitch, take a moment to reflect:

- How quickly did I respond when the moment tested me?
- What part of my mindset or game held up best when the pressure was loud?
- How did my presence help stabilize or elevate the people around me?

Hold the trophy high, not for the noise, but for the steadiness you earned.

CHAPTER 9

SEPTEMBER: LAMBEAU FIELD

"The measure of who we are is what we do with what we have."
Vince Lombardi

You do not stroll into Lambeau. You brace for it. The wind cuts, your breath hangs in the air, and the crowd feels close enough to hit you too. Opened in 1957, Lambeau has seen football at its rawest, including the 1967 Ice Bowl, when Bart Starr crashed over the goal line with seconds left. This place strips the game down to what holds up when comfort is gone.

Lambeau does not care how things look. It cares whether you can line up in the cold, take the hit, get back up, and do your job again. The footing gets tricky, the calls are imperfect, and momentum can swing without warning. What matters here is focus, reliability, and a standard that stays firm when conditions turn rough.

This chapter is guided by four champions who lived that truth in different ways. Lombardi brings relentless standards, Tomlin steadiness, Brady discipline, and Mahomes creativity built on preparation.

This chapter is about the brilliant basics. It is about raising your standard, playing forward without hesitation, and staying focused when the conditions stop being comfortable. Lambeau does not blink. Neither should you.

DAY 244: MENTAL TRAINING PARTNER

VINCE LOMBARDI

"The quality of a person's life is in direct proportion to their commitment to excellence, regardless of their chosen field of endeavor."
Vince Lombardi

When Vince Lombardi arrived in Green Bay in 1959, the Packers had won one game the year before and lost the habit of winning. He changed that fast. Meetings started on time, practices had purpose, and every detail mattered. On the first day of camp, he held up a football and said, "Gentlemen, this is a football." The message was clear. Greatness starts with the basics.

Lombardi believed discipline was commitment made visible. He studied film relentlessly, taught the smallest details, and expected full effort every day. The work did not rise and fall with mood, momentum, or excuses. Over time, that consistency became the team's identity.

Under Lombardi, the Packers won five NFL championships, including the first two Super Bowls. His teams played tough, sharp, and connected because they knew what was expected and took pride in doing it right. He made excellence feel like the job, not the exception. That is why his message still hits.

This week, Lombardi is your mental training partner. He will show you how to respect the fundamentals, honor the details, and bring discipline to your preparation and competition. The standard is built in what you do again and again. That is how winning starts to look like who you are.

DAY 245: CHASE THE RABBIT

"We are going to relentlessly pursue perfection, knowing full well we will not catch it, because nothing is perfect. But in the process, we will catch excellence."
Vince Lombardi

Lombardi treated perfection like a rabbit out in front of you. You do not chase it because you expect to grab it. You chase it because it keeps your feet moving and your standards high. The rabbit stays just ahead, and that is what sharpens you. In the chase, your habits get tighter, your focus gets better, and your game rises.

MORNING EDGE: PICK UP THE RABBIT

Choose one part of your day to chase a little harder. It could be your footwork, breathing, preparation, recovery, or the way you reset between reps. Picture the rabbit just out in front of you and say, "Go get a little better." Then bring that spirit into your first action.

FLIP THE SWITCH: KEEP CHASING

When you catch yourself easing up, wake yourself back up. Clean up one detail, lift your energy, and say, "Stay on the rabbit." The best reps are often the ones where you recommit after a drift.

CHAMPION'S WRAP: WHAT THE CHASE PULLED OUT OF YOU

Think of one moment today when you tightened something up instead of letting it slide. Maybe you sharpened your form, stayed with the rep, or brought more care to a small detail. That is how excellence sneaks up on you. You chase the rabbit, and one day you realize your whole game moved up.

DAY 246: STAY IN THE FIRE

"Mental toughness is essential to success."
Vince Lombardi

Lombardi is talking about what happens when the work starts biting back. Your breathing gets heavier, your body gets louder, and your mind starts looking for the nearest exit. That is the moment that tells the truth. Hard moments do not just test your standard. They give you a chance to live it.

MORNING EDGE: FIND YOUR HARD

Pick one part of today that is likely to test you. See it ahead of time and picture yourself stepping right into it instead of circling around it. Say, "This is where I grow." Then meet it with your eyes up and your effort on.

FLIP THE SWITCH: STAY IN THE FIRE

When fatigue, doubt, or discomfort shows up, tighten up your basics instead of backing off. Stand taller, breathe deeper, and say, "Right here. Stay with it." Then attack the next action with full commitment.

CHAMPION'S WRAP: WHERE YOU GOT STRONGER

Think of one moment today that asked something real from you. Maybe it was a hard rep, a tired stretch, or a moment when your mind wanted to fade. That was not just a hard moment. That was a chance to get stronger, and you took it.

DAY 247: SHOW UP FOR EACH OTHER

"Individual commitment to a group effort—that is what makes a team work."
Vince Lombardi

Lombardi is saying team success starts with personal responsibility. A strong team is built when each person brings commitment to the shared effort. That commitment shows up in how you practice, how you respond, and how you carry yourself when things get hard. Every player adds something to the group, and that something matters. The team improves when everyone contributes.

MORNING EDGE: BRING YOUR PIECE

Before practice or competition, think about what your team needs from you today. Maybe it is energy, focus, toughness, communication, or steadiness. Say, "They can count on me." Then show it with your effort, your body language, and the way you go about your work.

FLIP THE SWITCH: LIFT THE GROUP

When the energy drops or the group starts to fade, choose to bring something strong to the moment. Talk more, move better, compete harder, and give your teammates something they can feel.

CHAMPION'S WRAP: BE SOMEONE THEY CAN COUNT ON

Think of one moment today when your effort, attitude, or response helped the group. That is what trusted teammates do—they make the team better by how they show up.

DAY 248: GET BACK UP

"It's not whether you get knocked down, it's whether you get up."
Vince Lombardi

Lombardi is saying hard moments are part of the deal. Everyone gets hit, misses, slips, or has a day that goes sideways. What matters is how quickly you get your feet back under you. Toughness shows up in the response. The faster you get back up, the less power the moment has over you.

MORNING EDGE: READY TO RISE

Think of one challenge you might face today and picture yourself handling it well. See yourself taking the hit, steadying yourself, and getting right back into the fight. Say, "I rise fast." Then carry that into your first action.

FLIP THE SWITCH: UP AND INTO IT

When something goes wrong, take one steady breath and lift your posture right away. Say, "Up and into it," then step back into the next play, rep, or moment with purpose.

CHAMPION'S WRAP: BACK ON YOUR FEET

Think of one moment today when you got hit and answered well. That is what toughness looks like in real life.

DAY 249: WHEN YOU'RE TIRED

"Fatigue makes cowards of us all."
Vince Lombardi

Lombardi is saying fatigue changes more than your body. It can shrink your thinking, your confidence, and your willingness to stay aggressive. That is why tired moments matter so much. Anyone can look sharp when they feel fresh. The real edge shows up in how you carry yourself when your energy drops.

MORNING EDGE: PLAN FOR THE DIP

Assume you will get tired at some point today. Decide now how you want to look and act when that moment comes. Say, "Tired is a feeling, not a decision." Then bring that standard into your first action.

FLIP THE SWITCH: BACK TO ZERO

When fatigue hits, go to Return to Zero. Breathe in through your nose for four and feel your posture gently rise. Breathe out through your mouth for six and let your shoulders soften. At the bottom of the exhale, think, "Back to zero," then lock back in on the next simple thing you can do well.

CHAMPION'S WRAP: STRONG WHILE TIRED

Think of one moment today when you were running low and still held your standard. That is where grit starts to show up for real.

DAY 250: KEEP THE FAITH

"It's easy to have faith in yourself and have discipline when you're a winner. What you got to have is faith and discipline when you're not a winner."
Vince Lombardi

Lombardi is talking about the hard part of belief. It is easy to stay confident when things are going well and the results keep backing you up. The real test comes when the results are slow, mistakes keep showing up, or progress is hard to see. That is when faith becomes a daily choice. You keep doing the work right, even before the payoff shows up.

MORNING EDGE: STICK WITH THE WORK

Start the day by deciding what will matter most today. Choose effort, execution, and the way you carry yourself. Say, "I'm staying with it." Then bring that mindset into your first action.

FLIP THE SWITCH: KEEP THE STANDARD

When frustration hits, bring your focus back to the next simple thing you can do well. Let the moment be hard and stay with the work anyway.

CHAMPION'S WRAP: FAITH IN ACTION

Look back on one moment today when you stayed disciplined even though the result was not there. That is where real belief lives. It shows up in what you keep doing when nothing is handing it back to you yet.

DAY 251: MENTAL TRAINING PARTNER

MIKE TOMLIN

"It's not about what you're capable of. It's about what you're willing to do."

Mike Tomlin

Mike Tomlin led the Pittsburgh Steelers from 2007 to 2025 without a losing season. That kind of consistency did not come from talent alone or from everything breaking right. It came from a standard that remained firm through injuries, roster changes, and whatever noise was swirling around the team.

His message did not change with mood, momentum, or outside pressure. Everyone in the building knew what was expected. Tomlin believed talent might open the door, but willingness decides who keeps walking through it.

Willingness shows up in the unglamorous parts of the job. It shows up in how you prepare when nobody is watching, how you respond when you are coached hard, and how you compete when it would be easier to drift. Tomlin stripped performance down to choices that hold up in the moment.

Players trusted him because he was steady, clear, and real. He did not ride emotion, and he did not flinch at results. That is why his message carried weight. When the moment tests you, remember the lesson. It is not about what you could do. It is about what you are willing to do today.

DAY 252: NO SLIDING SCALE

"The standard is the standard."

Mike Tomlin

Tomlin is talking about a fixed bar. Your mood may change, the conditions may change, and the day may feel different than you hoped. The standard does not change with any of that. It stays there and asks the same question: Are you going to meet it? That is how consistency is built and trust is earned.

MORNING EDGE: SET THE BAR

Choose two standards for today. Keep them simple, clear, and behavioral, like strong effort, quick reset, good body language, sharp focus, or being on time. Say, "This is the bar today." Then let your actions rise to meet it.

FLIP THE SWITCH: RISE TO THE BAR

When you feel yourself drifting, ask, "Am I meeting the standard right now?" If the answer is no, make one clear adjustment right away and bring your behavior back in line.

CHAMPION'S WRAP: HELD THE LINE

Look back on one moment when you met the standard and one moment when you slipped below it. See both clearly and keep it honest. One shows you what to keep doing. The other shows you exactly where to rise tomorrow.

DAY 253: STAY OPPORTUNISTIC

"More grounded, more humble, more selfless makes us more opportunistic."
Mike Tomlin

Tomlin is saying humility helps you see what ego misses. Grounded people stay open, and open people keep learning. That is where opportunities show up. A correction lands, a pattern stands out, and a small edge appears for the athlete who is ready to catch it.

MORNING EDGE: KEEP YOUR EARS OPEN

Start the day by choosing one place where you will listen closely. It might be a coach, a teammate, your body, or the way a rep feels. Say, "There is something here for me." Then stay open enough to catch it.

FLIP THE SWITCH: CATCH IT QUICK

When frustration rises or feedback hits a nerve, pause and ask, "What can help me here?" Take the useful part and put it to work right away. Coachable athletes do not stay stuck in reaction. They turn the moment into an opening.

CHAMPION'S WRAP: FOUND THE OPENING

Look back on the day and name one thing you picked up because you stayed open. Maybe it was a correction, a detail, a tendency, or a better way to handle a moment. Small edges find people who are still listening.

DAY 254: USE THE RIGHT TOOLS

"Excuses are tools of the incompetent."
Mike Tomlin

Tomlin is saying excuses do not build anything. They may explain the moment, but they leave you in the same place. Strong performers reach for better tools. They own it, adjust it, and get back to work. That is how they maintain control over what happens next.

MORNING EDGE: PACK THE RIGHT TOOLS

Before the day starts, think of one situation where you usually explain, blame, or stall. Decide now that you will answer it with ownership, adjustment, and effort instead. Say, "Own it and fix it." Then carry that into your first action.

FLIP THE SWITCH: FIX, DON'T EXPLAIN

When something goes wrong, pause for a beat and ask, "What helps right now?" Go straight to the next useful action. Coaches, leaders, and competitors trust people who fix things faster than they defend themselves.

CHAMPION'S WRAP: WHAT YOU REACHED FOR

Look back on one hard moment from today and notice what you grabbed first. Did you reach for an excuse, or did you reach for a response? That choice matters. The tools you use under pressure shape your habits, your standards, and your future.

DAY 255: PLAY WITH DIRECTION

"We don't live in our fears. We live in our hopes."

Mike Tomlin

Tomlin is talking about where you aim your mind. Fear and hope can both show up in big moments, but they send you in different directions. Fear fixes your attention on what might go wrong. Hope locks you in on what you want to make happen. That is what gives your effort direction and your movement purpose.

MORNING EDGE: SET THE AIM

Start the day by naming one thing you want to make happen. Maybe it is attacking the first rep, trusting your shot, speaking up, or staying aggressive when it counts. Keep it simple and specific. Say, "This is what I'm bringing today," and let that aim guide your actions.

FLIP THE SWITCH: AIM FORWARD

When hesitation shows up, ask yourself, "What am I trying to make happen right now?" Let that answer pull you into the moment. Clear aim creates cleaner action.

CHAMPION'S WRAP: WHAT YOU WENT AFTER

Look back on one moment when you moved toward something instead of shrinking away from it. Notice what you were trying to create and how it changed your energy. That is what it looks like to compete with direction.

DAY 256: WIN THE DAY IN FRONT OF YOU

"I tend to attack the challenges that are right in front of me, the ones that I have today."
Mike Tomlin

Tomlin is talking about keeping your focus close. Big goals get heavy when you try to carry all of them at once. The challenge in front of you is enough. When you lock in on today, your energy gets sharper and your decisions get cleaner. That is how real progress is made.

MORNING EDGE: NAME TODAY'S WIN

Decide what would make today a win. It might be one practice, one workout, one meeting, one class, or one hard conversation handled the right way. Say, "This is the job today." Then go do it with full attention.

FLIP THE SWITCH: BACK TO WHAT'S HERE

When your mind jumps ahead, go to RTZ: In for four and out for six. Then say, "Handle today." Bring your eyes, breath, and attention back to the next thing in front of you and do it well.

CHAMPION'S WRAP: TODAY COUNTS

Look back on the day and name one thing you handled well. Maybe it was your effort, your focus, or your staying with the task at hand. That is how strong days stack up. Tomorrow can wait its turn.

DAY 257: NO RÉSUMÉ THINKING

"If there's a secret, the secret is I'm focused on the challenges and tasks at hand and not my résumé."

Mike Tomlin

Tomlin is talking about staying out of your own highlight reel. Résumé thinking pulls you into image, status, and how everything will look later. The task in front of you brings you back to what is real. That is where your best work lives. The more fully you give yourself to the job, the less you need to worry about the story it will tell.

MORNING EDGE: DROP THE CLIPBOARD

Before the day gets going, name one task that deserves your full attention. Picture yourself setting down the mental clipboard, the stats, the future, the image, and just going to work. Say, "Win the task." Then bring that into your first action.

FLIP THE SWITCH: BACK TO THE WORKBENCH

When your mind starts drifting to how you are being judged, what this means, or how it will look, go to RTZ: In for four and out for six. Then ask, "What does the work need right now?" Answer that question with your next action.

CHAMPION'S WRAP: LET THE WORK TALK

Look back on one moment today when you got out of your head and fully into the task. Maybe you were focused, steady, and all the way there. That is a real win. The best days are often the ones where you stop narrating and start working.

DAY 258: MENTAL TRAINING PARTNER

TOM BRADY

"To be great at something, you don't need to be special. You just need to be what most people aren't: Consistent. Determined. Willing to work for it. No shortcuts."

Tom Brady

Tom Brady built greatness the hard way. Drafted late and doubted early, he turned preparation, discipline, and consistency into one of the greatest careers in sports history. He won seven Super Bowls by doing the ordinary things better and longer than almost anyone else. That is how he separated himself.

At Michigan and in the NFL, Brady stayed patient while others looked for faster results. He studied until the game slowed down and practiced until execution felt second nature. When his chance came, he did not need to manufacture anything extra. He trusted what he had built.

Brady also protected his edge with discipline away from the field. He said yes to recovery, preparation, and habits that kept him sharp, and he let the rest go. Late nights, shortcuts, and distractions had no place in the standard he was trying to live. He understood that every choice either feeds your edge or chips away at it.

This week, Brady is your mental training partner. He will show you how to do the basics brilliantly, prepare like every rep matters, and build a standard you can trust under pressure. Stay consistent, stay disciplined, and let the work stack in your favor.

DAY 259: THE POWER OF NO

"I do too. But I think I was born with the ability to say no."
Tom Brady

Brady said that during a 2025 podcast interview with Shaquille O'Neal, after O'Neal admitted he liked burgers and club sandwiches and asked how Brady stayed so disciplined with food. Brady likes those things too, but he does not let every craving make the decision for him. That is where discipline starts. It is not about never wanting something. It is about being able to want something and still choose what serves you better. Great competitors are shaped as much by what they refuse as by what they choose. They build their edge by saying no to what pulls them away from their standard.

MORNING EDGE: DECIDE YOUR NO

Before the day gets going, name one thing that tends to pull you away from your best. Decide now how you are going to respond when it shows up. Tell yourself, "That may be available, but it is not for me today." A strong day gets easier when the decision is made early.

FLIP THE SWITCH: STRENGTHEN THE NO

When an impulse shows up that interferes with excellence, do not stand there and debate it. Take one Return to Zero breath and give yourself a clear answer. Say, "No, that is not who I am today," then move straight into the next action that supports your standard. Every time you do that, you strengthen your discipline.

CHAMPION'S WRAP: WHERE YOU SAID NO

Think of one moment today when you could have said yes to something that would have taken you off course, but you did not. That is how self-control is built. You are teaching yourself that your standard gets the final word.

DAY 260: SOMETIMES HARD IS THE WAY

"I think sometimes in life the biggest challenges end up being the best things that happen in your life."
Tom Brady

The hard road asks more of you, but it also gives more back. Being buried on a depth chart, working your way back from injury, or grinding without much recognition can feel frustrating, unfair, and lonely. Brady knew those stretches long before the rings and the spotlight. He was not handed much early, but that became part of his edge. Hard seasons build staying power. They sharpen your hunger, test your standard, and reveal what kind of competitor you become when nothing is being given away.

MORNING EDGE: MEET THE HARD THING WELL

Name one challenge you are facing right now and decide how you want to meet it today. Bring patience, grit, and discipline to what is in front of you. You do not need the whole path this morning. You need a strong response to today's resistance.

FLIP THE SWITCH: LET THE HARD BUILD YOU

When discouragement shows up, remember that this is where your edge is being built. Stay with the rep, the drill, the rehab, or the task in front of you. Hard does not mean wrong. Sometimes hard is the way.

CHAMPION'S WRAP: WHAT THE HARD REVEALED

Ask yourself, "What did the hard bring out of me today?" The way you answer that question is shaping the competitor you are becoming.

DAY 261: THE NEXT ONE IS THE BEST ONE

"You wanna know which ring is my favorite? The next one."
Tom Brady

That line has swagger, but it also reveals a championship mindset. The best competitors do not let success turn into comfort. Brady respected what he had earned, but he never let yesterday's win become today's hiding place. He kept his eyes on what was next, what was still possible, and what still needed to be built. That kind of hunger keeps you sharp, driven, and relentless.

MORNING EDGE: CHASE THE NEXT RING

Ask yourself, "What do I need to do today to move one step closer to the next ring?" Let that question sharpen your focus and raise your standard. Big wins are built by how you handle what is in front of you right now.

FLIP THE SWITCH: DON'T CAMP ON YESTERDAY

When your mind starts living off what you have already done, bring it back to what still needs to be built. Picture the next win, the next breakthrough, or the next version of you that is still taking shape. Then go back to the work in front of you with hunger.

CHAMPION'S WRAP: WORTHY OF THE NEXT RING

At the end of the day, ask yourself, "Did I work in a way that was worthy of the next ring?" That question keeps you honest, focused, and moving forward.

DAY 262: THE CHAMPION'S DIAL

"You can't pay attention to what others say about you.
What matters is what you say to yourself."
Tom Brady

High-level athletes live around noise. Praise, criticism, predictions, and opinions are always trying to get your attention. The dial is your ability to choose what gets turned up and what gets dialed down. Brady understood that the athlete who controls the inner voice controls the moment. When your own message is clear, outside noise loses its grip.

MORNING EDGE: SET YOUR FREQUENCY

Before the day begins, decide what voice you want leading it. Tell yourself, "My voice sets the tone today. Eyes on the task. Mind where my feet are." Turn that voice up before anything else gets a say.

FLIP THE SWITCH: DIAL DOWN THE NOISE

When outside voices start getting loud, do not argue with them or give them more airtime. Take one Return to Zero breath and say, "Dial it down. Back to the job." Then lock your eyes on the next specific thing that needs your full attention. The moment gets simpler when your focus gets clear.

CHAMPION'S WRAP: CHECK THE DIAL

At the end of the day, ask yourself, "What did I turn up, and what did I dial down?" Your answer will tell you a lot about who was really leading your focus.

DAY 263: YOUR BODY WRITES THE SCOUTING REPORT

"Body language is a big thing. I can't show fear. I can't show doubt."

Tom Brady

Before the play starts, your body has already said something. The way you walk, breathe, stand, and move tells people what kind of competitor you are. Hurried movement and restless energy make you look easier to shake. Calm eyes, steady breath, and strong presence send a different message. They say you are settled, ready, and here to compete. Under stress, your body writes the scouting report.

MORNING EDGE: SEND THE RIGHT MESSAGE

Walk into training or competition like someone who is ready for the moment. Let your eyes settle, let your breathing slow down, and carry yourself with strong presence. Decide what you want your body language to say today, then make sure your body says it before you do.

FLIP THE SWITCH: WEAR THE LOOK

When pressure hits, picture the most composed and confident version of yourself. See how that version stands, breathes, and moves, then step right into that look. Your body can help lead your mind back to where it needs to be.

CHAMPION'S WRAP: READ THE REPORT

Think of one pressure moment today and ask yourself, "What did my body say there?" Your body language is either building belief or leaking doubt, so make sure it is telling the right story.

DAY 264: FISH WITH INTENTION

"The fish just don't jump in the boat. If you want to catch them,
go catch them. Throw that line in the water and do some work.
If it doesn't work that day, do it again the next day."
Tom Brady

Brady was not casting at random. He knew what he was after and stayed with it. Greatness works the same way. You do not build it by being busy or available to everything. You build it by putting your time, energy, and attention where they actually pay off. That means saying no to distractions so you can keep saying yes to preparation, recovery, and repeatable work. Progress comes to athletes who keep casting in the right water, even on the days when nothing bites.

MORNING EDGE: CAST IN THE RIGHT WATER

Ask yourself, "What actually moves me forward today?" Then put your time and energy there first. Do not confuse motion with progress.

FLIP THE SWITCH: CAST AGAIN

When results do not come right away, do not drift off course. Take a steady breath and cast again with the same purpose. Stay with the kind of work that pays off over time.

CHAMPION'S WRAP: WHAT DID YOU CAST FOR?

Before bed, ask yourself, "Did I go after what mattered today, or did I just stay busy?" Your answer will tell you whether your effort had direction.

DAY 265: MENTAL TRAINING PARTNER

PATRICK MAHOMES

"Every day should be maximized by trying to be the best person and athlete. Taking things one day at a time and going out there to be the best possible player are key."

Patrick Mahomes

Patrick Mahomes grew up around big-league sports and learned early how competitors carry themselves. The son of former MLB pitcher Pat Mahomes, he developed in a world where preparation, feel, and adaptability mattered every day. At Whitehouse High in Texas, he starred in football, baseball, and basketball, even throwing a no-hitter with sixteen strikeouts. That multi-sport background still shows up in the way he plays: creative, poised, and ready for anything.

At Texas Tech, Mahomes lit up the field with one of the most explosive arms college football had ever seen. He tied an NCAA record with 734 passing yards in a single game and won the Sammy Baugh Trophy as the nation's top passer. When the Chiefs traded up to draft him tenth overall in 2017, he did not rush the process. He spent a full season behind Alex Smith, learning, preparing, and getting ready in silence.

When his chance came, he was ready for it. Since then, Mahomes has led Kansas City to multiple Super Bowl appearances, winning three championships and earning three Super Bowl MVP awards. What makes him so dangerous is not just talent. It is the calm, creativity, and trust he brings when the play breaks down and the pressure rises.

That is why Mahomes is the right training partner to close the month. He lives the daily game, prepares with purpose, competes with joy, and handles today the right way. This week, he will show you how to stay loose, think clearly, and trust yourself when the moment starts moving fast. Greatness gets built one day at a time, and Mahomes is proof.

DAY 266: GREATNESS IS A DECISION

"Every day is a new day. You have to come in with that mindset of being great."
Patrick Mahomes

Mahomes does not wait for the day to feel big before he brings something big to it. He shows up with intent, energy, and a clear decision about how he will compete. That is what keeps his game growing. Greatness is not reserved for game day or special moments. It is built on ordinary days when you decide that average is not getting a turn.

MORNING EDGE: BRING THE STANDARD EARLY

Before your first rep, decide what greatness looks like today. It might be your focus, your pace, your body language, or the way you finish. Say, "I'm bringing it today," and let that decision set the tone.

FLIP THE SWITCH: DON'T GIVE THE DAY AWAY

When your energy drops or a rep goes sideways, do not drift into average. Reset quickly, take one breath, and go attack the next rep with intent. Great competitors do not need a perfect day. They keep bringing something to it.

CHAMPION'S WRAP: DID YOU BRING IT?

Before bed, ask yourself, "Did I bring greatness to this day, or did I wait for the day to give me something first?" That answer will tell you a lot.

DAY 267: WIN THE NEXT SNAP

"I just try to go to the next play. That's the biggest thing.
You can't let one mistake define you."
Patrick Mahomes

Mahomes has a rare ability to stay on the attack when things go sideways. When a throw misses, a drive stalls, or a play breaks down, he does not stay there. He gets back to competing fast. That is one of the biggest separators in sport. The mistake costs what it costs, but holding on to it usually costs more. Great competitors keep the last play from stealing the next one too.

MORNING EDGE: OWN THE NEXT SNAP

Decide how you want to respond when something goes sideways today. Pick one simple reset phrase you can use anywhere, such as "Next snap," and pair it with a steady breath. Use it early so your mind and body know the move.

FLIP THE SWITCH: GET BACK ON THE ATTACK

After a mistake, give yourself a clear physical cue and move right into your reset. Clap your hands, nod once, or take one steady exhale. Say your phrase, bring your eyes back up, and step into the next play with intent. Your edge is in how fast you get back to attacking what is in front of you.

CHAMPION'S WRAP: BACK ON THE ATTACK

Before bed, ask yourself, "How quickly did I get back on the attack after something went wrong today?" That answer tells you a lot about the competitor you are becoming.

DAY 268: REHEARSE YOUR GREATNESS

"You see the no-look passes and all that, but those are just things you work on in practice. It's not just showing up in the game. It's the work you put in every single day."
Patrick Mahomes

People see brilliance in the moment and assume it appeared out of nowhere. Mahomes reminds us that greatness usually shows up where it has already been welcomed, pictured, and practiced. The best moments in sport are rarely accidents. They are often the visible proof of what an athlete has been building long before anyone was watching.

MORNING EDGE: SEE IT BEFORE YOU NEED IT

Before training begins, picture one thing you want showing up when the pressure is on. See yourself doing it with freedom, confidence, and clean rhythm, as if the moment has already arrived. Then step into the day determined to train that future into something real.

FLIP THE SWITCH: PRACTICE THE PLAYER YOU'RE BECOMING

When the session feels ordinary, remember that this is where tomorrow's breakthrough is being built. Bring your focus back to the quality, feel, and intention you want to own when it counts. Every strong rep is a message to your future self that says, "This is who we are becoming."

CHAMPION'S WRAP: MEET YOUR FUTURE SELF

Before bed, think about the athlete or performer you are trying to become and ask whether you trained in a way that would make that version of you proud today. Picture that future self looking back at this day and thanking you for how you showed up. Great moments are easier to trust when you have already started becoming the person who can handle them.

DAY 269: KEEP THE GOLD, DROP THE DIRT

"Every experience, good or bad, you have to learn from. I just try to learn from every mistake that I make so that I never make them again."
Patrick Mahomes

Great competitors know how to pan for gold. They can go through a messy day, a rough rep, a bad game, or a frustrating mistake and still come away with something useful. They do not keep the whole event. They keep the lesson. Mahomes has a gift for doing exactly that and moving on lighter.

MORNING EDGE: LOOK FOR THE GOLD

As you start today, remind yourself that every experience has something to teach you. Your job is not to carry the whole thing. Your job is to find the gold and leave the dirt.

FLIP THE SWITCH: LEARN IT AND LIGHTEN UP

When something goes sideways, ask one quick question: "What is this here to teach me?" Keep the lesson, take one steady breath, and let the rest fall away. You do not need to drag a whole mood into the next moment just because one thing went wrong.

CHAMPION'S WRAP: TRAVEL LIGHT

Before bed, think of one moment from today that did not go the way you wanted. Name the lesson, smile at what it taught you, and let the rest go. Tomorrow is easier to step into when you are not carrying extra weight.

DAY 270: PLAY FOR MORE THAN YOURSELF

"It's all about playing for my teammates."
Patrick Mahomes

Mahomes understands something a lot of athletes learn the hard way. It still has to be your game, your standards, and your responsibility, but the moment gets heavy when it becomes all about you. When you turn your focus to your teammates, your role, and what the group needs, you stop trying to prove something and start trying to deliver something. You still bring your own game, but playing for more than yourself often brings the best version of you out.

MORNING EDGE: BRING IT FOR THEM

Before the day begins, think about the people you are showing up with and for. Picture your teammates, your coaches, or anyone who counts on your effort and energy. Tell yourself, "I'll bring my best, and I'll bring it for them," and let that guide how you show up.

FLIP THE SWITCH: DO YOUR JOB FOR THE GROUP

When pressure hits, stop checking how you feel and come back to your job. Ask yourself, "What does my team need from me right now?" Then do that with focus and intent, and let everything else take care of itself.

CHAMPION'S WRAP: DID THEY GET YOUR BEST?

Before bed, think about the people around you and ask yourself if they got your best today. That question keeps it simple and honest. It is still your game, but it shows up strongest when you give it to something bigger than yourself.

DAY 271: PLAY WITH LOVE

"I love this game."
Patrick Mahomes

Mahomes plays like someone who is still in love with it. You can feel it in the freedom, the creativity, and the way he attacks the moment instead of shrinking from it. Love changes the whole experience of competition. It turns pressure into energy, effort into expression, and hard work into something worth doing again tomorrow. When you reconnect with what you love, the game opens back up.

MORNING EDGE: REMEMBER WHAT YOU LOVE

Before practice or competition, take a moment to remember what drew you to this in the first place. Picture the feeling of a clean rep, a great play, a perfect shot, or the joy of being fully locked in and alive. Let that feeling wake something up in you before the day begins.

FLIP THE SWITCH: COME BACK TO LOVE

When you feel disconnected and start going through the motions, come back to what you love about competing. Take one Return to Zero breath and tell yourself, "I love this game, and I'm here to play it fully." Let that thought wake your energy back up and help you compete with freedom, expression, and joy.

CHAMPION'S WRAP: KEEP THE LOVE ALIVE

Before bed, think of one moment today when you felt connected to the game in a real and energizing way. Hold on to that moment for a second and let it remind you what keeps you coming back.

DAY 272: WE'VE GOT AN ANSWER

"I feel like, even if something goes wrong, I have confidence in myself and my team that we'll fix it."
Patrick Mahomes

Something is going to wobble today. A play will break down, a rep will get messy, or a plan will need to be adjusted on the fly. Great teams do not waste energy acting surprised when that happens. They trust the repair, settle quickly, and get to work.

MORNING EDGE: EXPECT THE WOBBLE

Start the day by reminding yourself that problems are part of the job, not proof that anything is falling apart. Tell yourself, "When something wobbles, we steady it," and carry that calm into the day.

FLIP THE SWITCH: SHIFT INTO SOLUTION MODE

When something goes sideways, bring the group back together and go straight into solution mode. Slow it down, make the adjustment, and trust that steady teams repair faster than frantic ones.

CHAMPION'S WRAP: STEADY HANDS

Think of one moment today when something needed fixing and notice how you responded. The best teams are not remembered for avoiding problems, but for how quickly and calmly they put things back in place.

DAY 273: STAY ON THE OFFENSIVE

"Stay humble, stay hungry."
Patrick Mahomes

Early on, the game teaches you how to respond. Later, it teaches you how to lead. Once you start succeeding, the challenge is no longer just handling pressure well. The challenge is staying in command of your own tempo, mindset, and direction.

MORNING EDGE: CALL YOUR FIRST PLAY

Before the day starts, decide how you want to open. Picture your first rep, your first move, or your first interaction, and step into it like a quarterback who already has the play call.

FLIP THE SWITCH: KEEP THE DRIVE ALIVE

When the rhythm shifts, stay in command of the drive. Take one Return to Zero breath, reset your posture and eyes, and choose the next play with purpose.

CHAMPION'S WRAP: WHAT DID YOU KEEP DRIVING TOWARD?

Before bed, think about what you kept moving toward all day. The best competitors do not just stay active. They keep directing their energy, focus, and decisions toward what matters.

CHAMPION'S TAKEAWAYS: LAMBEAU

Lambeau showed you what is left when comfort leaves the field. Cold, fatigue, mistakes, and shifting momentum were all part of the test, and you learned how to stay with your work instead of getting pulled around by conditions. You went back to basics, reset quickly when things went wrong, and kept your effort and focus steady when the game got messy. That is the kind of game that travels anywhere.

As you step away from Lambeau, ask yourself:

- When conditions were uncomfortable, what part of my game stayed reliable?
- How quickly did I respond after mistakes or frustration?
- Where did I hold the standard instead of negotiating it?

Bring that steadiness, toughness, and trust with you into the next arena.

CHAPTER 10

OCTOBER: BOSTON MARATHON

"At the Boston Marathon, you run against the distance, not the other runners. And you run against yourself."

Joe Henderson

The Boston Marathon began in 1897, inspired by the first modern Olympic Games. It's the world's oldest annual marathon and one of the most demanding stages in sport. The course runs through eight Massachusetts towns—Hopkinton to Boston—and finishes at Copley Square, but the real test happens long before the finish line comes into view.

The opening miles feel easy with the downhill start out of Hopkinton. That's the trap. Spend too much too early, and the race collects its debt later. Wellesley's scream tunnel lifts you, then the Newton Hills take over—Firehouse Hill, Commonwealth Avenue, and finally Heartbreak Hill near Boston College. That's where patience, stamina, and mental discipline matter more than talent.

From there, it's downhill toward Brookline and into Boston, past the Citgo sign and into the roar at Hereford and Boylston. Boston isn't just about speed. It's about restraint, rhythm, and staying composed when fatigue stacks up, and relief is still miles away.

This month is about pacing your mind. You'll train yourself to stay calm when it hurts, focused when your body wants out, and steady when chaos creeps in. Every rep is a mile closer to Boylston. Your training partners—Meb Keflezighi, Des Linden, Shalane Flanagan, and Eliud Kipchoge—will demonstrate how champions build stamina, maintain composure, and go the distance.

DAY 274: MENTAL TRAINING PARTNER

MEB KEFLEZIGHI

"Winning Boston wasn't about time. It was about heart."
Meb Keflezighi

Meb Keflezighi built his life and career on discipline, endurance, and steady belief. Born in Eritrea and forced to flee with his family as a child, he eventually settled in San Diego and found running through a middle school PE class. A teacher noticed his engine, but Meb built the rest through work. That consistency carried him to UCLA, where he became a four-time NCAA champion and started building the kind of trust that shows up late in the race.

Meb went on to become a four-time Olympian and the only American man to win both the New York City Marathon and the Boston Marathon. His 2014 victory in Boston felt bigger than sport. One year after the bombing, at thirty-eight years old, he ran with the names of the victims on his bib and took command of the race with courage and purpose. He surged early, held his form through the Newton Hills, and never gave the lead back.

What made Meb so strong was the way he prepared for the hardest part of the day. He trained the details until they held under fatigue, breathing, posture, fueling, patience, and pace. When the pain rose and the margin got thin, he did not need to search for something new. He trusted what he had already built and kept running with purpose.

That is why Meb is such a powerful training partner for this week. He will show you how to stay disciplined, hold your rhythm, and keep your effort organized when fatigue starts asking hard questions. Purpose does not make the road easier. It gives your effort direction and helps carry you to the line.

DAY 275: WHAT'S POSSIBLE FOR YOU?

"Run to win, not just against others, but against your own limits."
Meb Keflezighi

This day is about curiosity, not pressure. Great athletes aren't obsessed with proving themselves; they're committed to finding out what they're capable of over time. You don't discover that on perfect days, but on ordinary ones where effort still matters. How you train there shapes how far you can go in your craft.

MORNING EDGE: SET THE INTENTION

Decide what skill or habit you want to improve today. Approach the session with the mindset of "Let's see how good I can get at this."

FLIP THE SWITCH: STAY ENGAGED

When things feel flat or tiring, don't check out. Stay present, stay patient, and keep executing with care.

CHAMPION'S WRAP: WHAT YOU LEARNED

Before bed, name one thing you learned about yourself today. That awareness is how growth actually happens.

DAY 276: HOW CLEAN CAN YOU STAY?

"I may not be the fastest, but I'll make the fewest mistakes."
Meb Keflezighi

Pressure doesn't test your talent; it tests your precision. When pace changes, fatigue builds, and attention starts to slip, most athletes tighten up rather than loosen up. The best do the opposite. They stay clean and free when it would be easy to rush or force things, and that's where separation happens.

MORNING EDGE: CHOOSE THE DETAIL

Pick one small detail that matters today, like breathing, posture, or rhythm. Decide to keep that detail clean and loose from the first rep to the last.

FLIP THE SWITCH: RETURN TO LOOSE

When you feel rushed or tight, slow the moment down. Settle your breath, soften your body, and return to clean execution.

CHAMPION'S WRAP: CLEAN FINISH

Before bed, replay one moment you stayed precise and loose under pressure. That's how your game shows up when it matters.

DAY 277: WHO ARE YOU RUNNING FOR?

"Every mile I run is a thank-you to those who helped me get here."
Meb Keflezighi

Gratitude isn't about being nice or sentimental. It widens your focus when pressure tries to shrink everything down to pain and doubt. When athletes remember they didn't get here alone, their breathing settles and their bodies stay looser under stress. That shift brings purpose back when effort starts to feel heavy.

MORNING EDGE: PICK THE PERSON

Choose one person who helped you grow or believed in you early. Picture them watching you train today and let that reminder steady how you move and compete.

FLIP THE SWITCH: RETURN TO ZERO

When fatigue or frustration sets in, take a Return to Zero breath to settle your body and clear your head. Inhale through your nose for four seconds and exhale through your mouth for six, imagining a warm light moving up your spine on the inhale and back down on the exhale as you quietly say, "Back to zero."

CHAMPION'S WRAP: CLOSE AT ZERO

Before bed, recall one moment you felt supported today. Let your breath slow and end the day calm and at zero.

DAY 278: DO IT FOR YOU

"Most of us have enough areas in our lives where we have to meet others' expectations. Let your running be about your own hopes and dreams."
Meb Keflezighi

In a world full of expectations, your sport has to stay yours. It is easy to start performing for approval because you want to make people proud, avoid letting them down, and show that all your work means something. But when your performance becomes more about proving something to others rather than expressing what matters to you, pressure builds and rhythm fades. The way back is to reconnect with what you want from the day, so the result matters to you first, and your effort comes from ownership rather than approval.

MORNING EDGE: MAKE IT YOURS

Name one result you want today that matters to you. Maybe it is running with rhythm, staying relaxed under pressure, or showing yourself how tough and composed you can be. Choose a goal that feels meaningful to you, not impressive to someone else.

FLIP THE SWITCH: RETURN TO ZERO (RTZ)

RTZ means Return to Zero, back to your center before outside expectations take over. Inhale for four seconds, exhale for six, and say, "My Game. My Way." Write RTZ on your shoe or wrist as a reminder to clear the noise, trust your training, and run your race.

CHAMPION'S WRAP: YOURS, NOT THEIRS

Take a moment tonight to notice when you were chasing something that mattered to you, not trying to impress everyone else. That is the kind of effort that keeps you grounded, steady, and free.

DAY 279: WIN THE EASY DAY

"One of the biggest differences between world-class runners and recreational runners is how slowly we elites sometimes run . . . a recovery day is much slower than race pace."

Meb Keflezighi

A lot of athletes know how to attack. Fewer know how to recover on purpose. Meb understood that easy days are not throwaway days or secret chances to prove you are in shape. They have their own job. When you turn recovery into a race, you usually miss the assignment and make tomorrow harder than it needs to be.

MORNING EDGE: KNOW THE ASSIGNMENT

Be clear about what today is for before you start. If the assignment is recovery, rebuilding, or rhythm, then that is what winning looks like.

FLIP THE SWITCH: DON'T RACE THE RECOVERY

When ego starts nudging you to speed up, compare, or turn the day into a test, cut it off. Hit RTZ, come back to the assignment, and remember that the goal is not to impress yourself today but to have more to give tomorrow.

CHAMPION'S WRAP: YOU PROTECTED TOMORROW

Think of one moment today when you stayed patient and followed the plan. That is discipline, and it is one of the reasons pros stay ready, durable, and sharp over time.

DAY 280: WIN THE SMALL CROSSROADS

"Long-distance running is not the sport for people who crave instant gratification."
Meb Keflezighi

The long game rarely gets won in dramatic moments. It's won in small crossroads that don't look like much at the time. A little extra scrolling, a little less sleep, a little shortcut here and there can quietly start moving you away from where you said you wanted to go. Meb understood that steady progress comes from seeing those moments early and making the long-term choice before impulse gets loud.

MORNING EDGE: SPOT THE SHORTCUT

Identify one moment today where you usually drift toward the easy option. Decide ahead of time what the long-term choice will be, so when that moment arrives, you are carrying out a plan instead of starting a debate.

FLIP THE SWITCH: CHOOSE LONG

When the urge hits to rush, snack, scroll, skip, or stay up, keep it simple. Tell yourself, "Choose long," and let that cue point you back to the version of you that you are building.

CHAMPION'S WRAP: TODAY COUNTED

Name one moment today when you chose the long-term option. One rep like that keeps the day moving in the right direction.

DAY 281: MENTAL TRAINING PARTNER

DES LINDEN

"Keep showing up."

Des Linden

Des Linden built her career the hard way. She grew up in San Diego, starred at Arizona State, and then joined the Hansons-Brooks Distance Project in Michigan, where the work was blue-collar, demanding, and relentless. That environment fit her. It shaped her into one of the toughest and most dependable marathoners of her generation.

She became a two-time Olympian, representing the United States in the marathon at the 2012 London Games and the 2016 Rio Games. Her defining moment came in Boston in 2018, when the weather turned brutal and the race became a test of grit. Cold rain and strong winds broke the field, and many top runners dropped out. Des stayed steady, managed the conditions, and kept moving until she turned onto Boylston Street alone in front, becoming the first American woman to win the Boston Marathon in thirty-three years.

What makes Des so powerful is that her story was never built on one perfect day. She finished second in Boston in 2011 by two seconds, came back from a stress fracture in 2012, and kept training through years that brought more work than attention. She kept showing up, kept building, and kept putting herself back in the fight. That is how toughness gets made.

This week, Des is your mental training partner. She will show you how to stay steady when conditions get tough, keep going when the day gets long, and trust the value of showing up again and again. Finish what you start, and let grit carry you the rest of the way.

DAY 282: DON'T WASTE THE BAD DAYS

"Some days it just flows and I feel like I'm born to do this. Other days it feels like I'm trudging through hell. Every day, I make the choice to show up and see what I've got."
Des Linden

Good days are fun, but they do not always teach you much. Bad days show you what holds up when the feel is missing and the mood is off. That is when you find out what is real in your game and what only works when everything feels easy. Des understands that a rough day is still a useful day. If you stay engaged, the day will usually tell you something worth keeping.

MORNING EDGE: CHANGE THE ASSIGNMENT

If today does not feel sharp, do not make the job harder by pretending it should. Decide instead that your job is to learn something useful about how you compete, move, or think when conditions are not ideal.

FLIP THE SWITCH: GET CURIOUS FAST

When things feel off, skip the self-judgment and ask, "What still works right now?" Build from that. Find the part of your game that is still there, and let it carry more of the load.

CHAMPION'S WRAP: FOUND THE GOLD

Name one thing today taught you about your game, your mindset, or your habits under strain. Days like this raise your floor, and that matters a lot more than people think.

DAY 283: DON'T ARGUE WITH THE MILE

"Some days are diamonds, some days are rocks. Just run the mile you're in."
Des Linden

Some days feel light and smooth right away. Other days feel clunky, heavy, or just a little off, and that is part of the deal. Trouble starts when you waste energy grading the day, searching for explanations, or acting like one rough stretch means the whole run is broken. Des understands that the mile does not need your opinion. It just needs your presence.

MORNING EDGE: EXPECT THE MIX

Go into the day expecting some miles to feel better than others. Meet each one as it comes, and let your job stay the same whether the legs feel like diamonds or rocks.

FLIP THE SWITCH: STAY WITH THE MILE

When a mile feels off, skip the audit and stay out of technical panic. Bring your focus back to your rhythm, your breath, and the ground right in front of you, then keep moving with quiet discipline.

CHAMPION'S WRAP: PRESENCE OVER OPINION

Think of one moment today when you stopped judging the mile and just ran it. That is how consistency gets built.

DAY 284: DON'T COAST TO THE GATE

"Some days, finishing is a win. So finish well."
Des Linden

A lot of athletes think they fade at the end because the body runs out. That is only part of it. More often, the fade starts when focus loosens, standards drop, and the mind begins negotiating with discomfort. Des understands that the finish asks a different question than the start. It asks who you are when the work is no longer exciting and your edge has to come from discipline.

MORNING EDGE: DECIDE WHO YOU ARE LATE

Before the day starts, decide what kind of finisher you want to be. Tell yourself, "When it gets late, I stay sharp, present, and professional," so you are not negotiating with fatigue when it shows up.

FLIP THE SWITCH: OWN THE FINAL REP

When fatigue hits and your standards start to slip, make the world smaller. Lock in on one thing you can still do well—your posture, your rhythm, your breathing, or your mechanics. Stay there and finish the rep like it still counts, because it does.

CHAMPION'S WRAP: NO FADE

Think of one moment today when it would have been easy to drift, coast, or get sloppy, but you stayed with it. That is the closer's edge. Anybody can start with energy. Finishing with intent is what separates people.

DAY 285: BE THE FUTURE NOW

"Will this help me become a champion? Act as if you are the thing you are trying to become."

Des Linden

You do not become your best in one big leap. You build it in the small choices that keep stacking in the same direction. Des understands that acting like the athlete you want to become is not fake. It is practice. The more often your habits, decisions, and self-talk match that future version of you, the less distance there is between who you are and who you are becoming.

MORNING EDGE: START WITH THE NEXT-LEVEL MOVE

Before the day gets moving, ask yourself one simple question: "What would the next-level version of me do first?" Then go do that before your current mood gets a vote.

FLIP THE SWITCH: TALK LIKE YOU MEAN IT

When limiting self-talk shows up, catch it before it gets too comfortable. Ask, "Would the athlete I'm becoming talk like this?" Then clean it up and move in a direction that matches the standard you are building.

CHAMPION'S WRAP: FUTURE YOU SHOWED UP

Think of one moment today when your actions matched the person you are working to become. That is how identity gets built. You do the rep first, and the belief starts catching up.

DAY 286: NO DRAMA MILES

"Tolerating what most people would consider intolerable is the flip side of endurance."
Des Linden

Endurance is not just the ability to handle discomfort. It is the ability to keep discomfort from draining extra energy through tension, commentary, and reaction. The moment gets harder when you add a story to it. Durable performers stay neutral, hold their form, and make the next good decision. They save their energy for the work itself.

MORNING EDGE: UNDERREACT EARLY

Go into today expecting discomfort, doubt, or fatigue to show up. Decide now that none of it gets a big reaction. No one gets through a hard stretch and wishes they had made it bigger.

FLIP THE SWITCH: UNDERREACT AND EXECUTE

When things get hard, get simple. Lock into rhythm, posture, breathing, and the next task. Save your energy for execution, not commentary.

CHAMPION'S WRAP: BANK THE COMPOSURE

At day's end, think of one hard moment you handled without adding drama. That is energy you kept, composure you built, and endurance you can trust.

DAY 287: PICK THE BETTER HARD

"Getting back in shape is never easy, but, as I kept reminding myself, being in shape is awesome."
Des Linden

Getting back on track is hard. So is feeling off, behind, and disappointed in yourself. Des understands that the choice is rarely between easy and hard. It is usually between two different kinds of hard. The better one asks for effort now and gives you your edge back later.

MORNING EDGE: RESTART SMALL

Pick one simple action that moves you back toward your standard and do it early. A small, clean restart beats another day of waiting for the perfect mood.

FLIP THE SWITCH: PAY NOW, NOT LATER

When resistance or guilt shows up, call the choice what it is. This is not hard versus easy. This is one kind of hard versus another, so fix one thing today and stop feeding the heavier one.

CHAMPION'S WRAP: THE BETTER HARD

Name one choice today that matched your standard. That is how trust in yourself starts coming back.

DAY 288: MENTAL TRAINING PARTNER

SHALANE FLANAGAN

"I've always had a fighter in me. I just needed to learn how to direct that energy."
Shalane Flanagan

Shalane Flanagan grew up around running and learned early what disciplined work looks like. Raised in Marblehead, Massachusetts, by two elite runner parents, she developed a strong foundation of belief and consistency. At the University of North Carolina, she became an NCAA champion and began building a career defined by toughness and precision. Her edge started with work, but it grew into something deeper.

She went on to become a three-time Olympian and won silver in the 10,000 meters at the 2008 Beijing Games. Over time, she moved to the marathon, where her competitive fire found its best expression. In 2017, she won the New York City Marathon, becoming the first American woman to do so in forty years. As she crossed the finish line, the emotion poured out, a release built over years of pressure, effort, and belief.

What made Shalane so strong was not just her fitness. It was the way she learned to channel her intensity. She brought structure to her training, precision to her pacing, and control to her emotions. Instead of letting that fire scatter her focus, she used it to sharpen her execution when the race got hard.

This week, Shalane is your mental training partner. She will show you how to direct your energy, stay composed under pressure, and compete with purpose when emotion rises. Bring your fire, then aim it. That is how intensity turns into performance.

DAY 289: SILENCE THE CHIRP

"Pain is inevitable. Suffering is optional."
Shalane Flanagan

Every runner knows the point where the body starts barking and the mind gets loud. The legs burn, the breathing gets harder, and suddenly your thoughts start offering all kinds of helpful little nonsense. Shalane understood that this moment is part of racing, not a sign that something is off. The key is learning how to keep your rhythm when the mind starts chirping.

MORNING EDGE: EXPECT THE CHIRP

Before the day begins, remind yourself that discomfort does not mean something is wrong. At some point, the noise will show up. Expect it, smile at it, and decide now: "When the noise shows up, I will stay with my rhythm."

FLIP THE SWITCH: RUN THE RHYTHM

When discomfort shows up today, treat it like normal race noise. Stay tall, stay loose, and remind yourself, "This is the work."

CHAMPION'S WRAP: STAYED WITH THE WORK

Think of one moment today when your mind got loud and you kept your rhythm anyway. That is a big-time skill. You stayed composed, and you kept moving forward.

DAY 290: SUFFER BETTER

"I love the idea that I can suffer better than anyone else."
Shalane Flanagan

Every athlete knows the point where the body starts making a serious case for stopping. The legs get heavy, the breathing gets rough, and the mind starts offering all kinds of creative exits. Shalane understood that this point is not a breakdown. It is where the race changes hands. When the easy feeling disappears, intention takes over.

MORNING EDGE: THE WALL IS THE TEST

Before the day starts, picture the point where things usually get hard. See yourself staying tall, keeping your rhythm, and meeting that moment like it belongs in the session.

FLIP THE SWITCH: WIN THE NEXT THIRTY SECONDS

When the wall shows up, stop thinking about the whole run. Bring it down to posture, rhythm, and breath. Tell yourself, "I do not need to feel good to keep moving," and win the next thirty seconds.

CHAMPION'S WRAP: BROKE THROUGH

Think of one moment today when the work got heavy and you stayed with it anyway. That is how this skill gets built. The wall showed up, and you answered it.

DAY 291: RACE DAY IS THE REWARD

"I prepare so well that the race is just the celebration of the work."
Shalane Flanagan

Some athletes get to race day and act like they are heading into court. Everything gets tight, careful, and overmanaged. Shalane sees it differently. The hard part was the training, the discipline, and the lonely work nobody saw. Race day is where you stop guarding it and let it out.

MORNING EDGE: THIS IS THE PAYOUT

Before the day starts, remind yourself that the work is already done. You are here to release it, enjoy it, and run with the freedom of someone who already paid the price.

FLIP THE SWITCH: OPEN UP

When nerves show up, resist the urge to get small. Lift your chest, take a fuller breath, and tell yourself, "Let it rip." Then go express what you built instead of trying to protect it.

CHAMPION'S WRAP: YOU LET IT OUT

Think of one moment today when you stopped managing and started expressing. That is the feeling to remember. The work was the struggle. The performance was the reward.

DAY 292: THE POWER OF NOW

"Sometimes, you have to be aggressive. You have to go when it's hard."
Shalane Flanagan

Too many athletes wait for the race to calm down before they commit. They wait for the pace to feel manageable, the legs to feel lighter, or the doubt to quiet down. Shalane understands that those moments rarely decide anything. The race changes when somebody acts while everyone else is still hesitating. You do not need the perfect moment. You need the guts to call your shot before the debate talks you out of it.

MORNING EDGE: PICK THE WINDOW

Think about the stretch of the race where you usually wait, second-guess, or hope the move will make itself. Decide now that when that window opens, you are going.

FLIP THE SWITCH: SAY IT AND SEND IT

When the mind starts bargaining, cut it off with one word: "Now!" Then drive your legs, stay tall, and commit hard enough that the body has no choice but to follow.

CHAMPION'S WRAP: YOU CREATED THE GAP

Picture one moment today when you chose action over hesitation. That is how races get broken open. Somebody always makes the move, and it is a very good habit when that somebody is you.

DAY 293: CARRY IT LIKE A CHAMPION

"I'm not afraid to hurt. That's where I find out who I really am."
Shalane Flanagan

Anyone can surge for a moment. The deeper test comes right after, when the effort settles into your legs, your breathing gets loud, and you still have to keep going. That stretch—the part after the move, when the work sits on you—is the carry. That is where races change shape and competitors separate. Shalane understood that who you are shows up in how you carry that part.

MORNING EDGE: CHOOSE YOUR CARRY

Before you start, decide how you want to look and feel when the effort gets heavy. Pick one word that has some backbone in it, like smooth, stubborn, calm, proud, or relentless. Carry that word into the day like it belongs to you.

FLIP THE SWITCH: WEAR THE WEIGHT WELL

When the work starts sitting on you, go back to your word and match your body to it. Let your posture rise, let your rhythm settle, and let your face say, "I know this part too." Keep moving in a way that makes the effort respect you.

CHAMPION'S WRAP: THE CARRY TOLD THE STORY

At the end of the day, replay one stretch where the work got long and you kept carrying yourself with intention. Notice the part of you that stayed tall, stayed honest, and stayed in it. That is the part people feel, even before they see the result.

DAY 294: RESPECT THE RHYTHM

"Running is about momentum. Once you've got it, protect it like hell."
Shalane Flanagan

Momentum is not always dramatic, but you know when it is there. Your breathing settles, your stride starts matching itself, and your mind quits poking at every little thing. Shalane understands that flow is less about creating magic than protecting alignment. Flow is a frequency. Once you've tuned in, don't touch the dial.

MORNING EDGE: TUNE THE DIAL

Start the day with one task done on purpose. Give it your full attention, clean effort, and enough patience for rhythm to show up before you ask for more.

FLIP THE SWITCH: BACK TO SMOOTH

When you feel yourself drifting, pressing, or getting emotional, stop reaching for extra. Settle your breathing, narrow your focus, and tell yourself, "Back to smooth," until your rhythm starts coming back under you.

CHAMPION'S WRAP: KEPT THE FREQUENCY

Think of one moment today when you protected your rhythm instead of breaking it with frustration or force. That is how momentum lasts.

DAY 295: MENTAL TRAINING PARTNER

ELIUD KIPCHOGE

"Only the disciplined ones in life are free."

Eliud Kipchoge

Eliud Kipchoge has built one of the most remarkable careers in endurance sport. Raised in rural Kenya, he developed his strength through daily movement, routine, and simple living. Over time, he turned that foundation into Olympic gold medals and a marathon world record of 2:01:09 in Berlin. His greatness is steady, quiet, and built over years of disciplined work.

In 2019, Kipchoge broke one of the sport's biggest barriers. At the INEOS 1:59 Challenge, he became the first human to run a marathon in under two hours. The conditions were controlled and the time did not count as an official record, but the performance changed what people believed was possible. It showed what can happen when preparation, belief, and execution line up.

What sets Kipchoge apart is the way he lives his discipline. His days follow a simple rhythm of training, recovery, nutrition, and rest, done with care and consistency. He pays attention to the small details and repeats them until they hold under fatigue. That is what allows him to stay calm, efficient, and focused deep into the race.

This week, Kipchoge is your mental training partner. He will show you how to stay disciplined, remove distractions, and do the small things well. Keep your focus simple, your effort steady, and your habits strong. That is how discipline turns into freedom.

DAY 296: DO NOT OBEY EVERY THOUGHT

"I want to show the world that you can go beyond your thoughts, you can break more than you think you can break."
Eliud Kipchoge

Kipchoge knows the mind loves to set limits before the body has actually reached them. It says slow down, this is enough, or maybe today is not the day. Those thoughts are normal, but they are not the boss. Great performers learn how to hear the thought, keep moving, and let action tell the real story.

MORNING EDGE: LET THE MIND TALK

Start the day by reminding yourself that your mind may complain, doubt, or try to bargain when the work gets hard. Decide now that you will notice the thought without letting it decide what happens next.

FLIP THE SWITCH: HEAR IT AND GO

When a limiting thought shows up, do not stop to argue with it. Take one Return to Zero breath, breathing in for four seconds and out for six, and say, "Noted." Then take the next strong step anyway.

CHAMPION'S WRAP: YOU DIDN'T OBEY IT

As you close out the day, think of one moment when your mind threw out a limit and you did not follow it. That is how freedom grows in the mental game.

DAY 297: BACK THE THOUGHT THAT HELPS

"Thinking positively and confidently changed my life. If you stay consistent and work hard, you can be successful for a long time."
Eliud Kipchoge

Kipchoge is not saying every thought deserves equal time. Some thoughts pull you backward, and some thoughts pull you through. Positive thinking is not pretending everything feels good. It is choosing the thought that helps you stay steady, committed, and moving in the right direction.

MORNING EDGE: PICK YOUR LINE

Before the day begins, choose one thought you want to carry with you when the work gets hard. It might be "One more good step," "Calm and keep going," or "Strong and smooth," but pick one that helps you work.

FLIP THE SWITCH: CHOOSE, THEN MOVE

When doubt, frustration, or negativity shows up, take one Return to Zero breath by breathing in for four seconds and out for six. Then replace the thought that weakens you with one that helps you, and move right away before the old thought settles in.

CHAMPION'S WRAP: KEEP THAT THOUGHT

As you close out the day, think of one moment when a better thought helped you stay with the work. That is how strong self-talk is built, one useful thought at a time.

DAY 298: TRAIN WITH LIONS

"If you train with fast athletes, it keeps you pushing. I know that good preparation is more important than everything else."

Eliud Kipchoge

If you want to be a lion, you need to train with lions. The people around you matter because standards, pace, and belief are contagious. Kipchoge understands that strong training groups can push you further, but he also knows you cannot depend on others to uphold your standards. At some point, the culture has to live in you.

MORNING EDGE: PICK YOUR PACK

Start the day by asking yourself who and what is shaping you. Choose the people, habits, and inputs that raise your standard, then decide how you want to train before the day starts training you.

FLIP THE SWITCH: BRING THE STANDARD

When the work gets hard and no one is there to push you, do not wait for outside energy. Take one Return to Zero breath by breathing in for four seconds and out for six, lift your posture, and tell yourself, "Be the lion today." Then do the next rep, drill, or task that way.

CHAMPION'S WRAP: YOU BROUGHT THE CULTURE

As you close out the day, think of one moment when you held the standard without needing someone else to create it for you. That is when culture becomes character, and that is when preparation starts to belong to you.

DAY 299: WHEN THE RACE TURNS MENTAL

"Athletics is not so much about the legs. It's about the heart and mind."
Eliud Kipchoge

Kipchoge is not saying the legs do not matter. He is saying that every hard effort reaches a point where the legs are no longer enough. That is when the race gets honest. When the body gets loud, the heart keeps you committed and the mind keeps your job clear.

MORNING EDGE: EXPECT THE HANDOFF

Before the day starts, remind yourself that if the work gets hard, nothing has gone wrong. Say, "When the legs fade, let the mind lead."

FLIP THE SWITCH: SHRINK THE JOB

When fatigue hits, do not ask your legs how they feel. Take one Return to Zero breath, breathing in for four seconds and out for six, lift your posture, and ask, "What is my job right now?" Then do that and only that.

CHAMPION'S WRAP: YOU STAYED IN IT

As you close out the day, think of one moment when your body wanted out and you stayed with the work anyway. That is the handoff Kipchoge is talking about, and that is where toughness starts to show.

DAY 300: BECOME THE ONE WHO CAN HANDLE IT

"If you have that belief—pure belief in your heart—that you want to be successful, then you can talk to your mind, and your mind will control you to be successful."
Eliud Kipchoge

Success has weight, and big moments ask you to carry it well. Belief is the inner conviction that aligns your mind, body, and actions when it matters most. When your identity is clear, you waste less energy negotiating and bring more energy to execution. Over time, you become someone who can carry pressure instead of being shaken by it.

MORNING EDGE: START AS THAT PERSON

Before the day gets moving, ask yourself, "What would the version of me who can handle this do first?" Then do that one thing right away and lock in with "Start like that person."

FLIP THE SWITCH: HOLD THE SHAPE

When doubt shows up, take one Return to Zero breath and come back to "Handle it like I do." Let that cue steady your body and sharpen your next action.

CHAMPION'S WRAP: BUILT TODAY

At the end of the day, think of one moment when you chose action over hesitation, composure over noise, or discipline over escape. Lock it in with "That one built me," because identity grows every time your actions match your standard.

DAY 301: RISE TO THE CHALLENGE

"The world is actually full of challenges and we need to challenge ourselves."
Eliud Kipchoge

Kipchoge treats challenges as something to meet, not something to fear. Hard moments are part of the path, and they are often where growth, separation, and self-respect are built. The key is to meet difficulty with a steady mind instead of a startled one. When you expect the hill, you can climb it with far less wasted energy.

MORNING EDGE: WELCOME THE TEST

Before the day begins, remind yourself that something today will ask more of you than is comfortable. Tell yourself, "When the challenge comes, I will meet it well."

FLIP THE SWITCH: STAY SMOOTH UNDER LOAD

When the challenge bites, blow out the junk with one hard exhale. Lift your eyes, loosen your hands, and give a slight grin as if to say, "Good. This is where it gets real." Then stay smooth and keep working.

CHAMPION'S WRAP: YOU MET IT WELL

As you close out the day, think of one moment when the challenge rose and you stayed steady anyway. That is how real toughness grows and how hard work starts to feel more natural.

DAY 302: THINK GOLD, NEVER SETTLE FOR SILVER

"I am just going to try to run my personal best. If it comes as a world record, I would appreciate it. But I would treat it as a personal best."

Eliud Kipchoge

Kipchoge keeps the standard inside the work. He is not chasing records as much as he is chasing his best. That is what thinking gold really means. Gold is not just a medal at the end. Gold is the standard you refuse to lower while the moment is still alive.

MORNING EDGE: SET THE GOLD STANDARD

Before the day begins, choose one place where you will not settle today. It might be your focus, your posture, your pace, or the way you finish your work. Tell yourself, "This is a gold moment," and meet it with full intent.

FLIP THE SWITCH: DO NOT TAKE THE SILVER

When the urge to ease up, cut a corner, or give yourself an out shows up, stop and take one Return to Zero breath. Then ask yourself, "What would gold look like right here?" and do that instead of the easier thing.

CHAMPION'S WRAP: YOU CHOSE GOLD

As you close out the day, think of one moment when you could have settled and did not. That is how a gold standard is built, one choice at a time.

DAY 303: RECOVER YOUR CLARITY

"I allow my body to recover, my mind to recover. I like to be with my family, to read books, and know what is going on in the world, to understand how people think."

Eliud Kipchoge

Kipchoge does not treat recovery like laziness. He treats it like part of the work. Without mental space, even good things start to feel heavy, and your mind loses the clarity to handle what matters well. Recovery creates margin, which is the space to breathe, think clearly, and handle one thing at a time.

MORNING EDGE: MAKE SOME ROOM

Before the day fills up, take five to ten minutes to do something that truly settles you. Read, walk, stretch, breathe, or sit quietly, and let your mind come back to one thing at a time.

FLIP THE SWITCH: CLEAR IT BEFORE YOU PUSH IT

When your mind gets crowded and everything starts feeling heavier than it is, do not just push harder. Take one Return to Zero breath by breathing in for four seconds and out for six, loosen your jaw, drop your shoulders, and ask, "What actually matters right now?" Then do only that.

CHAMPION'S WRAP: NOISE DOWN, PRESENCE UP

As you close out the day, think of one moment when you gave yourself enough space to reset instead of forcing your way through the fog. That is recovery doing its job, and it is one reason steady performers last.

DAY 304: QUESTION THE CEILING

"No human is limited."

Eliud Kipchoge

When Kipchoge ran under two hours, he did not just break a record. He challenged a story. A lot of ceilings are not physical walls so much as old beliefs, repeated doubts, or ideas that have started to sound like facts. The moment you stop treating every limit like the truth, growth opens up again.

MORNING EDGE: SPOT THE CEILING

Before the day begins, name one thought that tends to cap you. It might sound like "This is as far as I go," or "If I push harder, I will come apart." Write it down and ask yourself, "Is that true, or is that just a ceiling I got used to?"

FLIP THE SWITCH: TEST THE LIMIT

When resistance shows up, do not stand there arguing with it. Take one Return to Zero breath, breathing in for four seconds and out for six, and take one small step that puts the thought under pressure. A lot of limits get weaker the moment you stop obeying them.

CHAMPION'S WRAP: YOU RAISED THE ROOF

As you close out the day, think of one place where you gave yourself more room than you usually do. That is how ceilings start to move. Not all at once, but each time you stop treating an old thought like a final answer.

CHAMPION'S TAKEAWAYS: BOSTON MARATHON

Boston showed you that pressure doesn't always hit all at once—it builds. You learned how easy it is to get impatient, push too early, or drift when the work stays hard for a long time. This chapter asked you to stay steady when fatigue lingered and the finish felt far away. You practiced pacing yourself, managing your emotions, and trusting your preparation instead of forcing outcomes. That's what real endurance looks like: staying cool, calm, and committed until the job is done.

As you step away from Boston, ask yourself:

- Where did patience help my performance?
- How did I respond when the work stayed hard for longer than I wanted?
- What helped me to stay steady?

Carry that discipline forward. It applies to training, competition, and daily life.

CHAPTER 11

NOVEMBER: MGM GRAND

"Everybody has a plan until they get punched in the mouth."
Mike Tyson

The MGM Grand sits on the Las Vegas Strip, and it fits the chapter perfectly because this kind of arena strips performance down to the truth. When the lights hit and the door closes, there is nowhere to hide. No weather, no crowd excuse, no teammate to cover the moment for you. There is only your preparation, your choices, and your willingness to stand in it.

That is what November is about. Pressure gets personal here. Combat sports test everything at once—your discipline, your composure, your decision-making, and your belief—and they test it fast. The moment does not care what you meant to do. It reveals what is actually there.

This month, your mental training partners are George Foreman, Cael Sanderson, Claressa Shields, and Amanda Nunes. Each built an edge by taking full responsibility for the moment in front of them. They did not wait for comfort. They trusted standards built long before the spotlight showed up.

The question this chapter asks is simple. Can you stand alone, own your choices, and execute when it counts? The MGM Grand does not reward excuses. It rewards ownership.

DAY 305: MENTAL TRAINING PARTNER

GEORGE FOREMAN

"If you want it, leave your excuses behind and come and get it."

George Foreman

George Foreman did something almost nobody thought was possible. On November 5, 1994, at the MGM Grand Garden Arena, he knocked out Michael Moorer in the tenth round and reclaimed the heavyweight championship of the world. At forty-five years old, he became the oldest heavyweight champion in boxing history. It was one of the boldest comebacks the sport has ever seen.

What made it even more striking was how clearly Foreman saw it coming. In the days before the fight, he said he was going to knock Moorer out and described how it would happen. He did not hedge, soften it, or back away from it. He believed it, spoke it, and stayed with it.

That belief was built on a much longer road. Twenty years earlier, Foreman had lost to Muhammad Ali in the Rumble in the Jungle and walked away from boxing. When he came back, he was older, heavier, and more deliberate, but he also came back wiser and steadier. On the night he fought Moorer, he wore the same red trunks from earlier in his career and quietly sang "The Impossible Dream" to himself before the opening bell.

This week, Foreman is your mental training partner. He will show you what can happen when preparation, belief, and action line up. Get clear about what you are here to do, back it with real work, and step into the moment without flinching.

DAY 306: KEEP TURNING THE CRANK

"Many people fail not because they don't have talent, but because they quit too soon."
George Foreman

Foreman understood that a lot of success looks and feels like turning a crank. It is repetitive, often unglamorous, and not always immediately rewarding. You keep turning because that is how progress gets made, even when nothing exciting seems to be happening yet. To turn the crank means to stay with the work, especially when the payoff is not visible yet.

MORNING EDGE: RESPECT THE FLAT STRETCH

Before the day begins, remind yourself that not all progress announces itself right away. Some of your best work will feel ordinary, repetitive, and unrewarding, but that does not mean it is not working.

FLIP THE SWITCH: ONE MORE TURN

When your mind starts asking, "Is this even doing anything?" do not stop to debate it. Tell yourself, "One more turn," then do the next rep, drill, or task with care.

CHAMPION'S WRAP: STILL TURNING

At the end of the day, think of one ordinary thing you stayed with when it would have been easy to drift or check out. That is how gains are built, and that is why the people who keep turning the crank keep moving ahead.

DAY 307: STAY HUNGRY ON PURPOSE

"The question isn't at what age I want to retire; it's at what income."

George Foreman

Foreman was not really talking about money. He was talking about refusing to decide that he was finished. A lot of people retire long before they ever leave the arena. They get comfortable, start coasting on what they have already done, and stop asking more of themselves. Hunger is not something you wait to feel. It is something you choose.

MORNING EDGE: CALL YOUR NEXT CLIMB

Before the day begins, name one area where you have been doing just enough or living off old work. Decide what one notch higher looks like there today and go after it on purpose.

FLIP THE SWITCH: DON'T PUNCH OUT

When you catch yourself easing up, stand taller and take one sharp breath. Tell yourself, "Not done. Not yet." Then raise the standard on the next rep, task, or conversation.

CHAMPION'S WRAP: STILL CLIMBING

When the day is done, think of one moment when you asked more of yourself instead of settling into cruise control. That is how hunger stays alive, and that is why some people keep growing long after others coast.

DAY 308: FORWARD ON FAITH

"Faith is one of the most important things I have. Without faith, you can't go very far."
George Foreman

Faith is not waiting until everything makes sense. It is choosing to keep moving when the next step is clear but the whole path is not. Foreman knew there are stretches when doubt gets loud and certainty is nowhere to be found. In those moments, faith is what keeps your feet under you and your life moving forward.

MORNING EDGE: START WITH ONE STEP

Before the day begins, choose one clear action you can take even if you do not feel fully ready. Tell yourself, "I do not need the whole map. I just need the next step."

FLIP THE SWITCH: FORWARD ANYWAY

When uncertainty shows up, stop standing there trying to solve your whole future at once. Look up, nod once, and tell yourself, "Forward anyway." Then take the next best action without dragging your feet.

CHAMPION'S WRAP: FAITH IN MOTION

Take one last look at the day and name one moment when you moved instead of waiting to feel completely sure. That is what faith looks like in real life.

DAY 309: PATIENCE IS A POWER MOVE

"You don't have to knock everyone out. Sometimes you just have to wait them out."
George Foreman

Foreman understood that not every moment needs force. A lot of athletes lose position because they rush, press, and try to make something happen before it is there. Patience is not sitting back or doing nothing. It is staying calm enough to keep control of the moment.

MORNING EDGE: DO NOT FORCE THE OPENING

Start the day by reminding yourself that not everything needs to be attacked right away. Tell yourself, "Stay calm, see it clearly, and let the moment come to you."

FLIP THE SWITCH: WAIT STRONG

When you feel the urge to rush, press, or overdo it, take one steady breath, relax your face, keep your head level, and stay ready. Tell yourself, "I do not need to force this; I just need to stay ready."

CHAMPION'S WRAP: YOU DIDN'T BITE

As the day winds down, think of one moment when you stayed patient instead of forcing the issue. That is how rounds are won, because sometimes the edge goes to the one who stays composed the longest.

DAY 310: THE WINDOW IS STILL OPEN

"You're never too old to dream another dream or to fight for it."
George Foreman

People are quick to blame the calendar. They point to age, setbacks, missed opportunities, or the passage of time and decide the window has closed. But Foreman proved that the clock does not beat you on its own. More often, people stop because they stop believing, stop pushing, or stop answering the call. If the dream still lives in you, then the window is still open. Your job is not to wonder whether it is too late. Your job is to become the person that your dream requires.

MORNING EDGE: MAKE THE DECLARATION

Before the day begins, name the goal that still matters to you. Say to yourself, "I still want this." Then ask what that goal asks of you today and let the answer guide how you show up.

FLIP THE SWITCH: PUT A POINT ON THE BOARD

When doubt, fatigue, or discouragement shows up, do not try to figure out your whole future at once. Take a breath, straighten up, and do one thing that moves you forward. A small step is enough to keep you in the fight.

CHAMPION'S WRAP: CHECK THE TAPE

At the end of the day, ask yourself if you acted like someone who still wants it. Write down one thing you did that moved you closer. That is enough to carry into tomorrow.

DAY 311: LIVE IT TWICE

"Learning to enjoy today has two benefits: It gives me happiness right now, and it becomes a good memory later."

George Foreman

Foreman understood something that many driven people miss. If you keep racing toward the next thing, you miss the day you are actually in. Enjoying today is not a break from ambition. It is a way of getting more out of life now and more from it later.

MORNING EDGE: CASH THIS DAY

Before the day begins, remind yourself that this is not a throwaway day on the way to something else. Tell yourself, "I want to live this day well enough to remember it."

FLIP THE SWITCH: DO NOT RUSH PAST IT

When you catch yourself hurrying through the moment, slow your breathing, soften your face, and notice one thing worth being here for. Tell yourself, "Slow down enough to enjoy what's here."

CHAMPION'S WRAP: KEEP ONE GOOD MOMENT

When the day is done, hold on to one moment you fully enjoyed, appreciated, or felt alive in. That is how a good day pays you twice: once while you are living it and again when you remember it.

DAY 312: MENTAL TRAINING PARTNER

CAEL SANDERSON

"Pressure is nothing more than a challenge. You can either let it crush you or let it make you better."

Cael Sanderson

Cael Sanderson knows what it feels like to carry expectation every time he steps into the arena. Raised in Heber City, Utah, by a wrestling coach and sharpened alongside his brothers, he built one of the most remarkable careers the sport has ever seen. At Iowa State, he went 159–0 and won four NCAA titles, then followed it with Olympic gold in 2004. That kind of record brings pressure with it.

As the undefeated streak grew, so did the weight around every match. At one point, when the pressure started to feel heavy, his coach gave him a blunt reminder: If you do not like the pressure, there is an easy way out—just lose. That hit home because it exposed the trap. Sanderson had started protecting the streak instead of fully wrestling.

That was the shift. He stopped treating pressure as something to escape from and began seeing it as a sign that something meaningful was at stake. He got back to scoring, attacking, and wrestling his style. That decision changed everything because pressure stopped shrinking his game and started sharpening it.

This week, Sanderson is your mental training partner. He will show you how to meet pressure head-on, stay aggressive with your decisions, and compete your way when the stakes rise. Do not protect your game. Bring it.

DAY 313: DON'T CALL IT TOO SOON

"Sometimes losing a match can be a blessing. Sometimes winning a national title isn't. It's all just moving forward."

Cael Sanderson

Too often, athletes rush to define what a moment means. A loss can feel like failure, and a win like confirmation of success—but both are incomplete chapters in a story that's still unfolding. Champions know that time is the truest judge. Your job right now? Stay present, keep grinding, and trust that meaning will reveal itself when the time is right.

MORNING EDGE: STAY IN THE STORY

Before the day starts, remind yourself: "I don't need to decide what today means yet." Your mission? Show up, stay engaged, and keep moving forward.

FLIP THE SWITCH: SKIP THE COMMENTARY

When things go sideways, mute the inner dialogue. Tell yourself: "Keep going," then take the next clean, deliberate action.

CHAMPION'S WRAP: THE MEANING COMES LATER

As the day ends, resist the urge to label it as "good" or "bad." Instead, ask yourself: "Did I stay in it?"

DAY 314: CHOP WOOD, CARRY WATER

"If you're winning, chop wood, carry water."
Cael Sanderson

Winning can be one of the trickiest moments in the mental game. Success has a way of loosening people up in the wrong way. They get comfortable, start reading their own press, or drift from the habits that got them there. Champions do the opposite. They treat success as a cue to get even simpler, even sharper, and even more faithful to the work.

MORNING EDGE: STAY WITH WHAT YOU BUILT

Before the day begins, remind yourself that success does not change the standard. Say, "Wins do not change my work. Praise does not change my process. I stay loyal to what built me." Then lock back in on the habits, routines, and details that matter most.

FLIP THE SWITCH: RETURN TO THE BRILLIANT BASICS

When your mind starts wandering toward results, attention, or applause, bring it back to the next simple thing that deserves your full effort. Great performers keep doing the ordinary things with uncommon care.

CHAMPION'S WRAP: WIN, THEN WORK

At the end of the day, ask yourself, "Did success make me sharper or softer?" Then identify one moment when you stayed steady, disciplined, and true to your routine. That is how excellence holds.

DAY 315: MAKE YOUR BLESSINGS COUNT

"The foundation for success is based on gratitude."
Cael Sanderson

Sanderson is not talking about gratitude as a soft extra. He is talking about the way serious competitors stay sharp. Gratitude reminds you that training, competing, and chasing something meaningful are privileges. That perspective brings better energy to the work. It keeps hunger alive and stops opportunity from becoming ordinary.

MORNING EDGE: REMEMBER WHAT THIS IS

Before the day gets moving, name three parts of your life or sport that you once wanted and now get to live. Let that sink in for a moment. Then say, "What a gift to be here." Bring that mindset into your first action.

FLIP THE SWITCH: BRING RESPECT TO THE MOMENT

When fatigue, frustration, or boredom creeps in, go to RTZ. Take one Return to Zero breath and remind yourself, "You asked for this—answer with your effort." Then finish the rep, drill, or day with real respect for the opportunity in front of you.

CHAMPION'S WRAP: SHOW ME THE GRATITUDE

Look back on the day and find one moment when your effort showed appreciation for the opportunity in front of you. Maybe it was your focus, your response, or the way you handled a hard part of the day. Gratitude is not just something you feel. It shows up in how you compete.

DAY 316: SAME JOB, ANY ARENA

"We don't think a whole lot about the arena. Our job is the same wherever it's at."
Cael Sanderson

Sanderson is talking about portable focus. The arena may be loud or quiet, familiar or strange, but your job stays the same. Champions do not spend much time making the setting bigger than it is. They bring their habits, their standards, and their work with them. The more you tie performance to comfort, the more fragile it becomes. The more you trust your job, the steadier you stay.

MORNING EDGE: BRING YOUR GAME WITH YOU

Before the day begins, remind yourself what travels well: your breathing, your body language, your focus, and your effort. Picture yourself bringing those into any room, field, court, mat, or stage. Say, "Different place, same job." Then start the day like you mean it.

FLIP THE SWITCH: BACK TO THE JOB

When the environment feels off, go to RTZ. Take one Return to Zero breath and let the feeling be there without turning it into a story. Then say, "Same job." Bring your attention back to the next task and do it with purpose.

CHAMPION'S WRAP: TRAVEL WELL

Look back on the day and pick one moment when you stayed with your work even though the environment felt a little off. Replay how you carried yourself, what you focused on, and how you stayed steady. That is how you learn to bring your game anywhere.

DAY 317: FINISH WANTING MORE

"I love wrestling. I love the sport."
Cael Sanderson

Sanderson's quote sounds simple, but it contains real wisdom. Love for the sport is part of what helps great performers last. The best do not burn themselves out trying to prove how much they care. They train hard, but they also protect the part of themselves that still wants to come back tomorrow. If you want this to last, you have to leave some fuel in the tank.

MORNING EDGE: PROTECT THE FIRE

Before the day starts, ask yourself, "What helps me stay sharp and still want more?" Decide on one small way you will train with purpose today without draining yourself dry. Say, "I want to finish wanting more." Then carry that into your first action.

FLIP THE SWITCH: KEEP SOME FOR TOMORROW

When the grind starts to feel heavy, go to RTZ. Take one Return to Zero breath and ask, "What helps me stay strong and hungry?" Then make the choice that keeps your edge alive, whether that means a reset, a laugh, a lighter touch, or a smarter finish.

CHAMPION'S WRAP: STILL DRAWN BACK

At the end of the day, check in with your energy and your desire. Ask yourself, "Do I still want to come back tomorrow?" That question tells you everything.

DAY 318: EMPTY THE TANK WHEN IT COUNTS

"For me the question is: Did I honestly do enough with the ability I was born with?"

Cael Sanderson

Sanderson is not talking about working all the time. He is talking about honesty. When it is time to recover, recover. When it is time to work, work. The standard is not constant intensity, but full honesty with the moment in front of you. That is how you avoid regret and make sure your ability does not stay trapped inside you.

MORNING EDGE: CALL THE DAY CLEARLY

Ask yourself what this day is asking for. If it is a day to push, decide now that you will not meet it halfway. If it is a day to recover, do that with the same honesty.

FLIP THE SWITCH: NO HALF-REPS

When you catch yourself coasting, drifting, or protecting energy you do not need to protect, bring yourself back. Tell yourself, "If it is time to work, then work," and finish the rep, the drill, or the task with purpose.

CHAMPION'S WRAP: CHECK THE MIRROR

As you close out the day, ask yourself whether you were honest with the work the day required. That is the kind of answer you can live with, and it is how trust in yourself gets built.

DAY 319: MENTAL TRAINING PARTNER

CLARESSA SHIELDS

"I don't break. I punch back."

Claressa Shields

Claressa Shields came up in Flint, Michigan, and fought her way into the history books. At seventeen, she won Olympic gold in boxing at the 2012 London Games, becoming the first American woman to do it. Four years later, she won gold again in Rio and kept building one of the fiercest careers in the sport. Her rise has always carried the same message. She came to win.

Shields has never been shy about her goals. She says what she is coming for and then trains like she means every word. That kind of clarity brings pressure with it, but it also creates direction. When you name the standard out loud, you have to live up to it.

What makes Shields so dangerous is how she handles the hard part of the fight. When things get uncomfortable, she stays in the fire and answers back. She does not wait for better conditions or a softer round. She keeps competing, keeps adjusting, and keeps bringing force to the moment.

This week, Shields is your mental training partner. She will show you how to match bold belief with real work and how to respond when the fight gets tough. Be clear about what you want, back it with action, and punch back when pressure shows up.

DAY 320: CALL YOUR SHOT

"I know I'm the greatest woman of all time. I can't hide it."
Claressa Shields

Some people wait for the world to name them. Others name themselves and get to work. Shields talks like someone who already knows what she is here to be and has no interest in shrinking it. That kind of statement is not about showing off. It is about planting your flag before the results are finished catching up. Once you get that clear, your work stops wandering and starts hunting.

MORNING EDGE: PLANT THE FLAG

Before training, name the standard you are living into. Say it in a way that wakes you up: "This is who I am building," or "This is what my work stands for." Then choose one behavior today that puts your flag in the ground and makes the statement cost something.

FLIP THE SWITCH: LET THE WORK TALK

When doubt, hesitation, or drift show up, bring the energy back through action. Move with conviction, finish with purpose, and carry yourself like someone whose work has something to say. Your identity gets built by behavior, not by mood.

CHAMPION'S WRAP: YOUR FLAG WAS THERE

At the end of the day, look back on one moment when your standard showed without explanation. Maybe it was in the way you finished, responded, or stayed with the work when it got demanding. That is how a claim starts to feel lived-in.

DAY 321: THE WORK BUILDS THE ROAD

"Boxing saved my life. It gave me a future when I didn't think I had one."
Claressa Shields

Shields is talking about more than sport here. She is talking about what happens when the work gives your life shape. It gave her somewhere to put her pain, her fire, and her hope. It gave her structure before it gave her success, and direction before it gave her fame. Sometimes the greatest gift of the work is that it builds a road before you can fully see where it leads.

MORNING EDGE: RESPECT WHAT IT'S BUILDING

Before the day starts, remember that your work is doing more than sharpening your skills. It is building habits, direction, and a life you can stand on. Step into the day like this work matters beyond today.

FLIP THE SWITCH: WIN THE NEXT ROUND

When life feels heavy, messy, or uncertain, come back to what is right in front of you. You do not need the whole future mapped out. You need this round, this exchange, and this next honest piece of work. Stay with it and keep answering the bell.

CHAMPION'S WRAP: STAYED IN THE ROUND

Tonight, think of one moment when you stayed in the round and kept moving forward. It may have felt small, but it still moved your life in a better direction. That is how a future gets built, one round at a time.

DAY 322: FIGHT THE RIGHT WAY

"I don't fight dirty. I fight hard. There's a difference."
Claressa Shields

Shields is talking about standards under heat. Anybody can get loud, rushed, or out of control when the moment turns intense and emotional. Real toughness looks different. It brings force without losing form.

MORNING EDGE: BRING CLEAN FIRE

Before you start, decide what hard and clean looks like for you today. Maybe it is strong body language, aggressive focus, clean execution, or pressure with poise. Pick your version and step in like that is your standard.

FLIP THE SWITCH: TURN HEAT INTO PRECISION

When the moment heats up, narrow your focus instead of letting it scatter. Lock in on one sharp cue like "clean," "sharp," or "right here," and let your body organize around it. The goal is to make your fire more exact.

CHAMPION'S WRAP: FIRE WITH FORM

At the end of the day, replay one moment when you stayed disciplined under pressure. Notice how you kept your edge without getting messy. That is the kind of toughness that holds up.

DAY 323: VISIT IT BEFORE YOU ARRIVE

"I've already seen myself winning. Now I just make it real."
Claressa Shields

Shields treats the mind like a preview room. She sees the moment before it arrives, feels it before it gets here, and gives herself a chance to live there early. That changes everything. The big moment stops feeling like foreign territory and becomes a place she already knows. Confidence grows when the mind can say, *I've seen this movie, and I like how it ends.*

MORNING EDGE: RUN THE PREVIEW

Before practice or competition, take a few seconds and watch one moment go your way. See the setting, feel the rhythm, and picture yourself handling it with authority, timing, and presence. Give your mind a preview worth following.

FLIP THE SWITCH: STEP INTO THE SCENE

When the moment gets big, bring back the picture you already built. Let your body recognize it like a place it has visited before. Then move like you are arriving for something familiar, not trying to invent it on the spot.

CHAMPION'S WRAP: KEEP THE BEST CLIP

At the end of the day, hold on to one moment that looked or felt the way you wanted. Replay it like a personal highlight and let the image get brighter, sharper, and stronger. That is how you build a mind that shows up ready.

DAY 324: TRAIN LIKE YOUR NAME MEANS SOMETHING

"I say I'm the greatest because I train like I am."

Claressa Shields

Big words are easy to love on fresh legs and a good day. The harder and better move is giving those words something to stand on. Shields's quote is pure alignment. She is saying her standard shows up in the work, not just in the talk. When your reps carry your signature, your confidence stops feeling borrowed and starts feeling earned.

MORNING EDGE: SIGN THE WORK

Before training, decide what you want your work to say about you today. Maybe it says you are sharp, fierce, disciplined, or all in. Pick the quality, then stamp it on the session with the way you start. Let the first rep introduce you.

FLIP THE SWITCH: MAKE IT LOOK LIKE YOU

When a rep gets sloppy, casual, or forgettable, wake it up. Tell yourself, "Make it look like me," and put your standard back on it. The point is not more reps. The point is reps with your name on them.

CHAMPION'S WRAP: LEAVE YOUR MARK

When the day is done, think of one rep, one choice, or one stretch of work that had your full signature on it. Maybe it was the focus, the sharpness, the pride, or the way you stayed with it when it got tedious. That is the kind of work that leaves a mark long after the session ends.

DAY 325: KEEP THE REAL SCORE

"They see the wins. They don't see the hours. But I do."
Claressa Shields

The world usually grades the shiny part. It sees the result, the headline, the clean finish, and the part that photographs well. You see the whole thing. You see the early mornings, the heavy legs, the extra round, the missed rep you cleaned up, and the choice to stay with it when nobody was handing out applause. That is why your view has to carry weight. The people outside may see the outcome, but you know what the day was made of.

MORNING EDGE: KNOW YOUR SCOREBOARD

Before the day starts, decide what counts today. Maybe it is your effort, your honesty, your response, your presence, or the way you finish. Pick the scoreboard you respect, and let that be the one you play to.

FLIP THE SWITCH: CHECK THE REAL SCORE

When opinions, comparisons, or noise start pulling at you, come back to the only question that matters: *How am I doing on the things I said count?* Let that answer settle you. Then get back to work like someone who knows where the real game is being played.

CHAMPION'S WRAP: READ THE DAY RIGHT

When the day is done, give yourself the kind of read only you can give. Look at what was asked of you, how you answered it, and what carried real weight. That kind of honesty keeps you grounded on good days and strong on hard ones.

DAY 326: MENTAL TRAINING PARTNER

AMANDA NUNES

"I respect my opponents. I learned that from life. I used to think I would step in there, throw one punch, and the other girl would go down and not get up again. Every time I thought that, I lost."

Amanda Nunes

Amanda Nunes grew up in Bahia, Brazil, and learned early that fighting demands respect. She started with karate, added boxing, and stepped into mixed martial arts as a teenager. In those early fights, she saw what happens when you rush, force, or underestimate what is in front of you. That lesson stayed with her and shaped everything that followed.

She went on to become the first woman in UFC history to hold two titles at the same time. Her dominance came from range, not from a single strength. Some fights called for power, others for patience, control, or defense. Nunes prepared to solve the fight that showed up instead of trying to force the one she had pictured.

What makes her so strong is how she competes when things are not perfect. There were title defenses where injuries limited parts of her game, yet she stayed present and kept working with what she had. She adjusted, trusted her preparation, and stayed engaged from start to finish. That is what composure looks like in a real fight.

This week, Nunes is your mental training partner. She will show you how to respect the challenge, trust your tools, and stay composed when the fight gets hard. Step in ready, stay with it, and finish what you start.

DAY 327: GET BACK FAST

"All the things I went through, my losses, those really helped me."
Amanda Nunes

Nunes is saying her losses did more than humble her. They taught her how to come back stronger, clearer, and less rattled. Anybody can feel good when things are going well. Mastery shows up in how fast and how cleanly you return when they are not.

MORNING EDGE: TRAIN THE BOUNCE BACK

Go into today knowing something may feel off at some point. Your job is not to make a big scene out of it. Your job is to get back to your work quickly.

FLIP THE SWITCH: NO SCENE, JUST SOLVE

When you miss, hesitate, or get frustrated, skip the drama. Blow out the junk with one hard exhale and tell yourself, "Solve it and go again." Then take the next clean action.

CHAMPION'S WRAP: BACK ON TRACK

When the day is done, think of one moment when you came back instead of spiraling. That is how losses start helping you before the next loss ever comes.

DAY 328: YOU ALREADY KNOW

"I proved it. I'm the best. I proved it."
Amanda Nunes

Nunes is not talking herself into anything. She is drawing on what she has already lived, earned, and survived. In tight moments, confidence does not come from saying the perfect thing. It comes from remembering the hard days you made it through and the work you have already done. When doubt gets loud, the answer is not to create belief from scratch. It is to come back to what you already know.

MORNING EDGE: RECALL ONE HARD DAY

Before the day begins, bring to mind one hard moment you got through without backing down. Tell yourself, "I have been here before, and I came through it." Then begin from that place.

FLIP THE SWITCH: TRUST WHAT YOU KNOW

When doubt shows up, do not get pulled into it. Take one steady breath and tell yourself, "I know who I am in hard moments." Then get back to the rep, the play, or the next strong action.

CHAMPION'S WRAP: DON'T FORGET WHO YOU ARE

As the day comes to a close, remember one thing you have already overcome, earned, or grown through. Let that put a smile on your face, because the strength you need is not missing. It is already yours.

DAY 329: COME BACK TO CAPABILITY

"You know, whatever people say, nothing's going to change it. What I think, what I'm capable of."
Amanda Nunes

Nunes is talking about inner authority. People can doubt you, praise you, compare you, or misunderstand you, and none of that has to decide your direction. What matters most is what you believe about your own capability. The strongest competitors return to a simple truth when things get loud, tight, or uncertain: *I'm capable of meeting the demands of this moment.* That belief steadies you and keeps you moving forward.

MORNING EDGE: START FROM CAPABILITY

Before the day begins, remind yourself of what is already in you. Say it clearly: "I'm capable of meeting the demands of this moment." Let that shape how you step in and what you expect from yourself.

FLIP THE SWITCH: BRING SOMETHING STRONG

When doubt, comparison, or outside opinions start crowding the space, bring something strong to the moment. Bring your poise, your fight, your patience, your sharpness, or your presence. Let the moment feel what showed up in you.

CHAMPION'S WRAP: CAPABILITY HELD

At the end of the day, think of one moment when you came back to what you knew was in you. Notice how that steadied you and kept you engaged. That is how self-belief becomes something you can rely on.

DAY 330: WEAR THE STANDARD

"I'm a champion. I have to defend this belt."
Amanda Nunes

The belt is the part people see, but the standard is what holds everything up. Titles shine in public, while the habits, focus, discipline, and body language that protect them are built in private. A belt can sit on a shelf, but a standard has to be worn in the way you train, respond, and carry yourself on ordinary days. That is what keeps your edge alive.

MORNING EDGE: PUT IT ON EARLY

Before training, decide what the standard looks like today. Maybe it is sharp focus, clean execution, strong posture, or finishing with pride. Put it on before the day tests you, and wear it from the first rep forward.

FLIP THE SWITCH: DEFEND THE STANDARD

When the work starts feeling casual, flat, or too comfortable, bring the standard back into the room. Ask yourself, "Would this defend the belt?" Then raise the quality of the next rep, drill, or decision. Champions protect their edge by how they answer ordinary moments.

CHAMPION'S WRAP: THE BELT WAS ON YOU

At the end of the day, think of one moment when your standard showed without needing an audience. Maybe it was in how you finished, how you responded, or how you stayed sharp when it would have been easy to coast. That is how a title keeps living in you.

DAY 331: PREPARED IS POWERFUL

"You need to prepare for every fight."
Amanda Nunes

Preparation gives you something solid to lean on when the moment arrives. Every focused rep, every honest effort, and every standard you keep adds strength to your foundation. Readiness grows on ordinary days, long before the lights come on. When you prepare with purpose, pressure feels like a place you are ready to enter.

MORNING EDGE: BUILD THE FIGHTER EARLY

Before training, remember that today's ordinary work becomes tomorrow's edge. Carry this with you: "Train like the bell rings tomorrow." Then handle the little things like they matter, because they do.

FLIP THE SWITCH: NO CHEAP REPS

When you feel tempted to coast, rush, or cut a corner, bring yourself back to the standard. Lock in on this: "Future me fights with what I do right now." Then give the next rep the kind of honesty you will be proud to stand on later.

CHAMPION'S WRAP: YOU PUT SOMETHING IN YOUR CORNER

When the day is done, think of one thing you did that added to your readiness instead of taking from it. Smile at that, because you are not just getting through days like this. You are building someone strong enough to answer the bell.

DAY 332: GUARD YOUR ENERGY

"I've lost before. You need great people around you, your family, people giving you positive energy."
Amanda Nunes

Nunes understands that energy is not just personal. The people around you can calm your system or speed it up, steady you or shake you. In pressure situations, other people's fear, drama, and tension can get into you fast if you are not careful. That is why guarding your energy is not extra. It is part of staying ready to perform.

MORNING EDGE: SET YOUR INPUTS

Before the day begins, think about what will have your ear first. Choose your first conversation, your music, your message, or your quiet time on purpose, because your mind should not have to recover from your morning before the work even starts.

FLIP THE SWITCH: STAY THE STEADY ONE

When someone else gets dramatic, negative, or frantic, catch it before you absorb it. Tell yourself, "They can rush; I will stay steady," then slow your exhale and get back to your job.

CHAMPION'S WRAP: KEEP THE ANCHORS CLOSE

At the end of the day, think of one person, habit, or choice that helped you stay grounded when things could have pulled you off center. Keep moving toward what steadies you, because that is the kind of energy that helps you compete well.

DAY 333: KEEP SHARPENING THE SWORD

"I'm going to keep on making history."
Amanda Nunes

Nunes is not talking about holding onto the past. She is talking about staying hungry enough to build something new. A lot of athletes succeed once and then start protecting their name, their status, or their comfort. That is where growth slows down. History is not what you already did. It is what you are still willing to become.

MORNING EDGE: BE A BEGINNER AGAIN

Before training, remind yourself that success does not mean you are finished. Tell yourself, "I'm still building," and come into the day ready to learn, work, and sharpen your edge again.

FLIP THE SWITCH: BACK TO COMMITMENT

When you catch yourself leaning on what you have already done, stop and wake back up. Tell yourself, "Commit, don't coast." Then attack the next rep, drill, or task like your future is still being built.

CHAMPION'S WRAP: HISTORY IS STILL BEING MADE

At the end of the day, think of one way you chose growth over comfort. Smile at that, because the best part of your story may still be in front of you.

DAY 334: REPRESENT SOMETHING BIGGER

"I represent Brazil with the flag and the belt."
Amanda Nunes

You are never just competing for the result in front of you. You are also carrying your values, your people, your story, and the standard you want your life to stand for. That gives your effort more meaning and more strength. When the moment becomes about something bigger than proving yourself, you often compete with more pride, freedom, and heart.

MORNING EDGE: PLAY FOR THE NAME

Before the day begins, decide who or what you are representing today. It might be your family, your team, your city, or the younger version of you who dreamed of this chance. Lock in on that and carry this with you: "Play for the name."

FLIP THE SWITCH: HONOR THE NAME

When the work gets hard and your mind starts narrowing in on your own discomfort, come back to what you represent. Remind yourself, "Honor the name." Then attack the next rep with pride.

CHAMPION'S WRAP: BE PROUD OF WHAT YOU CARRIED

When the day is done, think of one moment when you showed up in a way that honored what matters most to you. Let yourself feel good about that, because effort hits differently when it comes from something deeper than ego.

CHAMPION'S TAKEAWAYS: MGM GRAND

The MGM Grand showed you what happens when everything is personal and exposed. This month you learned how to take ownership of your effort, your energy, and your decisions when there's nowhere to hide. You practiced staying composed, defending your standards, and trusting the habits you've built rather than reacting in the moment. That's real accountability—showing up steady, prepared, and responsible for how you compete.

As you step away from Vegas, ask yourself:

- Where did I take responsibility instead of making excuses?
- When pressure showed up, what helped me stay composed?
- What habits helped me feel ready and in control?

Carry that ownership forward. It travels well.

CHAPTER 12

DECEMBER: LOS ANGELES MEMORIAL COLISEUM

"For every athlete who steps into this stadium, the flame burns the same—a call to rise again."

From the Opening Ceremony of the 1984 Los Angeles Olympic Games

Your journey began in Olympia, where the Olympic spirit first took shape. Now, in December, you return to that same spirit on one of the biggest stages in sport. The arena is different, but the standard is the same.

The Los Angeles Memorial Coliseum has carried Olympic history before and will do it again. It hosted the Games in 1932 and 1984, and will welcome them back in 2028. This is a place where the spotlight grows and the pressure gets heavy. Your job is to carry your team, roots, and values into that light while still competing free.

Your mental training partners for this final chapter are Noah Lyles, Chloe Kim, Marie-Philip Poulin, and Armand Duplantis. Different sports, different styles, and the same ability to rise when it matters most.

This chapter is not about learning something new. It is about bringing everything you have built into the moments that ask the most of you. Your mindset, your habits, and your identity all come with you now. This is the final test, not of talent, but of who you have become.

DAY 335: MENTAL TRAINING PARTNER

NOAH LYLES

"I have asthma, allergies, dyslexia, ADD, anxiety, and depression. But I will tell you that what you have does not define what you can become. Why not you!"
Noah Lyles

Noah Lyles grew up handling real challenges that could have lowered the ceiling in other people's minds. Asthma, learning struggles, anxiety, and depression were all part of the picture. He faced them honestly, trained through them, and kept moving toward the athlete he believed he could become. He never let the labels write the ending.

The results have been electric. Noah holds the American record in the 200 meters at 19.31 and won Olympic gold in the 100 meters at the 2024 Paris Games. He has also won multiple world titles across the 100, 200, and 4×100 relay. Those performances grabbed the spotlight, but the real story was built long before the cameras found him.

What makes Noah so powerful is how deliberately he trains belief. He uses visualization like reps and treats self-talk like part of the job. He has said he runs drills in his mind throughout the day, sharpening the race before he ever steps onto the track. That kind of preparation turns confidence into something lived and trained.

This week, Noah is your mental training partner. He will show you how to see the moment clearly, speak with purpose, and keep building even after success. Race to express, not to protect. Bring your full self to the line and let the work show.

DAY 336: THIS MOMENT IS MINE

"I'm a true believer that the moment isn't bigger than me; the moment was made for me."

Noah Lyles

Big moments feel heavy because they matter. They start to feel too big when you step into them hoping to survive instead of expecting to belong. Noah flips that whole mindset. The moment is not here to scare you off. It is here to call out what your preparation built.

MORNING EDGE: CLAIM THE STAGE

Before training or competition, tell yourself, "This moment fits me." Let that show up in your posture, your breathing, and the way you begin.

FLIP THE SWITCH: STEP INTO IT

When pressure starts to make you hesitate or shrink, do not back off and wait to feel ready. Take one good breath, say, "This moment is mine," and move toward the rep, the play, or the shot with intent.

CHAMPION'S WRAP: YOU MET IT

As you close out the day, think of one moment when you stepped in instead of holding back. That is what preparation is for, and the more often you meet the moment, the more natural it becomes.

DAY 337: TRUST THE WORK THEY NEVER SAW

"To every athlete who is worried about what people say about you, just remember they can't tell you what workout you did yesterday. So they can't tell you if you are getting better or not."

Noah Lyles

Most people only see the race, the stat line, or the result. They do not see yesterday's workout, the extra reps, the rehab, the film, or the choices you make when no one is watching. That is why outside opinions can sound loud and still mean very little. Let people talk from the outside. You live on the inside of the work.

MORNING EDGE: RETURN TO THE EVIDENCE

Before practice, remind yourself that real progress is often private before it becomes obvious. Pick one part of the work you can respect today and do it with full intent.

FLIP THE SWITCH: BACK TO THE WORK

When a comment, comparison, or doubt gets in your head, come back to what is real. Tell yourself, "They did not see the work," then lock into the next rep, the next cue, or the next right choice.

CHAMPION'S WRAP: PRIVATE PROOF

As you close out the day, name one thing you did that moved you forward, even if nobody else noticed. That is the kind of proof that keeps you grounded and your progress moving.

DAY 338: DON'T TAKE ORDERS FROM FEAR

"There is no way that I am gonna lose to my fear."

Noah Lyles

Fear shows up to try to talk you out of the effort it takes to be great. It wants you to be cautious, quiet, and careful right when the moment calls for boldness. But fear does not get to decide how hard you push or how cleanly you execute. It can show up on the track, but it does not get a lane.

MORNING EDGE: BEAT IT TO THE PUNCH

Before practice or competition, expect your body to wake up if the moment matters. Take one Return to Zero breath by inhaling for four seconds and exhaling for six, unclench your jaw, drop your shoulders, lift your eyes, and tell yourself, "Fear doesn't call the shots. I do."

FLIP THE SWITCH: GO BEFORE IT GROWS

When nerves spike, do not stand there and let fear settle in. Take one Return to Zero breath, fix your posture, and tell yourself, "Fear doesn't decide this. I do." Then make a strong first move.

CHAMPION'S WRAP: YOU DIDN'T BACK DOWN

As you close out the day, remember one moment when fear showed up and you stayed with the rep, the play, or the pressure anyway. That is how courage gets built and how fear stops taking up so much space in your head.

DAY 339: WIN IT IN YOUR MIND FIRST

"When I'm in the blocks, I already see myself winning."
Noah Lyles

Big performances do not begin at the gun. They begin earlier, in the mind, where belief, rhythm, and trust start to take shape. Noah is not talking about wishful thinking. He is talking about giving his body a clear picture of success before the moment arrives. When you see it first, you stop walking into the moment like a stranger and start entering it like you have already been there.

MORNING EDGE: RUN IT BEFORE YOU RUN IT

Before practice or competition, take a moment to see the performance you want. Feel the setup, the rhythm, the response, and the finish, and let your body settle into that picture.

FLIP THE SWITCH: I'VE ALREADY BEEN HERE

When the moment gets big, do not act like it is brand new. Tell yourself, "I've already been here," and trust the picture you gave your mind before the pressure showed up.

CHAMPION'S WRAP: END WITH THE RIGHT PICTURE

As you close out the day, replay one thing you did well and let that image stay with you. The mind keeps practicing what you leave it with.

DAY 340: OWN YOUR GREATNESS

"I saw my name pop up and I said, 'Goodness gracious, I'm incredible.'"
Noah Lyles

After the photo finish in the 100 meters at the 2024 Olympic Games, Noah did not know he had won until his name appeared first. In that instant, his reaction was not ego so much as honesty in real time. Too many athletes are quick to own what went wrong and slow to own what they did brilliantly. You are allowed to think well of yourself and own what you did well.

MORNING EDGE: START WITH BELIEF

Before the day gets going, ask yourself, "What if it all turns out great?" Use that question to interrupt the doubts and negative what-ifs that usually show up before an important moment. Then tell yourself, "My best is already in me," and go.

FLIP THE SWITCH: DO NOT SHRINK IT

When you feel yourself backing off, downplaying, or getting small, stop right there. Stand tall, meet the moment, and tell yourself, "Let my best show." Then compete with the size of your ability, not the size of your fear.

CHAMPION'S WRAP: OWN ONE THING

As you close out the day, name one thing you did well and let yourself take it in. Tell yourself, "I did that well, and I give myself credit for it." Confidence grows when you give yourself credit for what you did well.

DAY 341: AMONG WOLVES

"I'm the wolf among wolves."
Noah Lyles

Noah was not talking about being louder than everyone else. He was talking about identity in a high-stakes moment. The best athletes do not step into big arenas hoping they belong there. They know they belong there because the work has already settled that question. When you stop auditioning and start trusting your place, your game gets freer, cleaner, and more dangerous.

MORNING EDGE: WALK IN LIKE YOU BELONG

Before practice or competition, remind yourself that you are not here to fit in quietly. You earned your place, so walk in like it. Let that show up in your posture, your eyes, and the way you start.

FLIP THE SWITCH: STOP PLAYING SMALL

When pressure hits, do not start shrinking, forcing, or trying to impress people. Settle down, trust your training, and compete like someone who knows he belongs in the fight. Let your game come out.

CHAMPION'S WRAP: THAT WAS YOU

As you close out the day, think of one moment when you looked, moved, or competed like the real you. Hold on to that feeling, because that is the version you want to keep bringing back.

DAY 342: MENTAL TRAINING PARTNER

CHLOE KIM

"Just because I'm young doesn't mean I didn't work hard to get to where I am."
Chloe Kim

Chloe Kim competes with a kind of freedom that makes the hardest tricks look light. That freedom is earned. It comes from showing up, putting in the work, and building trust long before the run begins. That is what makes her such a powerful training partner.

She was born in Long Beach, raised in Torrance, and supported by parents who believed in her dream enough to build life around it. Her father famously left his job so he could drive her to the mountains and help her train. Chloe started snowboarding at four and joined the US Snowboarding Team as a teenager. The foundation was built early, and it was built with purpose.

The results have been historic. Chloe won Olympic gold in the halfpipe in 2018 and again in 2022, then added silver in 2026 to become the first female snowboarder to medal in the halfpipe at three straight Olympics. She is also a three-time world champion, a multiple-time X Games gold medalist, and the first woman to land both a 1260 and a double cork 1080 in competition. Those runs look free because the work behind them is so deep.

This week, Chloe is your mental training partner. She will show you how hard work creates freedom and how preparation lets you compete light when the moment gets big. Do the work, trust what you built, and let yourself play. That is when your best stuff comes out.

DAY 343: THE HARD WAY

"When I was younger, me and my dad worked really hard. We did it the hard way."
Chloe Kim

Doing it the hard way means no shortcuts and no handouts. It's early mornings, long drives, packed weekends, dark bruises, and many reps you don't post online. That kind of work doesn't just build skill. It teaches you that you can stay with hard things and finish them. That's how everything was built here, step by step, long before Olympic gold. Most athletes say they want it. The great ones keep choosing the hard way when it would be easier not to.

MORNING EDGE: CHOOSE THE HARD WAY

Before practice, remind yourself that comfort doesn't make you better. Say, "I take the hard way," and start with intent, even if you don't feel ready yet.

FLIP THE SWITCH: NO SHORTCUTS

When training gets tough, don't pull back. Stay with the rep and finish it clean. That's usually where the separation happens.

CHAMPION'S WRAP: YOU POWERED THROUGH

Before bed, think about the hardest moment you didn't avoid today. That's how you learn you can be counted on.

DAY 344: FLIP THE PRESSURE

"For whatever reason, I'm pretty good with pressure. I kind of just flip it over and think of it as positive."

Chloe Kim

Pressure shows up when something matters. It is not a warning sign that something is wrong. It is a signal that your system is turning on. The key is to use that energy instead of trying to escape it.

MORNING EDGE: SET THE MEANING

Before practice, decide what pressure means today. Take one Return to Zero breath: Inhale for four, exhale for six, let your posture rise and your body settle. Then lock it in: "This feeling is fuel." Don't wait for pressure to define you. Define it first.

FLIP THE SWITCH: OWN THE MOMENT

When the surge hits, don't analyze it. That's where athletes lose it. Give a slight smirk, a small nod, and say, "Good. This is it." Then go. You're not trying to get rid of the feeling. You're using it to move with intent.

CHAMPION'S WRAP: TRAIN THE RESPONSE

At night, replay a big moment and feel the surge again. See yourself meeting it the same way every time: Steady eyes, loose body, and ready to attack. Pressure becomes predictable when your response is automatic. And when it's automatic, it's yours.

DAY 345: FINISH WITH PEACE OF MIND

"I knew if I went home with the gold medal knowing that I could do better, I wasn't going to be very satisfied."

Chloe Kim

The result is never the whole story. You can win and still know you left something on the table. You can lose and still walk away with peace because you gave it your all. Peace of mind comes from competing in a way that you can live with afterward.

MORNING EDGE: SET THE STANDARD

Before practice, decide how you want to leave today. Not with a certain score or result, but with the kind of effort, focus, and honesty you can respect. Tell yourself, "I want peace of mind tonight," and let that shape how you train. The best standard is one you can stand behind when the day is done.

FLIP THE SWITCH: FINISH THE REP CLEAN

After a rep, a run, or a drill, ask yourself, "Can I stand behind that?" If the answer is no, reset and do the next one with full intent. Peace of mind is built in those small moments when you choose not to cheat the standard.

CHAMPION'S WRAP: SLEEP WELL

Before bed, think about the moments when you stayed true to your standard. Let yourself feel the calm that comes from knowing you did not cut corners with your effort or your focus. That feeling is deeper than praise and steadier than a result. It is the kind of satisfaction that travels with you.

DAY 346: THEY EXPECT MORE FOR A REASON

"I always try to see it in a positive way, like, you know what, the people that are expecting so much of me know I can do it and believe in me."

Chloe Kim

Expectations do not come out of nowhere. They show up because people have seen what you are capable of. The mistake is hearing them as pressure instead of recognizing them as proof. High expectations are often a reflection of real ability.

MORNING EDGE: READ IT RIGHT

Before practice, remind yourself what expectations mean. They are not random, and they are not there to make you tight. Tell yourself, "They expect more because I can do more." Let that thought lift your posture, sharpen your focus, and sharpen your intent.

FLIP THE SWITCH: STAND UP TO IT

When expectations show up, do not rush or shrink. Stand tall and let them steady you. Other people saw something in you before you fully saw it in yourself. Let that recognition call you up instead of wear you down.

CHAMPION'S WRAP: SEEN CLEARLY

Before bed, think of one person who expects a lot from you. Do not picture that expectation as weight. Picture it as a sign that your ability is real and visible. There is peace in knowing you are not being asked for more by accident.

DAY 347: RESPECT THE ARENA

"I think, every time I'm on the mountain, I'm just so thankful to be there."

Chloe Kim

Gratitude is not pretending the work is easy. It is remembering that this is the life you chose and worked for. The pressure, the hard days, and the demands come with being in an arena that matters. When you respect the arena, you stop acting bothered by the very thing you came here to do.

MORNING EDGE: REMEMBER WHERE YOU ARE

Before practice, take a moment to think about what it took to get here. The early mornings, the repetitions, the sacrifices, and the discipline all helped build this life. Tell yourself, "This is the arena I earned," and step in with purpose. Respect starts with remembering.

FLIP THE SWITCH: CARRY IT RIGHT

When irritation, boredom, or pressure starts creeping in, check your body and your attention. Take one steady breath, stand tall, and lock back into the work. Do not move through the arena casually. Carry yourself like someone who knows where they are and what it means to be here.

CHAMPION'S WRAP: GRATEFUL FOR THE LIFE

Before bed, think about one part of the day that reminded you that this is the athlete's life. Maybe it was training while tired, competing under pressure, or staying with the work when it got hard. Let yourself feel grateful for the chance to live at this level. Gratitude keeps your perspective clean and your edge alive.

DAY 348: COMPETE LIKE ONLY YOU CAN

"I think the cool thing about snowboarding is that everyone has their own style."

Chloe Kim

The best athletes do not compete like copies. They compete with a rhythm, presence, and style that is their own. That does not come from forcing something special or trying to look a certain way. It comes from trusting your system enough to let your game come out the way it was built to.

MORNING EDGE: LET YOUR GAME SHOW UP

Before training, take one Return to Zero breath and settle into your body. Remind yourself that your rhythm is already there. You do not need to manufacture it. Tell yourself, "My job is to let my game show up," and step in ready to trust what is natural.

FLIP THE SWITCH: RETURN TO YOUR FEEL

When you get too mechanical, too careful, or too caught in your head, come back to feel. Lock into your timing, balance, tempo, and movement. Do not chase someone else's look or force a version of the performance that is not yours. The goal is not to look right. The goal is to be fully in your game.

CHAMPION'S WRAP: MORE YOU

Before bed, think about one moment today when you trusted your feel and let yourself compete freely. That is your style showing up. That is your game becoming more honest and more dangerous. The more you trust it, the more dependable it becomes.

DAY 349: MENTAL TRAINING PARTNER

MARIE-PHILIP POULIN

"Your mindset determines if you win or lose before the puck even drops."
Marie-Philip Poulin

Marie-Philip Poulin has earned the nickname "Captain Clutch" for a reason. She has built a career on showing up calmly and decisively when the game is on the line. That edge does not come from emotion or theatrics. It comes from preparation so thorough that pressure starts to feel familiar.

She grew up in Beauceville, Quebec, playing outside and battling with her older brother. Those early games helped shape her toughness, her feel, and her willingness to compete. From Boston University to the professional game and Team Canada, she kept growing into bigger roles and bigger moments. Over time, she became more than a scorer. She became the standard.

Her résumé tells the story. Poulin is a three-time Olympic gold medalist and a multiple-time world champion for Canada. She scored the game-winning goals in the 2010 and 2014 Olympic gold medal games and the overtime winner at the 2021 World Championship. When the game is hanging there, Captain Clutch has a way of stepping right into it.

This week, Poulin is your mental training partner. She will show you how to prepare so well that the biggest moments feel like part of the job. Stay clear, stay composed, and trust the habits you built. That is how clutch gets trained.

DAY 350: COMPETE WHERE YOU STAND

"Every practice feels like a game day. That's how you get better."
Marie-Philip Poulin

Great competitors do not wait for special moments to come alive. They bring game-day sharpness to ordinary moments. Practice is where you sharpen your instincts, raise your standard, and learn to compete right where you stand. When you train like that, the work gets more alive and improvement starts to move faster.

MORNING EDGE: COMPETE NOW

Walk into practice ready to engage, not just participate. Lock in with "Compete on this rep," and bring game-day sharpness to the first ordinary moment in front of you.

FLIP THE SWITCH: RAISE THE LEVEL

When the work starts to feel repetitive, flat, or automatic, wake yourself up and make the next rep matter. Come back to "Raise the level," and bring game-day sharpness to the moment instead of waiting for the moment to bring it out of you.

CHAMPION'S WRAP: FIND THE FIRE

At the end of the day, think of one ordinary moment where your edge came alive and the work started to feel sharp, competitive, and fun. Remind yourself, "That is the feeling," because that spark is part of what helps great performers keep growing.

DAY 351: WHEN HEART TAKES OVER

"Skill gets you started, but heart finishes the journey."
Marie-Philip Poulin

Skill can carry you a long way, but not all the way. There will be moments when your body feels heavy, your timing is off, and your best stuff does not come easily. That is not the end of the day. That is the moment heart takes over. Heart is what keeps you pressing, competing, and staying fully in it when things stop feeling smooth.

MORNING EDGE: DECIDE WHO SHOWS UP

Before practice, decide what is going to carry you today. Not comfort. Not rhythm. Not whether everything clicks early. Tell yourself, "If it gets hard, that's where I come alive," and step in ready to prove it with your effort.

FLIP THE SWITCH: GO TO HEART

When discomfort hits, do not back off or wait for perfect feelings. Smile, give a small nod, and say, "Go to heart." Then move with intent. Heart is the choice to stay aggressive and committed when the easy version is gone.

CHAMPION'S WRAP: HEART FINISHES

Think about one moment today when things did not feel easy and you stayed with it anyway. That is heart. Skill may open the door, but heart is what keeps you moving when the day asks more of you. That is the part of you that finishes.

DAY 352: LEAD ANYWAY

"Leadership is not just about wearing a letter; it's about inspiring your team."
Marie-Philip Poulin

Leadership is a choice you make in real time. It begins with how you respond when something needs to be lifted, steadied, or sharpened. Some moments call for energy, some call for honesty, and some call for someone to go first. Great leaders read the moment and give the group what it needs.

MORNING EDGE: SET THE TONE

Walk into practice ready to lead with your body language, your pace, and your intent. Make your focus visible. Make your effort clean. Teams are always reading what matters by how their leaders carry themselves.

FLIP THE SWITCH: STEP TOWARD IT

When the moment gets loose, quiet, or off track, step toward it. Raise the energy, tighten the standard, or give someone a lift. Leadership is not doing everything. It is giving the moment the one thing it most needs.

CHAMPION'S WRAP: YOU MOVED THE GROUP

As the day ends, think about one moment when your presence helped move the group in a better direction. That is leadership at work.

DAY 353: SEE IT ALL COMING

"Visualization is huge for me. I try to picture every play and scenario. Helps ground me when I'm on the ice. Plus, having rituals and routines adds a layer of comfort amidst the chaos."

Marie-Philip Poulin

Visualization works best when you use it for the full range of competition. You picture clean moments and difficult ones with the same steady presence. You see how you want to breathe, carry yourself, and respond in both. That is how readiness becomes more than a feeling.

MORNING EDGE: SEE THE FULL PICTURE

Before practice, picture one moment going your way and one moment that tests you. In both scenes, see yourself steady, composed, and ready to respond well. Tell yourself, "I'm ready for all of it," and let that settle into your body. Readiness grows when your mind has already been there.

FLIP THE SWITCH: TRUST THE REHEARSAL

When pressure hits, go straight to your response. Set your posture, steady your breath, and move with intent. You have already seen this kind of moment in your mind. Now let your body carry out what you rehearsed.

CHAMPION'S WRAP: ALREADY BEEN HERE

At the end of the day, think about one moment that felt familiar because you had already pictured it. Let that sink in. That is one of the great gifts of visualization. It helps the moment feel known before it ever arrives.

DAY 354: STEP INTO COMPETE MODE

"For me, it's listening to a specific playlist and making sure to lace up my skates just right. Also, I always tape my stick in a very particular way. It's like my moment of Zen before the storm."
Marie-Philip Poulin

Great competitors decide how they are going to enter the arena. That moment before the action starts is where you shift from everyday life into compete mode. Your routine helps you gather yourself, sharpen your focus, and step in with intent. Once you cross that line, your job is to trust it and go.

MORNING EDGE: BUILD THE ENTRY

Before training or competition, move through your routine with purpose. Music, gear, breath, or movement, do it in a way that helps you lock in. Tell yourself, "This is where I enter compete mode," and feel your focus rise. Strong routines help the mind and body arrive together.

FLIP THE SWITCH: STEP ACROSS THE LINE

When the moment arrives, carry yourself like someone who is ready. Stand tall, breathe steady, and step forward with clear intent. Let your routine do its job. You crossed the line ready, so now compete that way.

CHAMPION'S WRAP: YOU CHOSE THE STATE

At the end of the day, think about one moment when you deliberately shifted into your competitive state. That was you taking command of your mindset on purpose. The more clearly you make that turn, the more reliable your performance becomes.

DAY 355: LEAVE SOMETHING WORTH FOLLOWING

"To inspire the next generation is the greatest success."
Marie-Philip Poulin

Legacy is built in the ordinary moments people watch and remember. It lives in how you train, how you treat people, and how you carry yourself when the day gets hard. Every athlete is teaching something with their habits, attitude, and response. The question is whether your example is worth following.

MORNING EDGE: SET THE EXAMPLE

Walk into the day knowing your habits send a message. The way you warm up, listen, compete, and respond all tells people what matters. Tell yourself, "My example goes first," and carry that into the work. Strong influence starts with daily standards.

FLIP THE SWITCH: SHOW THEM THE WAY

When the moment gets frustrating, sloppy, or flat, stay steady and raise the standard. Someone around you is learning from how you handle this part. Show them what poise, effort, and discipline look like in real time. Legacy is often built when the moment gets tested.

CHAMPION'S WRAP: WHAT YOU TAUGHT TODAY

At the end of the day, think about one thing your actions taught the people around you. Maybe it was how to work, how to respond, or how to stay steady under pressure. That is how legacy grows. One day, one standard, and one example at a time.

DAY 356: MENTAL TRAINING PARTNER

ARMAND DUPLANTIS

"Ever since I started vaulting in my backyard, when I was in diapers, I wanted to be the best that's ever lived, to break the world record."

Armand Duplantis

Armand Duplantis was born into pole vault, but he still had to build himself into Mondo. His father, Greg, was a former vaulter who built a runway and pit in the backyard in Lafayette, Louisiana, and his mother, Helena, was a former heptathlete and volleyball player who gave him a strong athletic base. From the start, vaulting felt like play, exploration, and flight. That early joy became the foundation for something extraordinary.

By his teens, Duplantis was already clearing heights most athletes never touch. He won Olympic gold in Tokyo and again in Paris, where he also set a world record, and on March 12, 2026, he broke the men's pole vault world record for the fifteenth time, clearing 6.31 meters at the Mondo Classic in Uppsala, Sweden. He keeps raising the bar because he has been chasing that feeling his whole life. The dream stayed huge, and so did the work.

What makes Duplantis so special is the way he carries big ambition without letting it tighten around him. When he steps onto the runway, the task gets simple. Run fast, trust the plan, and go up. He competes with freedom because his preparation is deep, his rhythm is trained, and his curiosity is still alive.

This week, Duplantis is your mental training partner. He closes this book because he lives its core message. Excellence is playful, disciplined, and always reaching higher. The bar will keep rising, and so can you.

DAY 357: RETURN TO WHAT BUILT YOU

"Without the backyard, I'm not whatever I am today."
Armand Duplantis

Big moments are built on small ones. The early days matter because they gave you something real to stand on. The ordinary work, the repeated reps, and the love of the craft built your game from the ground up. When pressure rises, you return to what built you.

MORNING EDGE: REMEMBER THE ROOTS

Before training, think about where your game began. Picture the early reps, the simple joy, and the part of you that loved doing it before anyone was watching. Tell yourself, "What built me still carries me," and bring that grounded feeling into today's work.

FLIP THE SWITCH: BACK TO YOUR BASE

When things start speeding up, come back to your base. Settle your breath, find your rhythm, and trust the parts of your game that have been there all along. Pressure gets loud, but your foundation stays steady. The best response is often a return, not a reach.

CHAMPION'S WRAP: SOLID GROUND

At the end of the day, remind yourself that the foundation is still there. The work that built you did not disappear when the moment got bigger. It is still in your body, your rhythm, and your response. That is what gives you something solid to compete from.

DAY 358: THE GOLD STANDARD

"I just became a maniac. I had to be great at it, and I just didn't accept anything except excellence out of myself, even from when I was like five years old."
Armand Duplantis

The gold standard is not something you save for big moments. It is how you choose to do the small things every day. It shows up in your focus, your discipline, and the care you bring to the ordinary work. The more often you meet that standard, the more natural excellence becomes.

MORNING EDGE: SET IT TO GOLD

From the first movement of the day, carry yourself like the standard is already set. Warm up with purpose, stay sharp in the details, and treat the ordinary parts like they matter. Tell yourself, "Gold standard from the start." Let that show up in how you move, prepare, and work.

FLIP THE SWITCH: BRING IT BACK TO GOLD

When your posture, focus, or effort slips, clean it up right away. Bring the next rep back to your level. Tell yourself, "Bring it back to gold," and then show yourself the correction. Gold-standard competitors do not wait for the perfect moment. They bring the standard into the next action.

CHAMPION'S WRAP: GOLD IN THE ORDINARY

At the end of the day, think about one ordinary moment you handled the right way. Maybe it was your warm-up, your effort on a tired rep, or your response after a mistake. That is where the gold standard gets built. Excellence grows when ordinary moments get treated like they count.

DAY 359: RAISE YOUR BAR

"You have to go up there and jump high and clear whatever the bar may be. It's a competition within myself. That's how it was even before I was the best in the world, because that's the approach to every competition."
Armand Duplantis

Your best competition is with the standard you set for yourself. Each day gives you a new bar to clear in your effort, focus, and discipline. When that becomes the game, comparison loses its grip and progress gets cleaner. Greatness grows when your own bar keeps rising.

MORNING EDGE: SET THE HEIGHT

Start the day by deciding where your bar is today. Pick one thing you want to do with more care, sharpness, or discipline than yesterday. Tell yourself, "Set it higher." Strong days start with a standard that asks something of you.

FLIP THE SWITCH: CLEAR WHAT YOU SET

When the moment asks for more, answer it. Do the harder rep, stay with the detail, or hold the standard a little longer. Tell yourself, "Clear the bar." Your next level is built by how often you meet your own height.

CHAMPION'S WRAP: HIGHER THAN YESTERDAY

As the day ends, think about one place where you rose to your own standard. That is the real win. The bar does not have to move a mile. It just has to keep moving up.

DAY 360: STAY ON THE CLIMB

"It's not like I just grabbed the pole and I was jumping six meters. You just work your way up little by little."

Armand Duplantis

Big jumps are built through small climbs. Progress comes from stacking good work before the results look impressive. Every session adds something: timing, trust, rhythm, strength, or feel. That steady climb is what makes your game stronger and your confidence more solid.

MORNING EDGE: CLIMB ONE STEP

Start practice by choosing one thing you want to sharpen today. Keep it simple, specific, and reachable. Tell yourself, "One step up." Then give that step your full attention. Great progress usually starts with a small target handled well.

FLIP THE SWITCH: STAY ON THE CLIMB

When impatience shows up, come back to the next rep. Let go of the need for something dramatic and lock into what builds you. Tell yourself, "Stay on the climb," and take the next rep with purpose. Momentum grows when you keep meeting the day where it is.

CHAMPION'S WRAP: STILL RISING

At the end of the day, remind yourself what the work added. Maybe it was a cleaner rep, a steadier mind, or a little more trust in your rhythm. That is how progress works. You are building something, even when it grows quietly.

DAY 361: CARRY THE FIRE

"Everything's internal. You have to have that type of drive and motivation for it to work. Nobody else can want it for you."
Armand Duplantis

Drive starts with you. It shows up in how you train when it's quiet and how you compete when it counts. The best athletes do not wait for the right mood or moment. They bring intent, energy, and purpose with them. That is what separates showing up from showing up ready.

MORNING EDGE: LIGHT IT EARLY

Start the day by deciding how you will show up. Bring purpose to your warm-up and sharpness to your first rep. Tell yourself, "I bring the fire with me." Set the tone before anything else tries to.

FLIP THE SWITCH: SPARK IT NOW

When your energy dips, act first. Pick up your pace, lift your posture, and attack the next rep. Tell yourself, "Spark it now." Energy builds when you stop waiting and start moving.

CHAMPION'S WRAP: YOU CARRIED IT

At the end of the day, think about one moment when you created your own energy. That is a competitive edge. When you can generate your own fire, you are never dependent on the moment. You bring your own fire with you wherever you go.

DAY 362: ENTER THE BUBBLE

"I try not to worry about anything. It's me and the bar. It's just a competition between me and the bar."
Armand Duplantis

Great performers know how to step into a different world when it matters. The crowd, the clock, the noise, and the stakes are still there, but they stop being relevant. The moment becomes smaller, clearer, and more playable. It is just you and what is in front of you.

MORNING EDGE: STEP INTO IT

Before the day begins, choose what your "bar" is today and see it clearly. Picture yourself inside that space where it is just you and the task, nothing else competing for your attention. Tell yourself, "Just me and the bar," and step into that world early.

FLIP THE SWITCH: STEP BACK IN

When your attention drifts, step back into your bubble on purpose. Take one Return to Zero breath, bring your eyes to your bar, and lock in again with "Back to my world." Great competitors do not chase focus—they re-enter it.

CHAMPION'S WRAP: WHERE DO YOU COMPETE FROM?

Before sleep, notice the version of you that showed up when everything got quiet and clear. That is your competitive world. The more often you step into it, the more natural it becomes to compete from there.

DAY 363: DON'T PUT A ROOF ON IT

"I've always tried not to put a limit on myself. There are endless possibilities."
Armand Duplantis

A lot of limits start when people decide too soon what they are capable of. They set a ceiling, name their level, and start living inside it. The best at any craft refuse to put a roof on themselves before they have truly tested how high they can go. That is why they keep growing long after other people would have settled.

MORNING EDGE: LEAVE THE SKY OPEN

Start the day without putting a ceiling on what is possible. Train with ambition, range, and full intent. Tell yourself, "The sky is still open." Carry yourself like there is more in you waiting to come out.

FLIP THE SWITCH: UNDER OPEN SKIES

When doubt or frustration tries to shrink the moment, refuse to let it set the limit. Attack the next rep, stay in the work, and keep climbing. Tell yourself, "Higher is still there." Champions rise higher because they do not let one feeling decide the ceiling.

CHAMPION'S WRAP: STILL OPEN SKY

As the sun sets, remember one moment today when you refused to let an old limit speak for you. That is how champions grow, by rising past the ceilings that lesser minds accept. The sky is still open above you, so keep climbing until your effort touches it.

DAY 364: RISE WITH THE MOMENT

"If I go into years only thinking about medals, I'm missing the whole meaning of what I've always been trying to do, which is push myself and push the barriers of what is possible."
Armand Duplantis

Big moments ask for more. They ask for more focus, more belief, more composure, and more of your full presence. The best athletes do not wait for those moments to feel easier. They rise until their energy, poise, and intent match the size of what is in front of them.

MORNING EDGE: CALL UP MORE

Pick one part of today that will ask more from you, whether that is your focus, your composure, or your presence. Tell yourself, "There is more in me, and today I bring it." Step into the day like someone ready to rise.

FLIP THE SWITCH: MATCH THE MOMENT

When the moment gets bigger, do not back off or get smaller inside it. Take one Return to Zero breath, lift your posture, and bring your eyes back to what matters most. Tell yourself, "Match the moment." Then answer it with your best focus, belief, and presence.

CHAMPION'S WRAP: CARRY IT FORWARD

Before sleep, name the version of you that showed up when the day asked for more. Let that version be the one you carry forward into tomorrow. Big moments change you when you answer them with something worth keeping.

DAY 365: LIVE THE GOLD STANDARD

"Despite having been fortunate enough to experience some incredibly grand moments, the smallest and most intimate moments define me equally, as an athlete, a person, and a man."
Armand Duplantis

The biggest moments never tell the whole story. You are also defined by how you handle the quiet parts, the ordinary parts, and the hard parts nobody applauds. Greatness is not something you rise to once. It is something you live. It lives in your habits, your standards, and the way you carry yourself when nobody is watching. That is the gold standard. That is the daily champion's mind.

MORNING EDGE: WEAR THE STANDARD

Today, do not reach for something extra. Live what you have built. Bring presence to the ordinary, pride to the work, and heart to the people around you. Open the day with this: "I live the gold standard." Then let it show up in your effort, your body language, and the way you handle every moment.

FLIP THE SWITCH: RISE LIKE YOU BELONG

When the moment gets bigger, do not shrink or reach. Rise into it. Meet the pressure, meet the challenge, and meet the people beside you with your full presence. Say, "This is what I'm built for." The gold standard is not talk. It is the way you answer the moment with all of who you are.

CHAMPION'S WRAP: CARRY IT FORWARD

As Day 365 closes, see what you built. You built a mind that returns, a standard that holds, and a way of living that honors your best. The daily work was never separate from greatness. It was greatness, so carry the gold standard forward.

CHAMPION'S TAKEAWAYS: LOS ANGELES MEMORIAL COLISEUM

The Coliseum brought you back to the heart of the Olympic spirit, not as a distant dream, but as a way of living and competing. This final chapter asked you to trust what you have built when the stage gets bigger. You practiced meeting big moments with belief, freedom, and full presence. You learned to trust your preparation, stay grounded in who you are, and bring your whole self to the moments that matter most. That is the standard now. That is the daily champion's mind.

As you close the year and step forward, ask yourself:

- Where did I trust who I have become instead of questioning myself?
- When the moment got bigger, how did I stay present and fully engaged?
- What standard do I want to keep living by, both in competition and in life?

Carry that standard forward. It was built in the daily work, strengthened under pressure, and proven when the moment asked the most of you. The year may be ending, but what you built is ready for every arena still ahead.

ACKNOWLEDGMENTS

DR. JIM AFREMOW

This book came to life through the support, effort, and belief of many people, and I'm deeply appreciative of all of them.

First, thank-you to my coauthor, Phil White. It's always a pleasure to work together, and I'm grateful for his partnership, insight, and commitment throughout this project.

I'm also thankful for our literary agent, Helen Zimmermann, whose guidance, experience, and encouragement have meant a great deal throughout the publishing process.

We deeply appreciate the team at BenBella Books for their support and hard work, including Clara Tamez, Assistant Editor; Anthony LaSasso, Marketing Manager; Monica Lowry, Senior Production Director; Morgan Carr, Designer; Madeline Grigg, Senior Publishing Associate; Alicia Kania, Vendor Content Manager; and Glenn Yeffeth, Publisher and CEO.

A special thank-you to Victoria Carmody for her excellent editorial work and for helping us strengthen and refine the manuscript with such care.

I also want to thank the many athletes, coaches, leaders, and high performers I've had the privilege to work with over the years. You continue to remind me that the champion's mind is not built in comfort, but in the daily choice to show up, stay with it, and rise again. Your trust, honesty, and commitment to growth have taught me as much as I could ever hope to teach.

Finally, I'm profoundly grateful to my wife, Anne, and our daughter, Maria Paz, for their unwavering love, patience, and support. They have been my foundation throughout this journey.

PHIL WHITE

There are so many people behind the scenes of every creative endeavor, and you can always multiply that by ten for a book. So thank you to everyone who has inspired, encouraged, and contributed along the way.

This starts with my incomparable coauthor, Jim Afremow. Just writing one book with him would've been a peak experience, and so for this—our third collaboration—to come to life is a privilege. I've learned more from Jim over the years than just about anyone, and as talented as he is in psychology and writing, he's an even better friend.

I'd also like to thank our creative partners at BenBella Books. It takes countless hours behind the scenes to bring a book to life, and having this talented team behind us is essential. So a big thank-you to Glenn Yeffeth, Victoria Carmody, Adrienne Lang, Clara Tamez, Anthony LaSasso, Chloe Shields, Monica Lowry, Morgan Carr, Madeline Grigg, Alicia Kania, and the rest of the crew. And, as ever, thanks to our agent, Helen Zimmermann, for finding the perfect home for this book.

I'd also like to thank my wife, muse, and creative director, Nicole White—the most beautiful and talented woman in the world. She toils unheralded behind the scenes and her name should be on every project I've ever completed. And to my sons, Harry and Johnny, thank you for being who you are and for the basketball, movies, Coronado trips, and everything else we enjoy together.

I'd also like to acknowledge the wonderful friends and family members who make life richer—you know who you are. Finally, I thank God for the blessing of this book, my writing partnership with Jim, and every other blessing.

ABOUT THE AUTHORS

Photo by Maria Paz Afremow

Dr. Jim Afremow is a leading high-performance consultant and the best-selling author of *The Champion's Mind, The Champion's Comeback, The Young Champion's Mind, The Leader's Mind,* and *The Creative's Mind* (the latter two co-authored with Phil White). For more than two decades, he has helped elite athletes, coaches, teams, and business leaders strengthen their mindset, lead under pressure, and perform at their best when it matters most.

Dr. Afremow has worked with athletes and teams from the NFL, MLB, NBA, NHL, UFC, MLS, PGA Tour, LPGA Tour, and WNBA, as well as US and international Olympians. His experience includes serving as a sport psychologist for the Greek softball and Indian field hockey Olympic teams and as the peak performance coordinator and mental skills coach for the San Francisco Giants.

He co-hosts the *Champion Conversations* podcast with Phil White, and lives in Eugene, Oregon, with his wife, Anne, and their daughter, Maria Paz. To learn more, visit drjimafremow.com.

Photo by Nicole White

Phil White is an Emmy-nominated writer and the coauthor of *The Leader's Mind* and *The Creative's Mind* with Jim Afremow, *Unplugged* with Andy Galpin and Brian Mackenzie, *Waterman 2.0* with Kelly Starrett, *Game Changer* with Fergus Connolly, *The 17 Hour Fast* with Frank Merritt, and *True North* with former Navy SEAL Ryan "Birdman" Parrott. He also writes for leading human performance brands, including Momentous, Teamworks, TrainingPeaks, RAPID, Absolute Rest, Vitality Blueprint, and TRX.

Phil lives with his wife and two sons in Evergreen, Colorado. Connect with him @PhilWhiteBooks and at philwhitebooks.com.